The Aptitude Myth

*How an Ancient Belief Came to
Undermine Children's Learning Today*

Cornelius N. Grove

ROWMAN & LITTLEFIELD EDUCATION
A division of
ROWMAN & LITTLEFIELD PUBLISHERS, INC.
Lanham • New York • Toronto • Plymouth, UK

Published by Rowman & Littlefield Education
A division of Rowman & Littlefield Publishers, Inc.
A wholly owned subsidary of The Rowman & Littlefield Publishing Group, Inc.
4501 Forbes Boulevard, Suite 200, Lanham, Maryland 20706
www.rowman.com

10 Thornbury Road, Plymouth PL6 7PP, United Kingdom

British Library Cataloguing in Publication Information Available

Library of Congress Cataloging-in-Publication Data

Grove, Cornelius N.
The aptitude myth : how an ancient belief came to undermine children's learning today / Cornelius N. Grove.
pages cm
ISBN 978-1-4758-0435-5 (cloth : alk. paper) — ISBN 978-1-4758-0436-2 (pbk. : alk. paper) — ISBN 978-1-4758-0437-9 (ebook)
1. Academic achievement—United States. 2. Achievement motivation in children—United States. 3. Learning ability. 4. Education—United States. I. Title.
LB1062.6.G77 2013
153.9—dc23
2013002028

♾™ The paper used in this publication meets the minimum requirements of American National Standard for Information Sciences Permanence of Paper for Printed Library Materials, ANSI/NISO Z39.48-1992.

Printed in the United States of America

With apologies to Herbert Spencer,
I dedicate this book to American parents who
care far less about their children's experiencing
"pleasurable excitement" today, and far more about
their children's being highly skillful, knowledgeable,
and competently creative thirty years from now.

Contents

Foreword

Being an independent scholar comes with a disadvantage. I don't know a famous scholar whom I can ask to write this Foreword. But independent scholarship also has an advantage. I'm able to allow historical facts to endlessly percolate in my mind, uninterrupted by others' trains of thought. Thus unfettered, I gradually came to understand that many Americans have a *culturally* inherited a set of beliefs about *biologically* inherited fixed intelligence. These beliefs comprise an ancient myth that, today, is undermining our children's capacity to learn. In particular, I came to four insights that might well be unique scholarly contributions:

1. The deep cause of many Americans' assumption that inherited aptitude determines one's ability to learn is a belief in inborn mental "givens," traceable to Plato and Aristotle.
2. The Calvinist and Romantic views of child rearing, although diametrically opposed to each other, shared one fateful assumption: that each child has God- or Nature-bestowed "givens."
3. The belief in the superiority of "organic" mental development surreptitiously engenders a culture of relative *passivity* toward learning—passivity by parents, teachers, and pupils.
4. The popular notion of a child's "potential" is *not* an expansive principle but a constraining and limiting one. Col. Francis Parker put it best: "Thus far shalt thou go and no farther."

Whether or not these insights will stand scholarly scrutiny, I'd like to make this point: They came to me while, in my metaphorical garret, I turned over and over *and over* within my mind numerous historical facts. Yahoo recently recalled to its offices all employees working at home in order to cultivate more innovation through frequent face-to-face collaboration. But there's still much to be said in favor of the determined, persistent thinker, working alone.

Cornelius N. Grove

Acknowledgments

Whatever merit this volume might possess is due, in part, to the assistance and guidance I received from three individuals. First and foremost, my gratitude goes to my decades-long friend and professional associate Kay M. Jones, who edited and reedited drafts with her consummate eagle eye, discovered old original sources, alerted me to possible misleading interpretations by potential readers, expertly and almost single-handedly constructed the thorough index, and made countless thoughtful suggestions along the way. Kay, you have my enduring, heartfelt appreciation for treating this book as though it were your own.

Two other long-time friends and professional associates provided guidance and many applicable suggestions. Willa Zakin Hallowell, my Grovewell business partner for twenty-three years, read drafts of all eighteen chapters and back cover copy, offering many ideas about how I could express myself in ways that would have more "Velcro." Kathy Molloy, our consultancy's first senior associate, read drafts of all eighteen chapters and the front materials, offering thoughtful and useful observations. Kathy also suggested the title of this book. Willa and Kathy, thank you for your sustaining interest, support, and flow of worthwhile observations and cautions.

During my five years of research and writing, I came to deeply admire the painstaking research of the professional historians on whose publications I was relying. I feel especially grateful for the works of R. Freeman Butts, John Cleverley and D. C. Phillips, Lawrence A. Cremin, Merle Curti, Kieran Egan, Stephen Jay Gould, Gerald L. Gutek, Richard Hofstadter, Lynn Hunt, Carl F. Kaestle, Herbert M. Kliebard, Edward A. Krug, Denis Lawton and Peter Gordon, Dorinda Outram, R. S. Peters, Diane Ravitch, Bertrand Russell, Charles L. Sanford, Joel Spring, David Tyack and Elisabeth Hansot, Edgar B. Wesley, and Bernard Wishy.

Cornelius N. Grove

Introduction

This is a book for well-educated Americans who worry about how well today's young Americans are being educated. This is also a history book.

Now you might think that a history book couldn't possibly also be a book that addresses a persistent, even worsening, crisis facing our children today and into the foreseeable future.

But it can be. Here's how: Part of our crisis about how well young Americans are being educated derives from *Americans' customary ways of thinking* about children, parenting, learning, and teaching. These ways of thinking are customary because Americans absorbed them during their childhoods from their parents and neighbors, who in turn absorbed them during *their* childhoods from their parents and neighbors, who in turn absorbed them during *their*. . . well, you get the picture.

These customary ways of thinking did not originate in America. They did not originate in our lifetimes, nor in our parents' lifetimes. These ways of thinking originated far away and very, *very* long ago. It will prove useful to examine why these ways of thinking originated and how they gained wide public acceptance within the United States.

Perhaps you're wondering, "What *are* these customary ways of thinking?"

Instead of a direct response, here are a few questions in return.

Were you aware that many Americans assume that each newborn baby arrives with a fixed set of mental abilities? . . . and that those inborn abilities largely govern the ways in which, and the extent to which, that child will succeed in school? It's a fact: The abilities measured by aptitude and I.Q. tests are believed by many American adults to record the outer limits on what and how much each child can learn in classrooms.[1]

Were you aware that, in many other regions of the world including most of Asia, many adults assume that a child is born with mental abilities *plus* a capacity for perseverance and intense effort? . . . and further expect children to apply that capacity to study in school—and after school? This, too, is a fact: Many adults abroad believe that a child's success in learning is largely governed by his or her *intentional effort* rather than by his or her aptitude.[2]

Which assumption is more likely to equip a nation's children to master the knowledge and skills taught in schools? That *aptitude* governs learning? Or that *effort* governs learning?

WHY DO AMERICANS ASSUME THAT *APTITUDE* GOVERNS LEARNING?

Two questions worth answering are these: First: When, where, and why did the idea originate that a child's performance in school is a reflection, largely if not entirely, of *aptitude*—a fixed set of abilities bestowed at birth? Second: How did that assumption manage to gain such wide credibility that, today, many Americans regard it as the modern way to think?

These questions matter because we are facing an educational emergency. We have witnessed a slow, seemingly irreversible decline in our children's mastery of the critical skills taught in schools and needed to thrive in a world with an information-based, technologically ever-more-sophisticated economy in which low-end jobs are disappearing. It's a decline made more urgent by work opportunities that increasingly require *mastery* of math, science, engineering, technical skills, and critical thinking.[3] It's a decline tracked over decades by a variety of measures, some of which report educational outcomes within our nation, and others of which compare outcomes from several dozen nations.[4] This decline—or at best, persistent stagnation—adversely affects the economic future of each of our children, and of our entire nation.

Many explanations are being publicly aired for the decline in our children's mastery of critical skills, and for the "achievement gap" between students of different incomes, ethnic backgrounds, and zip codes. Competing camps advance a variety of recommendations for reversing our collective failure, with two leading perspectives being proposed. One holds that our schools will be improved through more teacher accountability, supported by frequent testing and more free-market principles (especially parental choice of schools). The other argues that change will begin only when poverty and other negative social conditions are addressed, which in turn will enable students to arrive at school with greater readiness to learn.

The purpose of this book is neither to support nor to rebut either of these points of view, which identify two *parts* of the explanation for the decline in American children's mastery.

A Part of the Explanation That Is Rarely Discussed

This book reveals a third part of the explanation for the decline in mastery, one that's rarely discussed. But it would be wrong to think of it as "the elephant in the room," which implies that the people in the room know of a nearby "elephant" but avoid talking about it. This third explanation for the decline in mastery lies outside the conscious awareness of virtually all Americans.

This book brings into awareness the third explanation. It concerns our beliefs about the aptitudes innately "given" to each child at birth, and the impact of these beliefs on our children's capacities for learning. This book traces the deep historical origins, the spread, and the eventual triumph of the archaic belief in the determining power of aptitude. Stated concisely, *The Aptitude Myth* says this:

> The third part of the explanation for the decline in mastery is the widespread belief in the power of inborn traits—aptitude—to determine each child's school performance. This supposedly modern mindset about children's learning, *actually inherited from long-gone European forebears*, is undermining our efforts to improve children's mastery of critical skills. If we want to improve *their* mastery, then we must transform *our* mindset. We must cast off old beliefs. We must think in new ways about children, learning, teaching, and—most of all—parenting.

The key belief that we inherited from long-gone European forebears is that *each child's mental ability is "given" at birth, and thus is fixed and inelastic.* Attempts by adults to compel a child to significantly expand his or her mental ability will be largely or entirely ineffective. In fact, such attempts might be counterproductive, for intense effort and long persistence in pursuit of academic mastery endangers a child's well-being. So adults simply should go with what each child has got.

Not Invented Here; Rather, Inherited *Here*

We assume that these ways of thinking are applicable because our parents, and their parents, and *their* parents also assumed it. We didn't invent these beliefs; we inherited them. The reasons why they came into being dozens of generations ago, and the paths by which they were handed down to us, are revealed within these pages. As you grasp what's being revealed, you'll come to understand that our American mindset about children's learning gradually emerged over 2,500 years for reasons that were almost totally separate and distinct from the goal of helping children to attain mastery of the skills and knowledge taught in schools. Mastery was rarely the chief goal. Today many of us perpetuate that obsolete mindset even though it deflects our urgent quest for solutions.

Our inherited mindset, embraced by many Americans as the modern, up-to-date way to think about parenting, teaching, and learning, is a relic. It's an ages-old way of thinking that arose to solve problems and realize values that, very long ago, were believed to have the highest priority. It's a mindset that, way back when, was believed to reliably guide people toward effective solutions. It was handed down from generation to generation to . . . us.

But we are not our long-dead European ancestors. *Their* urgent problems about children and learning, teaching and parenting, were different from *our* urgent problems. Their solutions might have been effective in bygone times and places, but in 21st century America those solutions are ineffective. Worse, they're diversionary. The old-fashioned mindset we inherited from this nation's European ancestors is not solving the educational crisis that our nation faces today; it's contributing to it.

THE "MODERN" MINDSET THAT'S ACTUALLY A RELIC: A PREVIEW

The story that will be told in parts I and II of this book concerns how we came to inherit an archaic mindset. It's a story about selected features of Western civilization beginning in the times of the ancient Greeks. It becomes more detailed as it describes events during the past six centuries, starting when Johann Gutenberg revolutionized printing. It's a story about the origins and spread of what, generations ago, was unquestionably a thoroughly modern mindset, which this book will label the "western-contemporary paradigm" (that's the one we've inherited).

Equally important, this book tells the story about what educated European parents and citizens long ago—people much like you—were thinking about how best to raise and educate children. It's about fascinating *dramatis personae* whose names you know such as William Wordsworth, Jean-Jacques Rousseau, and Aristotle. It's also about equally compelling but lesser-known characters such as Francis Bacon, Johann Pestalozzi, and G. Stanley Hall. And it's about a *very* influential 19th century public personality you might never have heard of: Herbert Spencer.

Here's a brief preview of what will be revealed by the story you're about to start reading.

Mastery Was Infrequently Anyone's Top Priority

Beginning with the ancient Greeks and on through the early years of the 20th century, cutting-edge thinking about child-raising, child-development, teaching, and learning was grappling with challenges and goals that had little or no relevance for children's mastery of the essential skills and knowledge taught in classrooms. Instead, cutting-edge thinkers were spending their time devising solutions for problems—theological, epistemological, philosophical, and psychological—that arose out of the assumptions they were imagining about the inborn "givens" conferred on each child at birth.

An example of an inborn "given" is Original Sin, a belief of countless Christians over many centuries. Whatever this might mean as a theological issue, the "fact" that each infant arrived in the world tainted by Original Sin formerly led adults to employ a draconian style of parenting and teaching, the goal of which was to save the child from Original Sin's awful consequences. This example makes a key point about such "givens": Although they are assumptions or beliefs that are based on ancient texts, they definitely are not inert or idle figments of the imagination. They motivate individual behaviors and community-wide practices with observable impacts.

Assumed "Givens" Generated Mastery-Averse Patterns of Thought

Through a chain of theological and mythopoetic reasoning about "givens," educated people in the West came to fear that, because children are mentally fragile (so they assumed), any sustained focus on academic learning would lead to permanent psychological debilitation—and even to physical debilitation! (For example, during the 19th century it was seriously argued that intense study by girls led to "enfeebled health," flat-chested figures, and sometimes a life of celibacy![5]) The popular preoccupation with "givens" also fostered the belief that each child is born with a *fixed, limited set* of mental abilities—his or her "potential"—that simply cannot be transcended.

The belief in fixed abilities was supported by two other beliefs that originated in ancient Greece. Plato wrote that knowledge is *inside* each person, having been acquired by him or her before birth. And the highly influential Aristotle taught that a child's mental development is spontaneous—like a plant's flowering—and cannot be strengthened or hastened by anyone's conscious effort—including the child's. Aristotle thought that a child's mental development simply *happens*. Child, parents, teachers—all must play merely *passive* roles.

"Givens" Were Embraced by Thought-Leaders, Including Scientists

By the early 19th century in the United States, inherited assumptions about children's innate "givens" had become well aligned with the pragmatic, increasingly efficiency-oriented values of the well-educated public. Elected officials, top educators, and even leading scientists consciously applied those ancient assumptions to resolve the urgent public policy issues with which they were grappling.

For instance, during the late 19th century, the huge educational challenge occasioned by the avalanche of immigrants was resolved by assuming that all of their children had been "given" very low intelligence. Then, early in the 20th century, the inherited belief that each child is born with fixed potential gained the *imprimatur* of science and joined the American establishment as the Scholastic Aptitude Test. Ignored or resolutely rejected as factors able to contribute to a child's attainment of mastery were family culture, parental directiveness, impactful childhood experiences, and teachers who settle for nothing short of mastery—not to mention the child's own spirited determination, intentional effort, and dogged perseverance.

That's a summary of what will be revealed. As for recounting of the historical story itself, part I of this book takes place in Europe and answers the question, "When, why, and how did Americans' current ways of thinking originate?" Part II occurs in our own nation and answers the question, "How did Americans apply the European ways of thinking, and why?"

REPLACING OUR ANTIQUE MINDSET WITH
ONE TAILOR-MADE FOR US TODAY

In part III, we'll leave history-telling behind in order to explore this question: "Can we transcend our inherited mindset to give mastery the highest priority?" This book replies, "Yes; here's how."

Our Need for a Fresh Mindset

This book argues that many Americans use an archaic mindset, or "paradigm" (framework for thought), that cannot solve today's educational problem. Merely disapproving of an outdated paradigm changes nothing[6]

With that in mind, part III comprises two chapters. Chapter 17 begins by reviewing nine features of the antique paradigm that we've inherited. That's followed by a brief recounting of highlights from the foregoing 16 chapters, underscoring the fact that during two and a half millennia of Western history *mastery was infrequently the top priority for anyone*—which is a key reason why many of us remain blind to the "how" of bringing our children to mastery.

Can a better paradigm be substituted for that ancient one? Can mastery be elevated to its rightful and necessary place as the top priority among all the worthy goals pursued in schools? This book says, "Yes, it can." These pages contend that *children's own perseverance and hard work is the best pathway to mastery*. Perseverance and hard work, often credited as decisive in making our nation great, today remain very much alive in school athletic programs, being touted by parents, coaches, fans, the media, and the players themselves. *Why not in academic programs?*

This book was written to address the question of why many parents and teachers are not insisting that children apply the All-American values of perseverance and hard work to their studies. In many cases the answer is fear—an *inherited* fear based on our *ancient* assumptions about children's innate "givens," especially about the imagined dangers of long and intense study. If we're going to give mastery its due, we must rid ourselves of this unrealistic fear.

A New, Mastery-Embracing Paradigm

Ridding ourselves of an unrealistic fear cannot, by itself, adequately overcome our current emergency. We must also replace other features of the out-of-date paradigm we inherited. What's needed is a comprehensive new paradigm.

Chapter 18 lays out such a paradigm. It takes the form of seven fresh assertions about "how the world works." It's a transformative set of beliefs, values, and goals to think *with* whenever we think *about* children, parenting, learning, and teaching. Each assertion promotes vigorous engagement with *today's* challenge, the decline of mastery.

The Challenge of Paradigm Change

Significant change in most Americans' paradigm about children, parenting, learning, and teaching will occur if, and only if, there's a broad, sustained effort to make that happen by concerned parents, educators, and citizens. That is why this book is addressed not only to American educators but also to the American public—and especially to American parents. A broad-based movement for change is needed now. In its absence, the gradual decline in American children's capacity to master the critical skills taught in schools will continue—irreversibly.

NOTES

1. The fact that Americans associate classroom success with *aptitude*, while people in Asia and many other world regions associate classroom success with *effort*, has long been known by anthropologists of education and other cross-cultural researchers. For example, a study widely discussed among concerned Americans during the early 1990s was *The Learning Gap*, by Harold W. Stevenson and James W. Stigler (Simon & Schuster, 1992), which compared American, Chinese, and Japanese primary education. See especially chapter 5, "Effort and Ability."

2. For example, during the early 1990s, cross-cultural researcher John Singleton reported that Japanese teachers regarded *gambaru* [to persist, to hang on] as the key to academic success. The teachers Singleton studied knew that the students' I.Q. scores were easily available in a nearby file cabinet, but regarded them as "not an item of interest or concern." John Singleton, "The Spirit of *Gambaru*," in Barbara Finkelstein et al., *Transcending Stereotypes: Discovering Japanese Culture and Education* (Intercultural Press, 1991), 119–22.

3. Consider the predicament of Traci Tapani, co-president of Wyoming Machine, a sheet metal firm in Minnesota. In 2009, she had ten openings for welding jobs that paid $20 per hour plus health care, paid vacations, and full benefits. Tapani had an extremely difficult time filling those positions, since job applicants trained in high schools did not understand metallurgical science, nor complex design drawings, nor how various metals, gases, pressures, and temperatures had to be combined for specific welds. Eventually, Tapani was forced to train her most promising job applicants in-house. This small vignette, repeated countless times, is why experts keep telling us that U.S. education is failing to provide the skill- and knowledge-mastery needed to keep up with 21st century global economic realities. Thomas L. Friedman, "If You've Got the Skills, She's Got the Job," *New York Times*, 18 November 2012, "Sunday Review" section, 1 and 11.

4. Noted educational historian Diane Ravitch reports that ". . . American students have never performed well on international tests. When the first such tests were given in the mid-1960s, our students usually scored at or below the median, and sometimes at the bottom of the pack." "School 'Reform': A Failing Grade," *New York Review of Books*, 29 September 2011, 32.

5. This claim, penned by Herbert Spencer in 1860, is quoted in context in chapter 10. Today, fears about physical debilities have been replaced by worries that too much study might make a child a socially handicapped "nerd."

6. Thomas S. Kuhn, *The Structure of Scientific Revolutions*, 3rd Ed. (University of Chicago, 1996), chapter VIII, "The Response to Crisis."

I

European Antecedents

The way many Americans think about children and learning is not modern. It was passed down to us from ancient Europeans, people who were dealing with parenting-related challenges totally different from those we face today. Part One conveys us to Europe back in deep historical time to discover when, why, and how those Europeans developed their mindsets.

Chapter 1 considers a pre-historical perspective on learning and teaching, which in turn was grounded in assumptions about communities, families, and children. Gradually, that perspective was eclipsed by newer patterns of thought. Chapter 2, set during the days of Plato and other Greek philosophers, begins our inquiry into why and how the newer patterns of thought first appeared and began to gain acceptance.

We then skip ahead 1,800 years to the middle of the 15th century, when the Renaissance dawned and eventually engendered the 18th century Enlightenment. Chapters 3, 4, 5, and 6 all examine that four-century stretch of time; each chapter explores an emerging perspective. Chapters 7 and 8 bring us into the 19th century: the first explores Romanticism's impact; the second visits a 19th century teacher who became the Western world's most influential educator.

Chapters 9 and 10 both discuss Herbert Spencer, the 19th century philosopher who had a huge following among the European and American public. More than any other individual except possibly Aristotle, Spencer shaped the mindset that many Americans, today, think *with* whenever they're thinking *about* parenting, children, learning, and teaching.

ONE

A Perspective on Teaching
Out of the Depths of Time

We can only infer that each group [among the ancient folk societies] tried to bring up its children in the image of its elders.

—R. Freeman Butts[1]

"What is the purpose of teaching?" is a question confronted by every society with children in classrooms.[2] Because it is abstract and philosophical, it's a question usually addressed as an adjunct to the much more down-to-earth one, "Who should become a teacher?" In some societies, the qualifications to become a teacher are stringent, and are framed in ways that don't necessarily emphasize a candidate's preparedness to teach skills or knowledge to the young. In other societies, the qualifications to become a teacher are relatively modest.

Why would a society set stringent qualifications for someone to teach? Stringent qualifications became important because the teacher's role frequently was not limited to knowledge transfer. This role also has been about, and in some cases has been *primarily* about, ensuring that the learners gain and maintain *virtue*, defined as conformity to the mores, values, social expectations, beliefs, and standards of behavior accepted in the local community.

To understand why virtue probably was of the utmost importance, let's peer back into deep history. Imagine a time long before the beginning of the Christian era, a time even before the days of the ancient Greek philosophers, a time when it's likely that no one was thinking about whether any child had enough aptitude to learn whatever he or she needed to know.

FAMILY-CENTERED SUBSISTENCE SOCIETIES IN PREHISTORIC TIMES

For thousands of years in the deep past, human beings lived in societies that were characterized by small villages, subsistence economics, and family relationships that were lifelong and very close. The intense and central role of family relationships is one of the sociocultural factors that clearly distinguish subsistence from urban-industrial societies.

In prehistoric subsistence societies, each family was dependent on the daily food- and shelter-producing labor of all family members, including children; everyone worked under the direction of the oldest parents (probably the grandparents of the youngest members). Parental direction was actively exercised, clearly hierarchical, and obviously

3

necessary in the sense that the family's physical survival could be observed to depend on everyone's coordinated efforts. Supporting these daily practices were deeply ingrained values—"virtues"—that called for children to respect and obey their parents.

Sociologists and anthropologists refer to this constellation of practices and values as "filial loyalty" (or "filial piety"). Filial loyalty in subsistence societies lasted a lifetime. It was a high moral obligation and an indispensable characteristic of virtue. As the world's great religions gradually developed, filial loyalty was enshrined as a matter of piety and sacred duty: "Honor thy father and thy mother that thy days may be long. . . ." To people living in subsistence societies, the idea of severing one's filial bonds couldn't even be imagined. For doing so would be proof at least of immorality . . . and possibly of madness.

The complexity of knowledge and skill needed to prosper in such a society was lower than, or at least very different from, what is needed in our urban-industrial society. (On the other hand, the survival skills routinely employed in subsistence societies would be hugely difficult for most of us modern folks to master.) Skills, practices, and their accompanying mindsets that had to be mastered for survival were passed down from parents to children.

It's likely that in those ancient days, no distinction was made between knowledge and virtue. Individuals whose behavior virtuously conformed to community mores and conventions were assumed to know what needed to be known. Let's use the term *virtue-via-conformity*. Those admired for exemplary virtue-via-conformity were deemed wise and therefore worthy of emulation.

Like the skills needed to survive, the virtues were passed down from generation to generation by precept and example. The notion that one could adjust community virtues for personal gain, or could attain his or her own unique aspirations, didn't occur. Absent were concepts that, in our nation today, begin with *self-* (self-expression, self-assertion, self-reliance, self-realization . . .).

SELECTING A TEACHER IN PREHISTORIC TIMES: A THOUGHT EXPERIMENT

For children in prehistoric subsistence economies, necessary learning was at least as much about virtue-via-conformity as it was about survival knowledge or skill. Because an increase in virtue-via-conformity was a critical learning objective for the young people, *virtue-via-conformity had to be an indispensable characteristic of the deliverer of that learning.* Over eons, one's parent, grandparent, or other close relative such as an older sibling or cousin was the deliverer of the learning, insuring that virtue-via-conformity would be demonstrated.

Let's do a thought experiment: Imagine what might have occurred in a subsistence village when it was found, for the very first time, that for some compelling reason (e.g., early deaths), the deliverer of learning for a family's children needed to be someone other than a close relative. The question faced by the family was, "Which individual who is not directly related to this family should instruct these children?"

I believe that all eyes would then turn to the few village members admired for their knowledge and skill, and even more so for their exemplary virtue-via-conformity. For they were the members who were deemed the wisest, who seemed to know best what was good for the community, who were thus most worthy of emulation and most deserving of respect, deference, and obedience. The children's teacher should be selected from among *them*.

THE "TIME-HONORED PARADIGM" FOR THINKING ABOUT TEACHERS

The characteristics viewed above introduce us to one end of a spectrum of values and beliefs that classifies the various ways in which teachers can be regarded.[3] This end is named the *time-honored paradigm*[4] for thinking about teachers, their students, the students' parents and kinfolk, and everyone's expectations about relationships among them.

At this "time-honored" end of the spectrum, a teacher is viewed as wise, morally good, skilled, and knowledgeable, and therefore as worthy of emulation, respect, deference, and obedience—in the classroom and out. Specifically:

- This way of thinking about a teacher is characteristic not only of the learners who come to his or her classroom but also of *all* the members of the local community, all the time.
- These desirable qualities—wisdom, goodness, knowledge, etc.—are conferred on a teacher "by ascription," i.e., by definition. The role of teacher is inseparable from these ascribed qualities. "Teacher" means one-who-teaches *and* all of those good qualities.
- The learners in the teacher's classroom are assumed by all community members to need whatever the teacher is dispensing. Learners are expected to acquire both the virtues *and* the knowledge and skills that the teacher possesses (or is assumed to possess).
- At the heart of the enterprise are virtue, knowledge, and skills; the teacher is the deliverer of these not only by instructional precept but also by day-to-day example.

This perspective on teachers and teaching is not merely a historical curiosity from ancient times. It is alive and well today. You need not journey into remote regions of the Kalahari Desert or Papua New Guinea to discover it in use. Across eons of time, the assumption that teachers are good, wise, and worthy of respect and emulation has been handed down from generation to generation. In many contemporary societies, it continues at a deep emotional level to influence the behavior of students, their parents, and other community members.

If you've ever taught or trained abroad, or if your work in the United States has brought you into sustained contact with learners recently arrived from abroad, it's possible that you have come face-to-face with the time-honored paradigm. You will have recognized this because of your students' or trainees' daily behavior: their expectations of you and their responses to you. Perhaps you evaluated their behavior favorably or unfavorably; perhaps you found it perplexing. In any case, now you understand why they behaved that way.

Figure 1.1.

THE SIX ELEMENTS OF THE TIME-HONORED PARADIGM

The time-honored paradigm is comprised of six elements. These are not statements about teachers. Rather, they are *statements about everyone's expectations of teachers*. The six are descriptions of key ways in which people in most world regions have viewed, and in some regions continue to view, anyone filling the role of classroom teacher at any level.

Virtue

The bedrock of the time-honored paradigm is high expectations and assumptions regarding the personal virtue of the teacher. Virtue means desirable qualities and behavior *as locally defined*. The local definition might refer to an external source such as a holy book, but the key feature is that the definition is locally subscribed to. Above we spoke of "virtue-via-conformity" to local standards.

Deference

Because the teacher represents and embodies virtue, he or she *by ascription* is deserving of deference and respect from all learners and other community members. The fact of the teacher's (expected and assumed) virtue automatically brings out deference in others; therefore—this is important—the teacher need not strive to "earn" their deference.

Guidance

Because the teacher represents and embodies community norms, he or she is expected to serve as a moral guide and mentor, and as what we today might call a lifestyle coach. This is an actively exercised role, very similar to a parental role; in some cultures even today a teacher of younger learners is called the "second parent." This guidance role may also be exercised in relation to adult learners.

Mastery

The teacher is instructing something, "content" in today's terms. He or she is assumed to have mastery of that content. In other words, he or she is regarded as *the one who knows all* with respect to the content. The deeply respectful words "sage," "guru," and "master" are appropriate and remain in daily use in some cultures. The point here is *not* that teachers literally know it all; they probably don't. Rather, it's that the expectations of the learners and all others are such that teachers are dealt with *as though* they know it all.

Criticalness

As the embodiment of virtue and the authority on content, the teacher is expected to ensure that learners get things right. Whenever a learner runs afoul of local virtue, whenever a learner falls short in mastering the content, the teacher is presented with an opportunity to heighten that learner's ability to live up to locally expected standards. So the teacher liberally applies verbal criticism and a variety of other disciplinary measures. As the recipient of ascribed deference from everyone, the teacher need not worry that his or her criticalness will upset learners, their parents, or other community members.[5]

Directiveness

As content master, deputy parent, and the recipient of ascribed deference, the teacher is expected to proactively tell the learners what to learn and how to learn it. The teacher actively and unapologetically directs the learners' efforts to learn. And here's a key fact: Learners and their parents perceive this directiveness as *positively supportive*. They do not perceive it as overbearing, nor as depriving students of opportunities to discover or create or express their unique individuality. The teacher is doing a critical job: actively aiding each student's efforts to master content and gain virtue.[6]

It's important to note again that, even though these six expectations of teachers arose in the depths of time, they continue to be honored in some parts of the world even now, during the second decade of our 21st century.

THE RISE OF THE "WESTERN-CONTEMPORARY PARADIGM" FOR THINKING ABOUT TEACHERS

The time-honored paradigm was observed in communities and places of learning throughout the Western world—probably the entire world—into the 15th century. Exceptions were few. After all, the time-honored paradigm worked well. *Why would anyone want to change it?*

It was, in part, to answer that question that I wrote this book. The question needs to be answered because, beginning in Europe during the 15th century, alternative assumptions and expectations about children, learning, parenting, and teaching began to be imagined. These new ways of thinking gradually coalesced into the opposite end of the spectrum of values and beliefs that classifies ways in which teachers and teaching can be thought about. I will refer to this alternative view as the *western-contemporary paradigm*.

As was true of the time-honored paradigm, the western-contemporary paradigm became applicable not only for thinking about teachers, but also for thinking about their students and the students' parents and kinfolk, and about the relationships among them. Here's the critically important point: As will be documented in the forthcoming chapters, *attention gradually came to be focused more and more on the students*, especially on the younger students. Attention to aptitude grew hand-in-hand with attention to students. Simultaneously, attention on what was being taught declined.

In 15th century Europe, the ages-old assumption about youngsters in classrooms had been that their role was totally receptive: to acquire virtue and knowledge under the authority and directive guidance of an esteemed teacher. Today, some 600 years later, the assumption shared by many parents and educators is that it's the *students*—that is, the students' aptitudes and other natural inclinations—that should drive classroom processes.

Central to the western-contemporary paradigm are two value propositions. Both derive from beliefs about young people and about how classroom processes for them should occur:

- Children learn best when encouraged to perform wholly within their natural inclinations.
- Classroom teaching is best when guided first and foremost by attention to the children.

I became curious about the *How?* and *Why?* of this momentous change in the Western perspective on teachers and teaching. I wondered: "What drove the gradual shift from 'time-honored' to 'western-contemporary,' from traditional knowledge- and skill-centered classrooms to modern student-centered classrooms?" What I discovered is informative and useful in better enabling us all to address the current predicament of American education.

MUSINGS AND SPECULATIONS

Of the six elements of the time-honored paradigm, one seems to have been more successful than the other five in surviving in our current American mindset: virtue. Teachers who are discovered to have violated community moral standards are in danger of loud condemnation by the press, open disapproval by members of the public, and swift disciplinary action by the school board.

WHY CHAPTER 1 IS IMPORTANT

Chapter 1 establishes a baseline—the time-honored paradigm for thinking about teachers—from which the story told in this book will unfold. It's important to grasp this paradigm because the questions being asked in this book are *Why would anyone want to change the time-honored paradigm?* and *How did the western-contemporary paradigm come into ascendance, especially here in the United States?* As related in chapter 2, answers begin to emerge in ancient Greece.

WHAT TO REMEMBER: BULLET-POINT LISTS OF
KEY LEARNINGS FROM CHAPTERS 1–16

Chapters 1 through 16 are each complemented by a bullet-pointed list of "What to Remember," organized under the headings "How Children Learn Best" and "Which Classroom Teaching Is Best" (for some chapters, only one of these two headings appears). The sixteen "What to Remember" lists are all found at TheAptitudeMyth.info.

NOTES

1. R. Freeman Butts, *The Education of the West* (McGraw-Hill, 1973), 28.
2. My historical inferences in this chapter were guided by Robert A. LeVine and Merry I. White, *Human Conditions: The Cultural Basis of Educational Developments* (Routledge & Kegan Paul, 1986), 24–50. Also useful was R. Freeman Butts, *ibid.*, 35–54. LeVine and White focus more on the preservation of virtue; Butts focuses more on the transmission of skill and knowledge.
3. I'm aware that this "spectrum" is a bipolar model, and I accept the possibility that there might be a third and maybe even a fourth set of values and beliefs about teachers.
4. "Paradigm" refers to assumptions, beliefs, and mental frameworks that members of a group characteristically *think with* when they are thinking about a certain topic.
5. For contemporary examples, see Farideh Salili, "Teacher-Student Interaction: Attributional Implications and Effectiveness of Teachers' Evaluative Feedback," in D. A. Watkins and J. B. Biggs, *Teaching the Chinese Learner*, CERC, University of Hong Kong, 2001, 77–114. See also her "Accepting Personal Responsibility for Learning," in D. A. Watkins and J. B. Biggs, *The Chinese Learner*, CERC, University of Hong Kong, 1996, 85–105.
6. For contemporary examples, see Sally Chan, "The Chinese Learner—A Question of Style," *Education + Training*, vol. 41, no. 6/7, 1999, 8. See also Irene T. Ho, "Are Chinese Teachers Authoritarian?," in D. A. Watkins and J. B. Biggs, *ibid.*, 99–114.

TWO

Greek Philosophers Focus on a World Beyond the Senses

The soul . . . having seen all things that exist, whether in this world or in the world below, has knowledge of them all . . . for all enquiry and all learning is but recollection.

—Plato[1]

When scholars of ancient Greece speak of classical ideas about education,[2] they're usually referring to matters such as the schooling of youth in Sparta and Athens, or philosophical prescriptions for education such as Plato's curricular ideals in *The Republic*, Book III.

For our purposes, though, it's more important to explore the ways in which leading Greek philosophers conceived of human beings, and especially the human mind. We need to begin here because Greek philosophers' speculations from more than 2,000 years ago have proved to be remarkably influential on how people in the Western world have come to think about the capacity for learning of young human beings.

THE CONTRIBUTION OF PYTHAGORAS TO THE PARADIGM OF PLATO'S TIMES

Let's begin with Pythagoras, who flourished in the 6th century B.C.E. If you ever studied plane geometry, you've heard of the Pythagorean theorem, and you've probably thought of Pythagoras as a mathematician. That's only half the story. Many historians of philosophy make a convincing case that many traditions of Western philosophy, some of which we're about to examine, owe their origins to Pythagoras more than to Socrates, Plato, or Aristotle. Aristotle himself said that Plato began his thinking within a paradigm that was based on the work of the Pythagoreans.[3]

The expression "music of the spheres" is from Pythagoras and his followers. It captured their conclusion that there are fundamental connections among arithmetic, geometry, music, and all celestial objects,[4] connections that seem not merely fascinating but basic to an understanding of all of nature. These insights went way beyond plane geometry. According to Aristotle:

> Contemporaneously with these philosophers and before them, the Pythagoreans . . . devoted themselves to mathematics; they were the first to advance this study, and having been brought up in it they thought its principles were the principles of all things. Since of these principles numbers are by nature the first, and in numbers they seemed to see many resemblances to the things that exist and come into being—more than in fire and earth

9

and water . . .; since, again, they saw that the attributes and the ratios of the musical scales were expressible in numbers. . .

    Since, then, all other things . . . seemed to be modelled after numbers, and numbers seemed to be the first things in the whole of nature, they supposed the elements of numbers to be the elements of all things, and the whole heaven to be a musical scale and a number. And all the properties of numbers and scales which they could show to agree with the attributes and parts and the whole arrangement of the heavens, they collected and fitted into their scheme. . . .[5]

Imagine being one of the Pythagoreans living in southern Italy during those days, centuries before the birth of Jesus. It was a heady experience indeed to realize that you and your associates had figured out some truly amazing things about the way the world works. (In our 21st century, physicists say they hope to come up with a "theory of everything"; in their own times, what the Pythagoreans accomplished was similar to that.) Although you and your fellow Pythagoreans hadn't discovered or invented *every-thing* from scratch—there's evidence that Pythagoras had visited Egypt and gained some of his insights there—you clearly had taken a giant leap forward.

The Pythagoreans' contributions were based on their observation by means of sight and hearing of events and things all around them and in the heavens; this is an empiricist point of view.[6] But note: *Their insights were mathematical, which required only contemplation,* and which yielded awareness that was certain, exact, and eternal. They experienced this process as yielding feelings of personal ecstasy. It was, in short, a *revelation from within.*

But who or what had done the revealing?

In order to pick up this thread, we must detour to explore some even more ancient history.

TRANSMIGRATION OF SOULS AND THE DAWNING BELIEF IN THE POWER OF INTUITION

Bacchus Worship and Feelings of "Enthusiasm"

During earlier times,[7] in the rugged Roman province known as Thrace northeast of the Greek peninsula, there lived a tribe of agriculturalists known as Thracians who worshipped a god of fertility known (in Latin) as Bacchus and (in Greek) as Dionysus. Their worship involved ecstatic rites.

When the Thracians learned how to make beer and wine, they soon came to love the intoxicated feelings; for this they honored Bacchus. Eventually Bacchus's function as a god of fertility became subordinated to his association with the wonderful madness of intoxication. Down to our present day, this ancient deity by either name is widely recognized as the god of wine as well as of fruitfulness and vegetation.

The worship of Bacchus produced "enthusiasm," meaning that the god was believed to have entered into the worshipper to become one with him or her.[8] It also involved savage practices such as tearing live animals to pieces and eating their flesh raw while engaging in wild, passionate dances all night long (which, by the way, was done by the women). The worship of Bacchus migrated to Greece, probably before the dawn of historical times; it was attractive to the Greeks, perhaps, because within that rapidly civilizing region some people were hankering after their recent primitive, unrestrained past.[9]

There were some Greeks, however, who experienced Bacchus-worship as repulsive.[10] A reform movement arose that practiced a more spiritualized, even ascetic, style of living and worshipping. The reformers believed that ecstatic feelings—enthusiasm—should arise from intoxication that was mental and arose from within spontaneously, not physiological and as an outcome of drinking wine. This new religion was associated with Orpheus.

Orpheus Worship and Transmigration of Souls

In Greek mythology,[11] Orpheus was a musician who used his lyre to enchant people, animals, and even trees and rocks. The principles of the Orpheus-worshippers are well known. They believed in the transmigration of souls, which meant that the extent to which you demonstrate virtuous behavior in this life will determine what happens to your soul during your next life. The next life usually finds your soul returning in a different host body, such as that of an animal.

If you were a deeply religious Orphic, your objective was to escape that cycle of death and rebirth. So you'd do your best to behave well and to gain purity through various rituals. You believed that virtuous behavior and outstanding purity would enable your soul to escape the confines of a series of physical hosts and to become one with the divine Bacchus. You'd become and forever remain "a Bacchus."

Was the idea of transmigration of souls original to the Orphic tradition? This question has kept scholars busy. Some say it was borrowed from the Egyptians, whose pyramids reveal belief in an afterlife; but their tradition never involved reincarnation. More likely is the possibility that transmigration of souls entered the West from India,[12] [13] where the concepts of *karma* (every deed has a consequence) and reincarnation had been established during the seventh century B.C.E. in the traditions and writings called *Upanishads*.

Indian Philosophy and Immediate Awareness of the "Real"

The Indian perspective makes a distinction between matter on the one hand, and spirit or self on the other. Spirit or self is distinguished by consciousness (not identical to mind, which Indians believed was material). It is one's spirit or self that is transferred in transmigration of the soul. Also in the *Upanishad* tradition is the possibility and desirability of emancipation from the cycle of rebirth by becoming united with ultimate Reality, with the "Real."[14] This is made possible by the assumption that the gods and all other beings are manifestations of a single Reality.

Important for us is the fact that Indian philosophy never thought ill of reason, logic, and analysis, seeing these as necessary, although insufficient, in one's search for unity with the Real. Indians saw the aim of philosophy as not merely theoretical understanding of the Real but rather immediate awareness of it. Reason can take one only so far; from that point on, *intuition* is required. Intuition is capable of yielding knowledge or awareness of the Real that is indubitable and self-certifying. Intuition, in this view, is highly similar to revelation.

"Intuition" and the related word "insight" are words that will reappear frequently in the following chapters, and in significant ways. In present-day speech, they suggest a quick and perceptive understanding of a person or situation, or perhaps a mysterious "sixth sense."

But in the context of this and following chapters, "intuition" and "insight" indicate a belief in something far more profound: that a person is able to grasp Truths or Realities that are not available to human beings' five senses. In chapter 9 (which discusses 19th century Europe), we'll see this belief carried to an extreme: *Only* by attending to one's private, internal, inborn intuition (it was claimed) can infallible Truth and scientific certainty be known.

In summary, the Greek founders of Orpheus worship might have been the source of this notion, but it's more likely that this idea was imported into Greece from India. The influential Pythagoras was personally associated with the Orphic tradition and strongly adhered to the belief in the transmigration of souls and reincarnation. It's said that he asked someone to stop beating a dog because in the dog's cries Pythagoras recognized the ghost, or *psychê*, of a deceased friend.[15]

As a religious Orphic, Pythagoras was a reformer. One of his reforms concerned the gaining of purity by abstaining from certain foods. Beans were at the top of Pythagoras's no-eat list!

ELEMENTS OF THE GREEK PARADIGM INTO WHICH PLATO WAS BORN

Ecstasy Via the Contemplation of Mathematics

Pythagorean reforms strengthened and redirected the Orphic's ascetic ideal. The empiricist perspective became merged with the motivation to attain ecstasy associated with Bacchus; in this merger, the ecstatic side dominated.

Pythagoras believed that the route to ecstasy was through a contemplative life, and that the greatest purification came from intensely and disinterestedly engaging in thought, especially of the mathematical kind, about the orderly, beautiful nature of all Reality. The outcome of such contemplation was "music of the spheres," an ecstasy-producing revelation of the beautiful, certain, eternal connections among arithmetic, geometry, music, and all celestial objects.

Earlier I asked, "But who or what had done the revealing?"

It wasn't a *who*. There is no evidence that any of the religious traditions discussed above yielded belief in a personal God of the kind we Westerners conceive today (even if we don't accept it literally). Nor was it a *what*, for the revelation had no specific material source. *The revelation arose from within, i.e., from the activity of the human mind*, in which a combination of rational thought and, especially, mystical intuition yielded insights about, and potentially "oneness" with, ultimate Reality. For Pythagoras, this insight was expressed as mathematical knowledge. Bertrand Russell puts it this way:

> Mathematical knowledge appeared to be certain, exact, and applicable to the real world; moreover it was obtained by mere thinking, without the need of observation. Consequently, it was thought to supply an ideal, from which every-day empirical knowledge fell short. It was supposed, on the basis of mathematics, that thought is superior to sense, intuition to observation.[16]

The Dawn of Deductive Reasoning

A significant fact about mathematical knowledge, especially geometrical knowledge, is that it is grounded in *deductive reasoning*. Pythagoras didn't invent deductive logic, but he used its processes.[17]

Deduction begins with "axioms" that are accepted as true either because they are based on empirical data, or because they are said to be self-evident. In a "syllogism," there are two axioms, a "major premise" and the "minor premise." The process itself is strictly logical: If the axioms are accurate, then the conclusion is accurate ("valid"). Syllogistic logic can be applied to reality. For example: (major premise) "All humans are mortal"; (minor premise) "Socrates is human"; (valid conclusion) "Therefore, Socrates is mortal."

It's very important to recognize that a deductive reasoning process *need not be grounded in empirical data*, neither in its major nor its minor premise. An example similar to the one above is: "All A are B; C is an A; therefore, C is a B." That's a logically true statement that has nothing to do with the world available to our five senses.

Geometric proofs are similar; they deal with statements about lines, angles, and so forth that we conceive in our minds (and perhaps draw on paper or on a screen to aid the mind's work). In spite of that fact—actually, *because* of that fact—logically and geometrically derived results have an ordered, exact, permanent beauty to them. The Greeks loved this.

Distrust of the Five Senses

One more historical detour will complete our awareness of the reigning paradigm that, to a considerable extent, was extant when Plato was coming of age.

There had developed in Greek philosophic thought a so-called negative doctrine that there is nothing permanent in the world that we humans perceive with our five senses. Everything was understood to be in a constant, if gradual, state of change; this notion was applied not only to things and events in the world available to the senses but also to the sense organs themselves.

The philosopher whose name is linked with this view, Heraclitus (4th century B.C.E.), famously remarked that, "you cannot step twice into the same rivers; for fresh waters are ever flowing in upon you."[18] This perspective convinced many Greeks that sense organ-based empiricism was a losing proposition. They asked themselves: What's the point of examining things if no conclusion that's based on observation can be trusted?

To complete this picture, we need to note one more philosopher who, almost certainly, exercised significant influence on Plato. In fact, one of Plato's essays is called by his name: Parmenides. Similar to Heraclitus, Parmenides (5th century B.C.E.) believed the five senses to be deceptive and condemned as illusory all sensed things and events. It's all *appearance*, he said. In the view of Parmenides, the only true being—the only thing that's *Real*—is "The One," infinite and indivisible.

Parmenides also had a parallel belief that, as one scholar has paraphrased it, "There can be no thought corresponding to a name that is not the name of something real."[19] In other words (my paraphrase): When you use a name, presumably any noun, it simply must be the name of *something*. That something, not its appearance to the illusory senses, can be found in that other world, the world of certainty, permanence, and deductive logic, the world of the Real.

Having explored the mental world of Pythagoras and other Greek philosophers, we can now state some of the key elements of the reigning paradigm into which Plato was born:

- The world that we humans observe with our five senses is not to be trusted because it is illusory (i.e., mere appearance) and/or constantly changing. Thus, empiricism is faulty.
- There's another world—perhaps we can think of it as a "parallel world"—that cannot be perceived by our five senses, but that nonetheless is "Real" (i.e., it exists).
- Access to the Real world occurs by means that are wholly mental and/or spiritual, that is, through contemplation; contemplation takes place *completely inside an individual*.
- The Real world may be accessed via mathematics, geometry, and other applications of deduction. A deduction's axioms *may* be, but need not be, empirically verifiable.
- The Real also may be accessed via intuition, which gives one direct, certain knowledge. Intuition has an outcome similar to that of revelation (the difference is that

revelation implies that a new idea is inserted into one's mind by an external deity or other source).

- Accessing the Real in all these wholly mental ways gives one a highly desirable ecstatic experience, sometimes referred to as "enthusiasm," meaning that the divine is believed to have entered into, or to have become one with, the individual doing the thinking.
- Transmigration of souls is a feature of life. A person may escape the endless cycle of death and reincarnation by living virtuously and taking steps to become and remain pure. Escape means becoming forever united with ("one" with) a certain deity or with the Real.

PLATO POSITS THAT THE MOST VALUABLE KNOWLEDGE IS *INSIDE* EACH PERSON

Plato the Popularizer

Plato (5th century B.C.E.) made huge contributions to philosophic thought in the West, but that doesn't mean that he was a thoroughly original thinker. It's more accurate to view Plato as, largely but not entirely, a popularizer of the ideas that had been passed down from the Bacchus cult and the mythical Orpheus, from Pythagoras, Parmenides, and Heraclitus, and perhaps even from the *Upanishad* texts in far-away India. This constellation of ideas comprised the philosophic paradigm within which Plato came of age. He ran with it.

But as we will see, Plato made his own contribution, editing and extending the wisdom that he had received. His contributions addressed what the reigning paradigm was positing about appearance vs. reality, about the nature of the "Real" and how to access it, and about what's presumably going on when a human being increases his or her store of knowledge.

Plato accepted the received wisdom: that the day-to-day world is actually a set of mere appearances, of which our senses are inaccurate witnesses; and that there is a parallel world that is "Real"—the world of true existence, a world of pure concepts that are certain and permanent.

To gain knowledge of our day-to-day world isn't worth much, said Plato, because it's ambiguous and transitory. Ultimate value comes from gaining knowledge of the eternal Real world. That knowledge, he said, is infallible; it's impossible for it to be mistaken in any detail. What's more, that knowledge is desirable and wonderful, and it is gained by mathematics and mystic insight.

Knowledge Is Seen as Inside *Human Beings*

The Pythagorean view of mathematics and its related mental process, deductive reasoning, offer a foundation from which to explore what Plato said about mystic insight, which will further acquaint us with the deep origin of a critically important belief: The most valuable knowledge is *inside* each human being, having been acquired by, or "given" to, him or her *before birth*.

Plato's reasoning process, consciously or subconsciously, seems to proceed along lines similar to the following. Be aware that the following numbered paragraphs rely substantially on what Plato wrote but are my own reconstruction of his step-by-step reasoning:

1. Besides our world of sense experience, there's another, "Real," world inhabited by pure concepts that have eternal existence. These concepts are "Forms," also known as "universals." Here's an example: There are many cats, all different from each other, all changing over time. But all of them share one attribute, "Cat," or "Catness." That attribute is a concept, a Form.

Put differently, there's one eternal and universal concept, Cat, shared imperfectly by each cat in our everyday world. The same applies to *anything* we want to talk about, including events (dance, soccer) and values (justice, beauty). Every individual thing that we sense in our daily lives is an imperfect copy of a pure Form.[20]

2. A feature of life is transmigration of souls, meaning that the essence of each human being—usually "soul" or "self," but sometimes "mind"—does not vanish when his or her body dies, but continues to exist and reincarnates, returning to earth in another body. In rare cases in which the person has lived a truly exemplary life, his or her essence escapes the cycle of death and reincarnation and becomes one with a deity, which probably is the same thing as uniting with the Real world, the eternal world of Forms.

3. The Real world of Forms is eternal, and each human being's soul or self is eternal. "Eternal" doesn't merely mean "existing from now forever forward into the future." It also means "having existed from now *forever backward into the past.*"

In turn, that means that on at least one occasion each person's soul or self must have been united with the Real world of Forms. In any case, each person's soul or self is *of* or *from* the eternal, unchangeable, Real world of Forms. And that means that *each individual, within him- or herself, already possesses complete and thorough knowledge of the Real world of Forms.*

4. And *that*, in turn, means that human learning, at least insofar as it concerns itself with gaining knowledge of the Real world, is a process of drawing out from each individual that which is already inside of him or her. *That knowledge was acquired by, or "given" to, the individual before birth.* Thus, learning is a process of becoming consciously aware of things that, deep down inside, one already knows. In short: What's worth learning is inside you.[21]

5. How do we learn? To the extent that mathematics and reasoning are not sufficient for all purposes, we learn by taking thought and gaining mystical insight. Mystical insight reveals direct *foreknowledge* of the Forms; it's infallible. As well, it's an ecstatic experience.

Plato in His Own Words

Writing in *Phaedrus*, Plato uses "universals" to mean "Forms":

> But the soul which has never seen the truth will not pass into the human form. For a man must have intelligence of universals, and be able to proceed from the many particulars of sense to one conception of reason;—*this is the recollection of those things which our soul once saw while following God,* when, regardless of that which we now call being, she raised her head up towards the true being.
>
> For . . . *every soul of man has in the way of nature beheld true being*; this was the condition of her passing into the form of man. But all souls not easily recall the things of the other world; they may have seen them for a short time only, or they may have been unfortunate in their earthly lot, and, having had their hearts turned to unrighteousness through some corrupting influence, they may have lost the memory of the holy things which once they saw.[22]

Plato's written works often relate dialogues in which Socrates is portrayed as conversing with his students. Plato uses Socrates to express his—Plato's—own ideas, as we see in *Meno*:

> *Socrates.* [Some priests, priestesses, and poets] say—mark, now, and see whether their words are true—they say that the soul of man is immortal, and at one time has an end,

which is termed dying, and at another time is born again, but is never destroyed. And the moral is, that a man ought to live always in perfect holiness.

The soul then, as being immortal, and having been born again many times, and having *seen all things that exist, whether in this world or in the world below, has knowledge of them all*; and it is no wonder that she should be able to call to remembrance all that she ever knew about virtue, and about everything; for as all nature is akin, and the soul has learned all things, there is no difficulty in her eliciting or as men say learning, out of a single recollection all the rest; if a man is strenuous and does not faint; *for all enquiry and all learning is but recollection*.[23]

ARISTOTLE ADJUSTS PLATO'S CONCEPTS AND STATES HOW MENTAL DEVELOPMENT OCCURS[24]

Aristotle on Forms and Movement

Aristotle (4th century B.C.E.) was Plato's pupil. His collected works are an encyclopedic analysis of virtually everything, including every concept, believed to exist during his times. "How Everything Works" would be a good title for it all. Aristotle's worldview, in broad strokes and in details, became the paradigm for influential Roman Catholic churchmen and other thought leaders in the West for well over 1,000 years, including the Middle Ages. To this day, Aristotle's perspective influences the way we in the West, and especially in the United States, think about the development of the human mind.

Aristotle didn't agree with all of Plato's ideas about "Forms." He agreed that Forms exist and are critically important, but he argued that Plato's view of the Forms erred in that it was unable to account for change, including physical movement and natural growth.

Aristotle's catch-all term for all kinds of change and development was "movement." Plato's idea of fixed, perfect Forms existing in a separate world couldn't deal with movement. So, said Aristotle, instead of Form being separate from matter and confined in another world, form[25] is *embodied in* the matter that we actually perceive with our five senses.[26]

Consider a house. Its form is "house"; its matter is wood or stone. A thing is defined by its form; its essence is its form, not the material out of which it is made. We look at an object and call it "house" because of its form, not because it's made of wood or stone.

In the case of living things, flesh is the matter, said Aristotle, and the soul is its form. (In Greek times, each human, animal, and plant—was believed to have a *psychê*, translated "soul" or "life"; in those days, *psychê* did not imply consciousness.) A corpse is matter without a soul.

Of course, Aristotle had much, *much* more to say about all this; but for our purposes we must acquaint ourselves with only one of his elaborations.

Aristotle's understanding of "movement" concerned ways of answering the question, "Why does movement occur?" Aristotle spoke of four answers, the four "causes" of movement. As explained in *Physics*, Book II, chapter 3, he posits:

- a material cause, because that's what something is made of.
- a formal cause, because that's the essence of something, "what it is."
- an efficient cause, in which case Aristotle is using "cause" as we do today: A house is brought into being (caused) by a carpenter; a living thing is brought into being and given the means to grow into a mature example of its species (caused) by its parents.[27]

- a final cause, the ultimate goal of the entire process, i.e., "that for the sake of which" the process occurs. This is the only cause with which we must acquaint ourselves.

The Teleological Cause and Human Mental Development

In positing a "final cause," Aristotle was stating that all processes leading to "move-ment"—change of any kind including growth and development—have a goal or purpose. The final cause of a process explains why it happens. Aristotle used the Greek word *telos*, meaning "end" in the sense of goal or objective.

Aristotle's students and legions of admirers, during his own times and far beyond those ancient times, learned to believe that all processes are *teleological*, i.e., that each one has as its objective the completion of a purposeful action or the attainment of a final state of being.

For us, here's the key point: In the case of a living thing, attaining its ultimate objective through growth and development is synonymous with attaining its form. At the begin-ning of its life, a living thing carries the potential to reach full maturity, which is its essence or form. The inherent potential to attain its mature form is part of the essence of each living thing.

That's our key point for two reasons: First, it's a perspective put forth by the philoso-pher who, far more than any other, supremely dominated Western thought, and especial-ly Roman Catholic thought, for over a thousand years. Second, this dominant point of view was applied not merely to physical and physiological growth and development of all "living things," *but also to the mental growth and development of human beings.* This is a critical fact that will reappear again and again throughout this book.

Aristotle in His Own Words

In translation, *telos* (purposeful final objective) becomes "end."

> If then it is both by nature and for an end that the swallow makes its nest and the spider its web, and plants grow leaves for the sake of the fruit and send their roots down (not up) for the sake of nourishment, it is plain that this kind of cause is operative in things which come to be and are by nature. And since "nature" means two things, the matter and the form, of which the latter is the end, and since all the rest is for the sake of the end, the form must be the cause in the sense of "that for the sake of which."[28]
>
> The necessary in nature, then, is plainly what we call by the name of matter, and the changes in it. Both causes must be stated by the physicist, but especially the end: for that is the cause of the matter, not *vice versa*; and the end is "that for the sake of which," and the beginning starts from the definition or essence; as in artificial products, since a house is of such-and-such a kind, certain things must *necessarily* come to be or be there al-ready....[29]
>
> For those things are natural which, *by a continuous movement originated from an internal principle*, arrive at some completion: the same completion is not reached from every principle; nor any chance completion, but always the tendency in each is towards the same end, *if there is no impediment.*[30]

Aristotle implies that each human is born with an internal principle—a potential acquired by, or "given" to, him or her *before birth*—that will purposefully, inexorably, automatically convey his or her *mental capacity* to attain its mature essence or "form," if there is no impediment.

A Fateful View of Child Development

Aristotle's view has two powerful implications:

- Externally applied help or encouragement is not needed for a child's mind to attain its mature form. Parents, teachers, and mentors can relax, for the process is inexorable.
- Internally applied effort is not needed, either. Intentionality, "will power," and deliberate exertion by the child simply aren't useful. Again, the process is inexorable. Just wait!

These two Aristotelian points of view are extremely important for us to keep in mind.

Finally, take special note of the phrase "if there is no impediment." At another point in this same discourse, Aristotle uses another phrase, "if nothing interferes."[31] These phrases underscore Aristotle's belief that attainment of the mature form *will occur*. He allows only the possibility of negative effects, i.e., the possibility of impediments or interferences.

MUSINGS AND SPECULATIONS

The Greeks viewed learning very largely as a process involving thought, yielding awareness. Little is said about the acquisition of behavioral skills or gains in practical adaptation to one's environment. I speculate that Greek philosophers became fascinated by the human capacity for *internal* (unvoiced) thought and the astonishing ability of a human being's thought, as it were, to "stand outside" of the individual and contemplate him or her as an object.

WHY CHAPTER 2 IS IMPORTANT

In this chapter, you have been introduced to two historical facts of transcendent importance for your understanding of the deep origins of the aptitude myth.

First, you've encountered Plato's belief that each person enters this world *already possessing* extremely valuable knowledge. And you've encountered Aristotle, who argued that attainment of the mature human form necessarily occurs, driven by a purposeful internal principle "given" before birth, and that this applies to biological *and mental* development. This process *will occur*, depending neither on external support *nor on the person's own intentional effort*.

In chapters 3 through 16, you'll see these ancient Greek views surface again and again, and you will come to understand that they remain a strong, persistent undercurrent within today's western-contemporary paradigm for thinking about children's learning and classroom teaching.

The "What to Remember" list for chapter 2 is found at TheAptitudeMyth.info.

GENEALOGICAL CHART: TRACING THE PATH TO A MODERN AMERICAN PARADIGM

Chapters 2 through 16 are each complemented by a genealogical chart, "Tracing the Path of a Modern American Paradigm." Each chart integrates the "Key Beliefs" discussed in its chapter; these are then traced throughout the subsequent charts. All the charts are found at TheAptitudeMyth.info.

"Tracing the Path of a Modern American Paradigm" enables the reader to gain greater awareness of the historical origins, and the development over many centuries of the beliefs or value propositions, that supply the paradigm that many Americans apply today when thinking about and discussing children, learning, parenting, and teaching.

Viewing these charts will significantly increase the reader's overall comprehension of the history and centuries-long impact of the beliefs that are being related in *The Aptitude Myth*.

NOTES

1. Plato, *Meno*, in B. Jowett, *Dialogues of Plato*, 3rd ed. (Macmillan, 1892), vol. II, 40.

2. For this chapter I have been guided primarily by Bertrand Russell's *History of Western Philosophy* (Simon & Schuster, 1945). Also useful was Charles H. Kahn, *Pythagoras and the Pythagoreans: A Brief History* (Hackett, 2001). I consulted other works but found that most have little to say about the deep origins of Platonic Realism.

3. See Aristotle, *Metaphysics*, Book I, chapters 5 and 6. After discussing the views of earlier philosophers, primarily the Pythagoreans, in chapter 5, Aristotle begins chapter 6 saying, "After the systems we have named came the philosophy of Plato, *which in most respects followed these thinkers*, but had peculiarities. . . ." In J. A. Smith and W. D. Ross, *The Works of Aristotle, Volume VIII Metaphysica* (Oxford: Clarendon Press, 1908), no page numbers [italics added].

4. One way these connections survived in educational practice is in the medieval "quadrivium," a curricular grouping that linked arithmetic, geometry, music, and astronomy. (The other medieval curricular grouping was the "trivium," which linked grammar, rhetoric, and logic, inspired by Greek philosophers known as sophists.)

5. Aristotle, *Metaphysics*, Book I, chapter 5, in J. A. Smith and W. D. Ross, *op. cit.*, no page numbers.

6. Empiricism also traces its beginnings to ancient Greece; it is said to have originated in Miletus, a city in Ionia (on the western coast of Asia Minor).

7. For this account I am relying on Russell, *op. cit.*, 14–24. For basic information about Bacchus (Dionysus), I'm relying on George E. Duckworth, "Dionysus," *Collier's Encyclopedia* (Collier's, 1997), vol. 8, 240.

8. *Ibid.*, 16. Russell says that, etymologically, this is the meaning of "enthusiasm."

9. I repeat here the opinion of Russell, *ibid.*, 17.

10. Some Romans did, too. In Rome, "Bacchanalia" were festivals said to include gross immoralities; they were prohibited by the Roman Senate in 186 B.C.E. H. J. Rose, "Bacchanalia," *Collier's, op. cit.*, vol. 3, 432.

11. For the account in this paragraph and the next I have relied on Russell, *ibid.*, 17–19; Kahn, *op. cit.*, 3–4; and George E. Duckworth, "Orpheus," *Collier's Encyclopedia* (Collier's, 1997), vol. 18, 230.

12. For this account of Indian philosophy I have relied on Kahn, *op. cit.*, 19; Joseph W. Elder, "Hinduism," *Collier's Encyclopedia* (Collier's, 1997), vol. 12, 132; T. M. P. Mahadevan, "Indian Philosophy," *ibid*, vol. 12, 639–40; and Clarence H. Hamilton, "Buddha and Buddhism," *ibid.*, vol. 4, 661.

13. It is possible for Indian beliefs to have made their way eastward prior to Pythagorean times. After the military campaigns of Cyrus (died 530 B.C.E.), the Persian empire extended from Greek-speaking Ionia eastward all the way to the Indus River. Some scholars believe that Greeks and Indians met annually at a New Year festival at Persepolis. Legend has it that Pythagoras himself visited India. Kahn, *op. cit.*, 19, including note 36.

14. The capitalized word "Real" in the context of this discussion and others designates a belief that something unperceivable by human beings' five senses nevertheless has objective existence. Another way of expressing this belief is to say that whatever is Real is "independent of experience"; it is not imaginary or phenomenal.

15. Kahn, *op. cit.*, 11; Kahn, in turn, cites an account of Pythagoras's near contemporary, Xenophanes.

16. Russell, *op. cit.*, 34–35.

17. Deductive logic was invented by Aristotle, who lived two centuries after Pythagoras. Aristotle is discussed later within this chapter, but here seemed to be the most advantageous place to bring up the process and implications of deductive reasoning for the first time (because it's closely related to mathematical reasoning).

18. John Burnet, *Early Greek Philosophy*, 2nd ed. (Adam and Charles Black, 1908), 150.

19. Russell, *op. cit.*, 49 note; Russell attributes this paraphrase (of a *very* confusing statement from antiquity!) to John Burnet, *Early Greek Philosophy* (no date, no page).

20. A clear discussion about this notion appears in Plato's *Republic*, near the beginning of Book X.

21. Plato's essay *Theatetus* is devoted to demonstrating that knowledge is neither a product of, nor dependent on, sense perception. For example, ". . . for we no longer seek for knowledge in perception at all, but in that other process, however called, in which the mind is alone and engaged with being." Plato, *Theatetus*, in *Great Books of the Western World*, vol. 7, "Plato" (Encyclopedia Britannica with the editorial advice of the University of Chicago, 1952), 536 [paragraph at mark 187].

22. Plato, *Phaedrus*, in B. Jowett, *op. cit.*, 455–56 [italics added].

23. Plato, *Meno*, in *ibid.*, 40 [italics added].

24. For this discussion I am indebted to Philip Cary, "Lecture Seven: Aristotle—Metaphysics," *Great Minds of the Western Intellectual Tradition, Part I: Classical Origins* (The Teaching Company, 2000), 31–34. I'm indebted, too, to Kieran Egan for alerting me to the critical importance, and enduring impact, of Aristotle's way of thinking about "Forms"; Egan, *Getting It Wrong from the Beginning* (Yale University Press, 2002), 46, 69, 76, 80–82.

25. The word "form" will not be capitalized when the reference is to Aristotle's conception.

26. Because Aristotle took this position, he is often claimed to be an empiricist or at least a forerunner of empiricism.

27. Aristotle spoke of the third answer only as "cause," not as "efficient cause." The latter term was applied by later Aristotelians. "Efficient" has its original meaning: "bringing about an effect." Cary, *op.cit.*, 33.

28. Aristotle, *Physics*, Book II, chapter 8 [near end of 199a]; in vol. 8, *Great Books of the Western World*, 276.

29. *Ibid.*, chapter 9 [end 200a, beginning 200b], 277 [italics in original].

30. *Ibid.*, chapter 8 [199b], 277 [italics added].

31. *Ibid.* [199a].

THREE

New Views of the Natural World

And all depends on keeping the eye steadily fixed upon the facts of nature and so receiving their images simply as they are. For God forbid that we should give out a dream of our own imagination for a pattern of the world. . . .

—Francis Bacon[1]

Near the mid-point of the 15th century, in 1440 to be exact, an invention appeared that had an incalculable impact on the course of western history, and eventually on world history.[2] I refer, of course, to Johann Gutenberg's interchangeable type. Soon it became possible to print reading materials infinitely more efficiently and less expensively than ever before.

Within 300 years, books in vernacular languages (instead of Latin) become available as well as affordable for members of the monied classes, and later for people of modest means. By the middle of the 18th century, popularizations of science, accounts of explorers, and works of fiction (among many other topics of books) become so widespread that works by well-known painters began to include depictions of a solitary individual reading a book.

Around the beginning of the 16th century, it began to become practical and economical for reading, thinking people in one geographical location to exchange ideas with similarly-minded people in other locations. Inexpensively printed words[3] collected in books made this possible. From that beginning, the story we're following slowly got underway during the 16th century and began to gather speed during the 17th century. By the 18th century, affordable documents were transforming the views and day-to-day lives of ever more people, not only throughout Europe but also in the fledgling United States.

LIFE, LEARNING, AND LOGIC IN 15TH AND 16TH CENTURY EUROPE

Our lives today are so infused with the concepts and products of science that it's difficult to imagine that, 600 years ago, *none* of this was even remotely foreseen. To the extent that people in the 15th century took time to contemplate their environment at all, they accepted the pronouncements of authorities, virtually all of whom were Roman Catholic leaders.

Among those religious figures, and among the very few others with the leisure and the inclination to devote time to simply thinking, the dominant philosophy for hundreds of years had been scholasticism.[4] This name is derived from *scholasticus*, applied to the people who administered the schools attached to cathedrals. The main characteristics of scholasticism were that it concerned itself largely with issues related to Christianity, that it drew heavily on the Greek classical traditions, and that it made use of specific approaches to thinking and teaching.

Although they were churchmen, the scholastics never thought of rejecting classical learning as pagan; on the contrary, they drew heavily on Platonic Realism. Then, around the beginning of the 13th century—and this is important—Aristotle's major treatises finally became available in Latin translation. Thereafter, the churchmen seem to have become mesmerized by the application of Aristotelian deduction and similar approaches to strictly logical thinking.

As explained in chapter 2, deductive logic basically involves a precise mental process of constructing a "syllogism" such that, if its premises are accurate, then its conclusion *must* be accurate (and the argument is said to be "valid"). What's important is that *deductive logic need not necessarily depend on empirical observation using the five senses.* It is entirely possible to construct elaborate, erudite deductive arguments about concerns such as how many angels can dance on the head of a pin and other wholly ethereal matters.

Relying on Aristotelian approaches, then, the scholastics developed a rigid framework for intellectual inquiry that remains today as a key connotation of "scholasticism": formally posing a question and stating two possible answers, analyzing it in the light of various authorities, considering all arguments in favor of one side and then the other side, deciding which answer is correct, and refuting point-by-point the arguments on the losing side. This process was called a *disputation.* Most questions addressed in this way concerned Christian belief and practice.

The disputation process was carried over into classrooms, where a lecturer might argue both sides of a question or hold a disputation with a student or another lecturer. Candidates for advanced degrees had to prove their learning via a lengthy disputation; this is the origin of today's doctoral dissertation defense.[5]

The Methods of the Scholastics and the Jesuits

For our purposes, the significance of scholasticism is that its methods were highly verbal and intellectual, relying on the received wisdom of classical and religious authorities, and proceeding largely by means of syllogistic reasoning and other forms of deductive logic. The "truth" of any proposition rarely depended on observational references but rather on its being in harmony, often explicitly, with unquestioned doctrine. Issues and their resolutions took place within the context of Christian belief and Aristotelian logic.

Thus, the products of scholasticism were much more about *verbal* distinctions among *otherworldly* beliefs than about generating fresh factual discoveries or useful real-life practices. Knowledge of the natural world stagnated where Aristotle had left it two millennia earlier.[6]

We cannot take leave of this topic without noting that, during the 16th century, the disputation and many other methods of scholasticism were adopted by the Jesuits, who systematized classroom instruction to a degree rarely equaled before or since. Their rules and precepts were all written down in the *Ratio Atque Institutio Studiorum Societatis Jesu*—or simply the *Ratio Studiorum*—first disseminated to all Jesuit schools in 1586, then revised in 1599.

Drawing on the works of the Roman philosopher Quintillian and the Italian humanist Vittorinoda Feltre, the *Ratio Studiorum* set forth an instructional approach emphasizing thorough and systematic repetition of the material to be learned. It made use of lectures, dictations, disputations and debates, exercises, dramas including both tragedies and comedies, competitions, examinations, and demonstrations of public approval for the most accomplished learners.

The Jesuits wrote guidelines for student motivation, classroom presentation, assessment, punishment, practice, and the general treatment of learners. They made use of emulation and rivalry. They even planned for physical education and periods of relaxation; it's said that the good fathers tolerated the young men's pub visits and the occasional resulting disturbances.[7]

NEW VIEWS BEGIN TO EMERGE LATE IN THE 16TH CENTURY

As the 16th century drew to a close, scholasticism's grip on religious and conceptual thought, and its preoccupation with Aristotelian patterns of thought and debate, began to loosen. Fresh perspectives on the natural world and, more significantly, new approaches to learning and thinking about that world, began to appear in Europe. Three thought leaders stand out as taking giant steps in this direction: Francis Bacon, René Descartes, and Isaac Newton.

Francis Bacon

Bacon (1561–1626) got his start as a student at Trinity College, Cambridge, with which he became totally unimpressed. He compared his professors to "becalmed ships; they never move but by the wind of other men's breath," and observed that they were "shut up in the cells of a few authors, chiefly Aristotle their dictator." He criticized the disputation, referring to its intricate logical gambits as "the ostentation of dispute," and adding that he came as a guest and not as an enemy.[8] Eventually becoming Lord Chancellor of England, Bacon is remembered today as a philosopher who made people's mundane concerns his central interest, challenging the wordiness and otherworldliness of medieval thought.[9]

Bacon wasn't particularly interested in education, but his influence on people's thinking about education was great because he emerged as a leading philosopher of knowledge. Bacon advocated that the objective of all knowledge acquisition was to enable humans to gain control over nature. The way to acquire practically useful knowledge, he said, was to (1) set aside all preconceptions about how the world works; (2) stop thinking exclusively by means of deductive reasoning; (3) employ all five senses to directly observe facts and gather data from the surrounding world of nature; and then (4) think about them using a mental tool that wasn't new but had lain dormant for 2,000 years: *inductive reasoning*.[10]

Induction—from the Latin *in* + *ducere*, "to lead in"—is the mental process of gradually attaining a generalization (or "law") about how a portion of the world works *after* using the five senses to carefully observe many individual cases of the relevant phenomenon.[11] This process is also known as "summative induction" and "induction by simple enumeration." The resulting generalization is held *tentatively* because future observations, if any, might lead to an adjustment in the original generalization.

In other words, any generalization is viewed as "very probably true." Inductive thinkers tend to be—and *need* to be—open-minded due to this necessity to remain tentative about their conclusions. Observation-based inductive reasoning became, and to this day remains, the principal method of experimental science.

Let's briefly consider the roles of inductive and deductive reasoning in modern science. (The two reasoning styles are often confused; this could be due, in part, to Arthur Conan Doyle's widely read novels in which Sherlock Holmes makes many "amazing deductions" that are, in fact, fine examples of *inductions!*) From a scientist's perspective, the critical question about any deduction is, *What is the basis of its axioms or first principles?*

In the scientific enterprise, they must come from observations by the senses (i.e., they must be *empirical* in origin). If they do, then deduction has a critical role to play because it provides indispensable support for clear thinking about the individual cases and the generalization.

What concerned Francis Bacon, however, were instances (extremely common in his day) in which the axiom or first principle had been handed down from an authoritarian source—a tribal or family elder (e.g., grandfather), an oracle (e.g., Delphi), a book (e.g., the *Koran*), a sage (e.g., Confucius), a political or ideological leader (e.g., Julius Caesar), or a revelation received from a superior being (e.g., by St. Paul on the road to Damascus). The prototype for all authoritative sources was Aristotle, whose voluminous pronouncements about how everything in the world works had been accepted without question, and without verification, for some 2,000 years.

In all of these cases, the handed-down axiom or principle was assumed to be *The Truth*, i.e., to be accurate and applicable—not the same as being observable by the five senses. Beginning with *assumed* Truth, a deductive process is capable of proceeding to arrive at a *logically valid* conclusion—not the same as arriving at an empirically verifiable conclusion.

Bacon put it this way: "And all depends on keeping the eye steadily fixed upon the facts of nature and so receiving their images simply as they are. For God forbid that we should give out a dream of our own imagination for a pattern of the world. . . ."[12]

René Descartes

Descartes (1596–1650) also broke from religious and classical authority; he advocated reliance on reason to distinguish truth from error. In his influential *Discourse on Method* (1637), he argued that people should doubt all of their beliefs, excepting only those of which they are absolutely certain. Descartes advocated that one should remain permanently skeptical about whatever he or she believes true in spite of the source of each belief.

Like his partial contemporary, Bacon, Descartes didn't address education, but his views were influential among the brothers of two teaching congregations who operated schools in France during the early 1600s, including the innovative Little Schools of Port Royal. The founder of the Little Schools, the Abbot of St. Cyan, was influenced by Descartes's call for clear thinking. The Abbot guided the brothers' effort to understand child nature and to find instructional methods that would "remove every avoidable difficulty from the way of their pupils."[13]

Although Descartes was similar to Bacon in some respects, he was very much unlike Bacon in others. So dedicated to the promotion of systematic doubt was Descartes that he distrusted human beings' five senses as a means of verifying statements. He was *not* an empiricist; he trusted only thought. Sounding like a Pythagorean, Descartes wrote, "The only principles which I accept, or require, in physics are those of geometry and pure mathematics. Those principles explain all natural phenomena."[14]

Preoccupied with the indubitable,[15] Descartes was a thoroughgoing deductivist. We remember him today as the originator of *Cogito ergo sum*, commonly rendered in English as "I think therefore I am." But that rendering is misleading. A more accurate interpretation is, "It is only through *thought*, not sense experience, that one can say that he or she has existence."[16]

Isaac Newton

The third thought leader espousing new views of the natural world was, according to most commentators, one of the most brilliant and influential thinkers in all of recorded history: Sir Isaac Newton (1642–1727).[17] You've probably heard the story of Newton and the apple. It's true. When he was in his early 20s he really did observe an apple falling from a tree just as he happened to be pondering what type of force could hold the moon in its course around the earth. That led to his establishment of the laws of universal gravitation. In addition, he developed the fundamentals of optical physics and invented calculus. In many ways Newton reorganized the study of all physical phenomena.

Newton (1) began with observed facts; (2) reasoned inductively to a hypothesis (a tentative generalization) that was expressed in mathematical terms and that *seemed to* explain those facts; (3) figured out the likely consequences if the hypothesis were true; then (4) determined through more observations and experiments whether the predicted consequences actually occurred. From Newton's methods there eventually emerged a fundamental and permanent reconceptualization of how scientifically-minded people should go about trying to understand the natural universe.

NEW VIEWS ENCOUNTER SCHOLARLY
SKEPTICISM BEFORE GAINING CREDIBILITY

Bacon, Descartes, and especially Newton enjoyed prominence in their own time, but it's important to recognize that their pronouncements did not suddenly change minds. Quite the contrary. What was then known as "natural philosophy" was widely held in low esteem, even subjected to public ridicule, well into the 18th century.

As with all new ways of understanding the world, natural philosophy began by being adopted by a tiny number of thought leaders. Academies of science had been founded in London, Paris, Berlin, and St. Petersburg beginning in the mid-17th century; operating under royal patronage, they had almost no popular impact. Newton's *Principia Mathematica* (1687) impressed some members of the academies and other intellectuals, who often were called "philosophes."

But there were other philosophes, most notably the German Gottfried-Wilhelm Leibniz, who attacked Newton as merely dabbling in "occult power." Leibniz's accusation resonated with some because, as the 17th century was drawing to a close, many thought leaders were beginning to be openly suspicious of anything that, like religion, even remotely resembled superstition.

Gradually, the triad of René Descartes's systematic doubt, Francis Bacon's observation-based inductive method, and Isaac Newton's law-governed view of nature began to prevail among the tiny sliver of the population with the ability to read and enough leisure to attend to such matters.

But the times were right for this mindset to gain traction, especially in northern Europe. The Reformation there had championed the notion that each individual was responsible for interpreting the Bible on the basis of his or her own reasoning; people were not totally reliant on the mediation and authority of priests. Non-theological thinkers such as John Locke were emphasizing a way of being in the world that focused on not only the autonomous individual but also his or her own experience and observation. And the philosophes had become wary of total reliance on a glorious historical past—the primary focus of classical humanists as well as of religious leaders—for wisdom and guidance.

As a result, the perspectives of Bacon, Descartes, and Newton began to gain adherents. Even though many of the philosophes were unable to penetrate the complex mathematical equations of *Principia Mathematica*, they did grasp that Newton was positing a mechanistic, *law-governed* universe comprehensible by human beings.

To the philosophes, the idea of a law-governed universe translated into a belief that similar methods could be used to understand humans and their society—and perhaps even to *improve* humans and their society. Thought leaders began to speak of "natural law" and to direct their attention, not backward to glorious antiquity, but forward to a time when daily life would be transformed by the application of reason.

Three widely known occurrences during the 18th century—the century known to us, and to contemporaries, as "The Enlightenment"—helped impel the growth of interest among the public in "natural philosophy." First, an earthquake struck Lisbon in 1755 and took the lives of some 10,000 inhabitants. The philosophes, especially François-Marie Voltaire in his novel *Candide,* used this event to pillory those who believed in the goodness of God, or even that God exists.

Second, during 1783 in Paris, and later elsewhere, a "philosophical experiment" became one of the most heavily attended, widely discussed, and ultimately iconic events of the century: the ascent, with passengers, of hot-air balloons. Benjamin Franklin, one of the attendees, spoke of the mass enthusiasm generated by this spectacle.

Finally, significant explorations of distant lands and peoples were carried out during the 18th century. James Cook made three voyages to the Pacific, and Vitus Behring visited the Aleutian islanders. They and others brought back plants, artifacts, and amazing stories of encounters with very different kinds of human beings. The new passage to the East Indies around the Cape of Good Hope began to bring exotic goods into coastal cities.

With details flooding in about alternative ways of living, thinking, deciding—ways of *being* in the world—Europeans in ever growing numbers began to take the advice of Descartes and questioned the eternal verities by which they and generations of their forefathers had been living.

EUROPE IN THE 15TH AND 18TH CENTURIES: COMPARING OLD AND NEW PARADIGMS

As the 18th century ended, "natural philosophy" was exciting the interests, and even the passions, of a rapidly growing number of Europeans. Middle-class people spoke often and approvingly of "nature" and "natural law." Books, ever more widely available, did their best to make difficult concepts accessible to the public (including *Newton for Ladies*). The lavishly illustrated, multi-volume *Encyclopaedie* was completed by Denis Diderot and Jean D'Alembert, as was another multi-volume *Histoire Naturelle*, about all living creatures, by Georges-Louis Buffon. An elaborate system of classification of plants was developed by Carl Linnaeus. The study of anatomy made huge advances. Interest in personal and public health burgeoned, including the revolutionary notions that illness was not a punishment from God and that individuals could proactively take steps to improve their own health. Many additional examples could be given to demonstrate that "reason" and what we now call "science" were overtaking European thought.

In comparison with Europe throughout the 15th century, Europe at the close of the 18th century harbored a small but highly influential fraction of the population with the capacity, the curiosity, and the leisure to inquire about and categorize the natural world. This new mindset was sharply different from the one that had prevailed during the medieval era, when everything worth knowing was assumed to be known already, to be complete and stable, so that society's objective was to insure that important knowledge was passed, intact and unchanged, from one generation to the next. That perspective likely was responsible, in part, for the prevalence of memorization as an instructional method in the very few schools in existence throughout the Middle Ages.[18]

But by the end of the 18th century, Europeans who were able to read and had the leisure to do so were all abuzz about the methods, discoveries, and potentials of science. In most of their social circles, one got respect by demonstrating awareness of science . . . or at least by pretending to do so. In the following chapters, we will see the growing influence of an inquiring mindset on the ways in which the influential Europeans thought about the rearing and education of children.

MUSINGS AND SPECULATIONS

Inductive reasoning is "evidence-based" whereas deductive reasoning *of the type that does not begin with observation-established facts* is "belief-based." The latter term is not usually applied to deductive thinking. But whenever deduction begins with an axiom or first principle that was handed down by an authoritarian source, then "belief-based" or even "faith-based" is accurate.

WHY CHAPTER 3 IS IMPORTANT

The inductivist or empiricist method is the foundation of modern science, a highly influential force in our own times. In subsequent chapters we will explore (a) how the empiricist view helped to spawn a new perspective on classroom teaching and (b) how it also was marshaled as "objective science" into the service of those who were promoting ideas about the human mind that were not evidence-based, being traceable back to Greek speculations.

At TheApitudeMyth.info are the genealogical chart and "What to Remember" list for chapter 3.

NOTES

1. James Spedding et al., eds, *The Works of Francis Bacon, Volume III* (Hurd and Houghton, 1864), 53.
2. Useful in my preparation of this chapter was R. Freeman Butts, *The Education of the West* (McGraw-Hill, 1973), 183–220. Also influential were Tim Blanning, *The Pursuit of Glory: Europe 1648-1815* (Viking, 2007), 456–521; Gerald L. Gutek, *A History of the Western Educational Experience*, 2nd ed. (Waveland, 1995), 159–73; Denis Lawton and Peter Gordon, *A History of Western Educational Ideas* (Woburn, 2002), 87–100; and Dorinda Outram, *Panorama of the Enlightenment* (Getty Publications, 2006), 8–21 and 238–77.
3. The words needed to be printed inexpensively and stated in a language other than Greek or Latin. Innovators found they could prosper by writing in the vernacular. Timothy Ferris, *The Science of Liberty* (Harper, 2010), 40.
4. For these paragraphs on scholasticism I have relied primarily on Gutek, *op. cit.*, 102–3; Butts, *op. cit.*, 168–70; Bertrand Russell, *The History of Western Philosophy* (Simon & Schuster, 1945), 428–39; and Harry S. Broudy and John R. Palmer, *Exemplars of Teaching Method* (Rand McNally, 1965), 59–70.
5. Broudy and Palmer, *ibid.*, 64–68, 88–92.
6. The following quote illustrates scholasticism's dependence on authority: "At the time when the discovery of spots on the sun first began to circulate, a student called the attention of his old professor to the rumor, and received the following reply: 'There can be no spots on the sun, for I have read Aristotle twice from beginning to end, and he says the sun is incorruptible. Clean your lenses, and if the spots are not in the telescope, they must be in your eyes!'" Gabriel Compayré, *The History of Pedagogy* (D. C. Heath, 1889), 74, note 1. Compayré in turn cites Naville, *La Logique de l'Hypothèse*, no date, no page.
7. Broudy and Palmer, *op. cit.* 64–68, 88–92; and Ivana Čornejová, "The Jesuit School and John Amos Comenius," in *Homage to J. A. Comenius* (Karolinum, 1991), 84–89.
8. The Francis Bacon quotes were all found in Timothy Ferris, *The Science of Liberty* (Harper, 2010), 46–48. Ferris, in turn, cites for "becalmed ships," Basil Montagu, *The Life of Francis Bacon, Lord Chancellor of England* (Pickering, 1833), 10; for "shut up in the cells of," *ibid.*, 7; for "the ostentation of dispute," Bacon, *Novum Organum, Book 1*, no date; and for "came as a guest," Thomas Babington Macaulay, *The Life and Writings of Francis Bacon, Lord Chancellor of England* (Edinburgh Review, 1837), no page.
9. This overview of Francis Bacon's philosophy relies primarily on William Boyd and Edmund J. King, *The History of Western Education*, 12th ed. (Barnes & Noble Books, 1995), 234–37.

10. Inductive reasoning was recognized by Aristotle—in *Prior Analytics, Book II,* for example, he writes, "For induction proceeds through an enumeration of all the cases" (chapter 23)—because he was interested in how the premises of a deductive argument can be known. Aristotle viewed induction as, at best, a contributing factor to the overall excellence of deduction.

11. This explanation of inductive reasoning partially relies on Ferris, *op. cit.,* 13, 45; Russell, *op. cit.,* 199; and Richard DeHaan, "Induction," in *Collier's Encyclopedia* (P. F. Collier, 1997), vol. 12, 729. Note that the Latin term for induction, *a posteriori,* means "from the latter," i.e., from thought following a previous process (observation).

12. Spedding et al., *op. cit.,* 53.

13. Boyd and King, *op. cit.,* 256–59; quote from p. 259. They see the Abbot's efforts as the origin of "child study," which emerged in the late 1800s as an international movement (see chapter 15).

14. Ferris, *op. cit.,* 53; Ferris in turn cites Peter Dear, *Revolutionizing the Sciences: European Knowledge and Its Ambitions, 1500–1700* (Princeton, 2001), 88.

15. "Preoccupied with the indubitable" paraphrases a Ferris quote of Bernard Williams, found in "René Descartes," in Paul Edwards, ed., *The Encyclopedia of Philosophy* (Macmillan, 1967), vol. 2, 346.

16. This insightful interpretation closely paraphrases Outram, *op. cit.,* 14.

17. For basic facts about Isaac Newton and his contributions to science, I've relied on Robert Schlaap's entry about Newton in *Collier's Encyclopedia* (Collier's, 1997), vol. 17, 467–71.

18. Frederick Eby and Charles F. Arrowood, *The History and Philosophy of Education Ancient and Medieval* (Prentice-Hall, 1940), 929–30.

FOUR

New Views of Human Consciousness and Learning

. . . All knowledge begins by sensuous perception; then through the medium of the imagination it enters the province of the memory; then, by dwelling on the particulars, comprehension of the universal arises; while finally comes judgment on the facts that have been grasped. . . .

—John Amos Comenius[1]

During the Middle Ages, only a miniscule fraction of Europe's inhabitants had the leisure or the interest to reflect on the nature of human beings.[2] But among the very few who did, shifting perspectives appeared as early as the 15th century. We've already noted the focus on individual autonomy engendered by the Protestant Reformation. This attention to the individual was matched by southern European teachers who called themselves Humanists (*umanista* in Italian).

HUMANISM AND REALISM DURING THE RENAISSANCE

The 15th, 16th, and 17th centuries in Europe are known as the Renaissance—from the French *re* + *naissance*, "again born"—a rebirth of interest in art, music, literature, and philosophy from the classical past. The Renaissance figure with the greatest name recognition in our own time is Leonardo da Vinci, who possessed an astonishing breadth of artistic and intellectual abilities.

Some historians caution that it's misleading to conceive of the Renaissance as being wholly about the fine arts. More significant, they say, is the "attainment of *self-conscious freedom* by the human spirit" in Europe.[3] One way that self-awareness of human capacities came about was that Humanists revived interest in Greek and Roman perspectives on human beings, then formulated beliefs about human excellence that are still with us today.

This focus on human capabilities is nicely captured by the Italian prodigy Giovanni Pico della Mirandola (1463–1494), in whose influential work *De hominis dignitate* [Oration on the Dignity of Man] appears this imagined statement by God to Adam in the Garden of Eden:

We have given you, O Adam, no . . . endowment properly your own, in order that whatever . . . gifts you may . . . select, these same you may have and possess through your own judgement and decision. The nature of all other creatures is defined and restricted . . . ; you, by contrast, impeded by no such restrictions, may, by your own free will . . . trace for yourself the lineaments of your own nature. We have made you . . . the free and proud shaper of your own being. . . . It will be in your power to descend to the lower, brutish forms of life; you will be able, through your own decision, to rise again to the superior orders whose life is divine.[4]

Humanistic ideas had very little to do with science. Their significance was that they pointed to human uniqueness, to the possibility of free will and self-assertion, and to the supremacy of human beings over the natural world—at least potentially.

One scholar has argued that a key link between the renewed interest in classical antiquity and the new interest in individual potential is that some people had a ". . . yearning toward antiquity . . ., a burning aspiration to be numbered with the mighty men of old. It was the universal object of the humanists to gain a consciousness of self distinguished from the vulgar herd, and to achieve this by joining the great company of bards and sages, whose glory could not perish."[5]

Thanks to the printing press, such ideas began to infiltrate the worldview of the middle and aristocratic classes, very small in number but very large in influence. And the middle class was growing because of the revival of city life and the increase in profitable international trade.

We can gain insight into the newly emerging views of human nature by tracing a shift in the meaning of the word "realism." Realism had been strongly linked with the philosophy of Plato; it was he, you'll recall, who posited a parallel world of the "Real"—a place inhabited by perfect concepts, or "Forms." Plato maintained that *this alternate reality is waiting inside each person to be released.* Plato's acceptance of universal, perfect Truths made his ideas deeply appealing to Roman Catholic theologians; thus, Platonic "Realism" was very influential across two millennia.

The meaning of "realism" evolved during the 16th, 17th, and 18th centuries. The ground for this change had been prepared by Renaissance humanism, which was shifting the focus of philosophers away from Platonic intangibles and toward the wonders and potentials of actual human beings, not only in themselves but also within their social and physical environments. Two thought leaders contributed to this shift in the perspectives of educated Europeans.

COMENIUS, LOCKE, AND THE RISE OF *SENSE* REALISM

John Amos Comenius (1592–1670) was the bishop of a small Protestant sect as well as being, arguably, the most widely influential educator of the 17th century. I deliberately say "*widely* influential" because Comenius, whose native place was Moravia (now a region of the Czech Republic), became an active contributor to educational endeavors in Sweden, Hungary, Poland, and England, usually because the civil or religious authorities invited him to come.

Comenius was the author, among many other publications, of *Orbis Sensualium Pictus* (roughly, "The World Sensed via Pictures"). This was a textbook for children that, from its appearance around 1650 until the early 1800s, was used all across the Western world— it eventually appeared in 14 languages—as the only schoolbook with drawings of a wide range of objects. Comenius prepared this book because, influenced by Francis Bacon's observation-based inductive method, he advocated that *instructors encourage learners to use their own five senses* to study objects, illustrations, and other realia found wholly in the external world.

In Comenius's influential 1657 publication for educators, *Didactica Magna* ("Great Didactic"), he offered a fresh perspective on classroom instruction in which the learners

. . . be made to exercise, first their senses (for this is the easiest), then the memory, then the comprehension, and finally the judgment. In this way a graded sequence will take place; for all knowledge begins by sensuous perception; then through the medium of the imagination it enters the province of the memory; then, by dwelling on the particulars, comprehension of the universal arises; while finally comes judgment on the facts that have been grasped, and in this way our knowledge is firmly established.[6]

The second thought leader might need no introduction, for the political philosophy of John Locke (1632–1704) played a major role in the thinking of the North American leaders who declared independence in 1776; we'll focus on that side of Locke in chapter 6. Locke also thought and wrote about knowledge, its acquisition, and its uses. In fact, among his 17th century contemporaries, Locke's claim to fame was largely due to his brilliant *Essay Concerning Human Understanding* (1690, published after 17 years of labor).

Only three years later, Locke completed *Some Thoughts Concerning Education.*[7] Here Locke wrote that children are like the fountains of rivers, which may be directed in various courses by "a gentle Application of the Hand." His opinion was that "of all the Men we meet with, nine Parts of ten are what they are, good or evil, useful or not, by their Education."[8] By "education," Locke meant all of the formative experiences throughout a young person's environment, only one of which is classroom learning. He concluded that in order for a child's behavior to become permanently guided by whatever is being learned, the learning must be practiced multiple times:

> But pray remember, Children are *not* to be *taught by Rules* which will be always slipping out of their Memories. What you think necessary for them to do, settle in them by an indispensable Practice, as often as the Occasion returns; and if it be possible, make Occasions.[9]

Locke Emphasizes the Malleability of the Young

These quotes, among many others, reveal Locke as convinced that environmental influences including deliberate practice sessions and all sorts of sensory experiences during infancy and childhood (that is, *not* innate ideas "given" at birth) are very largely responsible for the qualities exhibited by adults. Although Locke didn't totally discount heredity, he did put far more emphasis on the malleability of the young, popularizing the Latin phrase *tabula rasa,* or "blank slate," to refer to the openly receptive human mind at the moment of birth.

This externally oriented, evidence-focused point of view, which had been pioneered by Francis Bacon, began to gain popularity during the 17th century. It came to be termed "*sense* realism." (Some people referred simply to "realism," but that risked confusion with its Platonic meaning.) This trend gradually led to a shift in the way many educated people conceptualized classroom teaching. Schools began to be founded upon the principles of sense realism; this was especially true in Germany, where such institutions were called *Realschulen.*

This trend also contributed to the growing interest in natural philosophy (i.e., science) in Europe during the 18th century. And as we shall discover in chapter 11, sense realism was found appealing by some people in the American colonies and later in the fledgling United States.

Before we leave John Locke, we must attend to two other features of his widely influential views on education. First, he advocated that adults take into account the capacities of children. He argued, in effect, that *children will be children* . . . and should be allowed to be so. He said that reasoning is understandable by children, adding "But when I talk of *Reasoning,* I do not intend any other but such as is suited to the Child's Capacity and Apprehension."[10] Addressing instructional styles, he strongly disapproved of any kind of corporal punishment or "breaking the mind," advocating kindliness simply because it's effective. He noted that children have an appetite for experience and love variety.

Second, Locke's view of the purpose of education was completely practical. He argued that it enables young people to adapt themselves to life's daily requirements. An empiricist in the mold of Francis Bacon and Isaac Newton, Locke was convinced that *experience* molds character and capacity. He saw education as neither a divine plan, nor homage to ancient ideas, nor wholly dedicated to the inculcation of moral virtues. Locke viewed the educational process as a way for a young boy to be transformed into a civic-minded, well-informed, socially gracious English gentleman. He also believed that self-denial belonged in the repertoire of an English gentleman.

PHILOSOPHIC TRENDS IN EUROPE BETWEEN THE 16TH AND 18TH CENTURIES

Here, in summary, are the key trends in philosophy that were being discussed by tiny but growing numbers of educated, influential Europeans between the 16th and 18th centuries:

- Realism. This term designates the philosophy passed down over some 2,000 years from Plato, who believed that, beyond the day-to-day world that each individual perceives by means of touch, taste, smell, hearing, and sight lies an unseen, "Real" world of perfect universal "Forms." The Forms were also said to be "ideals," which gives this philosophy its alternative name: "Idealism."
  What's worth learning? The Realists' answer was that one should attain awareness of the Reality not available to the senses. Significantly for us, that awareness is "given" to each human at birth, and it awaits inside him or her to be drawn out in one way or another.
- Protestantism. At the beginning of this chapter, we briefly took note of *Protestantism*—its root word is "protest"—conceived in opposition to Roman Catholicism, the long-reigning Christian persuasion. The Protestants disagreed with the Catholics on various theological details. What's important for us is the Protestants' emphasis on individual autonomy. And it's also significant for us that both types of Christianity posited that each and every human being is born with a soul, something "given" that is unavailable to the five senses.
  What's worth learning? The Protestants' reply was that one should learn the Bible's Truth (which encouraged reading). Two varieties of Protestantism will be discussed in chapter 8.
- Rationalism. Very much alive as a European philosophic trend is rationalism.[11] Its origins lie in the views of René Descartes, who in turn seemed to be influenced by the Pythagoreans. Rationalists posit that humans' faculty of reason needs to be developed through the discipline of intense study, similar to the way one's muscles can be made to strengthen by heavy exercise. Once fully developed, a person's reason can be applied in a wide variety of ways. Rationalists rarely spoke of using one's five senses or of adapting to daily life via experience.
  What's worth learning? The rationalists said that supremely disciplined exercise of one's faculty of reason comes from the study of Greek, Latin, mathematics, and philosophy—which reveals their community of interest with the humanists. Rationalists relied on contemplation, and thus were favorable to "given" intuition and deductive reasoning.

- Sense Realism. The focus of this chapter has been on sense realism, very closely related to Francis Bacon's inductive reasoning, and thus to John Locke's evidence-based philosophy of empiricism. Empiricism, the direct opposite of Platonic Realism, focuses its attention on things that can be directly perceived by touching, tasting, hearing, seeing, and/or smelling.

  What's worth learning? Sense realists such as Comenius respond that young people should use their five senses to study objects, illustrations, and other realia, then move on to develop memory, judgment, and so forth. Locke's response would be that young people should learn about their own environment through experiences of all kinds, the goal being full adaptation to all of the practical exigencies encountered in daily life.

- Humanism. This school of philosophy gave the Renaissance its name by reviving interest in the Greek and Roman classics. The Humanists devoted much thought (mythopoetic rather than scientific in nature) to human beings and their various capacities to attain excellence and greatness. Besides sharing a community of interest with rationalists, humanists can be viewed as harbingers of romanticists, whose philosophy will be the focus of chapter 7.

  What's worth learning? The Humanists' reply was that one should strive for excellence, and should do so by gaining familiarity with the works of Greek and Roman fine artists.

Humanism, sense realism, rationalism, and Protestantism were differing philosophies, but their trajectories nonetheless combined, gradually, to enable a startling new idea to be voiced: Individuals can shape or reshape themselves in order to depend less on others, express their respective personalities, make decisions informed by verifiable facts, and attain a better future.

During the late 18th century, this fresh perspective was captured by Immanuel Kant. In his essay *"Was ist Aufklärung?"* (What Is Enlightenment?), Kant answers his own question by stating that Enlightenment is "man's throwing off his self-incurred immaturity." Defining immaturity as the inability to apply one's intelligence without another's guidance, Kant boldly unfurled the Latin maxim *Sapere aude!*—Dare to know![12]

Slowly, the new views of human nature reduced the powerless, dependent perspective with which almost everyone during the 15th century had been viewing his or her life. By the end of the 18th century, people could entertain this possibility: With self-initiated forethought, with reliance on information provided by their own five senses, with their capacity to apply reason to that information, and with intentional effort, they could expect to approach the ends of their lives in better circumstances than fate had decreed when their lives began.

MUSINGS AND SPECULATIONS

The most significant view of human consciousness to emerge during this era concerned the self-conscious, self-directed ability and effort of human beings. This is beautifully captured in Giovanni Pico della Mirandola's *De hominis dignitate,* quoted early in this chapter.

WHY CHAPTER 4 IS IMPORTANT

Introduced in this chapter were the foundations of three perspectives on classroom teaching. One says that what's worth learning is internal to the learner. The second says that what's worth learning is external to the learner. These perspectives will reëmerge in chapter 11. The third perspective says what's worth learning is whatever best disciplines the rational mind by being intensely studied; this perspective will reëmerge in chapter 13.

At TheAptitudeMyth.info are the genealogical chart and "What to Remember" list for chapter 4.

NOTES

1. M. W. Keatinge, *The Great Didactic of John Amos Comenius* (Adam and Charles Black, 1896), 287.

2. Useful in the preparation of this chapter was Gerald L. Gutek, *A History of the Western Educational Experience*, 2nd ed. (Waveland, 1995), 34–56 and 114–73; R. Freeman Butts, *The Education of the West* (McGraw-Hill, 1973), 183–220 and 335–66; Frederick Eby and Charles F. Arrowood, *The History and Philosophy of Education Ancient and Medieval* (Prentice-Hall, 1940), 837–56; Denis Lawton and Peter Gordon, *A History of Western Educational Ideas* (Woburn, 2002), 57–100; Tim Blanning, *The Pursuit of Glory: Europe 1648–1815* (Viking, 2007), 456-521; and Dorinda Outram, *Panorama of the Enlightenment* (Getty Publications, 2006), 8–21 and 238–77.

3. John Addington Symonds, *Renaissance in Italy: The Age of Despots* (Henry Holt, 1883), 4 [italics added]. Eby and Arrowood, *op. cit.*, posit the Renaissance as "the adolescence of modern European civilization" (838).

4. Found at www.cscs.umich.edu/~crshalizi/Mirandola/ (paragraph 6). For an extended discussion of Pico della Mirandola, visit plato.stanford.edu/entries/pico-della-mirandola.

5. John Addington Symonds, *Renaissance in Italy: The Revival of Learning* (Henry Holt, 1888), 32. Eby and Arrowood, *op. cit.*, note that humans' rational *and emotional* natures were liberated during the Renaissance (854).

6. Keatinge, *op. cit.* Basic information about Comenius is from Boyd and King, *op. cit.*, 241–54. When visiting Prague, visit the excellent Pedagogical Museum of J. A. Comenius.

7. My exposition of Locke's pedagogical views relies primarily on Peter Gay, *John Locke on Education* (Teachers College, 1964), especially 4–12.

8. John Locke, *Some Thoughts Concerning Education* (Macmillan, 1902), §1, 2.

9. *Ibid.*, §66, 39.

10. *Ibid.*, §81, 60.

11. This explanation of rationalism is partially based on R. Freeman Butts and Lawrence A. Cremin, *A History of Education in American Culture* (Holt, Rinehart, & Winston, 1953), 55.

12. Outram, *op. cit.*, 29; original source of quote not cited.

FIVE

New Views of Children and Childhood

Tout est bien sortant des mains de l'Auteur des choses, tout dégénère entre les mains de l'homme.
Everything is good as it comes from the hands of the Author of Nature; but everything
degenerates in the hands of man.

—Jean-Jacques Rousseau[1]

The first historian of childhood, Philippe Ariès, concluded in his 1960 book that during
the Middle Ages, people regarded infants and young children as having no personality,
no moral sensibility, and no significance.[2] Children were expendable. This lack of regard
for the young continued until each was weaned (later than today), at which time the child
was viewed as a sort of miniature adult and slipped into community life without fanfare.
This approach to children, said Ariès, protected parents from grief during an era when
many children died at a tender age.[3]

Later historians have disagreed with some of Ariès's conclusions; among other things,
they have found evidence that medieval parents actually did show warmth toward their
young.

YOUNGER CHILDREN ARE BETTER CHILDREN

What concerns us here, however, is not changes in parent-child relationships over the
past centuries, but rather changes in the way Europeans and, later, Americans thought
about the minds and souls of young people. If we consider the era when Johann Gutenberg invented interchangeable type in the mid-15th century, we can recognize with reasonable certainty that:

- At that time the image of Jesus Christ as an infant and child was an object of
  veneration, as it already had been for centuries, and as it still is for some people.
- Among the handful of thought leaders (almost all theologians) who paid attention
  to such matters, young children were viewed, simultaneously, in two totally different ways:
  - They were born in sin, participating from their first breath in this earthly vale
    of tears.
  - They were exceptionally pure along the lines suggested by Christ in *Matthew*
    18:3, "Except ye . . . become as little children, ye shall not enter into the
    kingdom of Heaven."

- The reason why these opposite views could coexist apparently is that little children were presumed *innocent*—not yet aware of, and non-participants in, actual sinful acts.
- These two seemingly contradictory ways of thinking about the very young—inherently sinful versus inherently pure—seem to have had very little impact on anyone's daily life.

An early sign that ideas were changing occurred in the 15th century when a French churchman named Gerson, who played a leading role at the grammar school of Notre Dame de Paris, wrote a treatise to advise priests serving as confessors about how to encourage children around the ages of 10 to 12 to feel guilt. Why? As noted above, the notion of children as exceptionally pure meant that they were "innocent." And the idea that they were innocent meant, very largely, that they knew nothing of the "fouwle dede," i.e., sex.

So in the interest of saving their souls, Gerson wanted children to learn to suffer guilt about any early sexual explorations. And in the interest of preserving their precious innocence, Gerson wanted to delay for as long as humanly possible even the wish to explore sex. So he also proposed changes in the way adults behave toward children as well as changes in the way Notre Dame de Paris administered discipline.

During the next 200 years, the view represented by Gerson was elaborated upon by influential European churchmen, both Catholics (including the Jesuits) and Protestants, and by secular moralists. I say "elaborated upon" because by the 17th century, the conception of children as innocent had been joined by a parallel conception of them as lacking reason and knowledge.

In the common mind, children were linked with angels. Painters and sculptors of that era depicted angels as *putti* or what we might call cherubs, small naked children. It was acceptable to show them naked, presumably, because they were pure. Assumed to be 99 percent soul (innocent) and 1 percent mind (ignorant), children were widely viewed as the dwelling place of the spirit of Jesus.

A long-term change in Europeans' views of children and childhood was occurring in parallel with the long-term change in how they viewed human nature and consciousness. The old outlook of powerless dependence, which was founded on the Christian conceptions of Original Sin and inherent human depravity, was being eclipsed if not fully replaced by an optimistic, humanistic perspective that saw humans as basically good, as possessing a natural capacity for increased excellence, and as capable of self-direction in pursuit of the possibility of a better future.

The Younger the Child, the Better the Child

But a curious twist occurred in how this paradigm shift was applied to children. Within the mindset that said "humans are good," there surfaced the belief that the *younger* humans are, the *better* they are. As they mature, they become less and less possessed of goodness.

Over hundreds of years churchmen, plus a handful of educators, secular moralists, and educated parents, came to view their responsibility toward children in two ways:

- Preserve innocence. On the one hand, adults had a responsibility to preserve the natural goodness of the very young—their miraculous purity and complete innocence—for as long as possible. Thus, they needed to guard children from people, activities, places, and ideas that could corrupt their innocence. (This view remains alive and well today.)
- Reduce ignorance—carefully. Because the young were ignorant, adults also needed to provide them with mental strengthening through the application of knowledge

and reason—but only of a sort that would not corrupt them. One glimpses this outlook today in the Roman Catholic rite of First Communion, which celebrates the miraculous purity and innocence of childhood while simultaneously instilling Church-approved knowledge and reason.

An Educational Blockbuster by a Celebrity Author

As we might well expect, someone eventually captured these thought trends, elaborated on their implications, and wrote them all down in a very long book—a book that quickly became widely available, including in translation. That book was *Émile, or On Education*; its author was Jean-Jacques Rousseau (1712–1778).[4] Its first sentence has gained a measure of fame:

> Everything is good as it comes from the hands of the Author of Nature; but everything degenerates in the hands of man.[5]

The impact of *Émile* across Enlightenment Europe was huge. Rousseau had been well known as a writer for more than a decade; in fact, Rousseau in the 18th century was what today we would call a celebrity. Just one year previously, he had published the world's first novel, *Julie, or the New Héloïse*, an instant and immense success. And in the very same year—1762—in which *Émile* was published, so was another Rousseau blockbuster: *The Social Contract*.

Without even trying, Rousseau attained the surest path to skyrocketing readership when, in Paris and Geneva, both *Émile* and *The Social Contract* were condemned and publicly burned by the authorities. (In the case of *Émile*, the problem was religious: The book defended deism.)

Émile is not a how-to book for classroom teachers; the scene throughout is of what we would call "home schooling" by a paid tutor. Rousseau himself never taught at the front of a classroom, and he had given up after a brief attempt at one-on-one tutoring. Upon the births of his own five children, Rousseau deposited each of them in a public institution, never to see them again.

In spite of these facts, known by contemporaries, *Émile* very quickly became a sensation among upwardly mobile parents, a few of whom went so far as to relocate to the countryside in order to protect their innocent children from the degenerating effects of urban civilization!

THE ENDURING IMPACT OF ROUSSEAU'S *ÉMILE*

Émile captured the interest and commitment of contemporary Europeans for two reasons. First, as noted in chapter 3, explorers of distant lands were returning to Europe bearing both artifacts and stories of previously unimagined kinds of human beings. Among educated Europeans, alternative ways of living, thinking, and deciding were being discussed with great interest.

Rousseau himself was among those captivated by tales of "savages" (not a pejorative term in those days) and the resulting possibilities. It is said that the play *Arlequin sauvage* made a great impression on young Jean-Jacques, who set about in 1742 to write an operetta on the discovery of the New World.[6] Twenty years later, Rousseau in *Émile* used the savages' ways of life as the basis of a stinging critique of contemporary schooling, drawing attention to what he viewed as the damage inflicted by European society on its children.

For Rousseau, the savage stood for uncorrupted Nature, a being who had *not* "degen-erated in the hands of man." This view drew the rapt attention of Rousseau's educated contemporaries.[7]

The second reason why Rousseau captured people's interest is that he portrayed a way of dealing with children that stood in stark contrast to the practices that were customary in the homes and schools of that time. He posited that each child should be given a full and free opportunity to grow according to his or her own emerging natural tendencies, following whatever interests were active at the moment. Rousseau's stance, known as "negative education,"[8] recommended that little attention be paid, especially early on, to the knowledge and skills that, in the past, adults had believed important for children to learn.

The emerging of each child's interests, argued Rousseau, should occur not with teach-er-delivered lessons, not with printed words, but spontaneously as he or she interacts with uncorrupted nature and with tangible objects in the manner advocated by Comenius and the sense realists. Books, he said, taught children to agree uncritically with the ideas of others.

Rousseau's views were not original. For example, similar views had been expressed earlier by the French writer Michel de Montaigne (1533–1592). A nobleman by birth and education, he was distrustful of those wielding authority. Instead of amassing power, he took a sustained interest in education. He recommended that the first object of study should be nature; that learning should involve practice, not memorization, and should be as pleasant as tennis, dancing, or other recreations; and that pedagogy should not be authoritarian. "Away with this violence! away with this compulsion! than which . . . nothing more dulls and degenerates a well-descended nature."[9]

An emerging thought trend was the deification of "Nature." What is natural is Good: It is God's creation, untainted by human civilization. For children, natural growth is Good, forced growth is Bad. The word "organic" began to be applied to natural develop-ment, from the simplest plants to humans, and within humans to physiological *and mental* processes.[10] Implied is spontaneous development that relies neither on internal intention-ality nor on external help.

These notions originated in Aristotle's teleological "final cause," which also had ap-plied to both growth processes. *This equating of all types of growth generated misunderstand-ing*. The resulting confusion is critical for our purposes; we will revisit it in chapters 7, 10, 17, and 18.

Today, the paradigm that many Americans reach for when discussing children and childhood is one that evolved over centuries, emerging in recognizable form during the Enlightenment. Parents, educators, and policy makers today are no strangers to the as-sumption that, within any one lifetime, the most wonderful and beloved period is *infancy*, which is naturally good because it is pure and innocent, and which is full of potentials that, in the fullness of time, *will* emerge.

In our 21st century language, Jean-Jacques Rousseau was a celebrity author who championed child-centered education of the kind that admires natural, organic growth and opposes classroom teaching that is book-oriented, curriculum-driven, teacher-cen-tered, and spontaneity-dampening.

THE EMERGENCE OF CHILDHOOD AND TWO VIEWS OF HOW TO REGARD IT

The American scholar Neil Postman has turned his interpretative mind to the topics we have been considering in this chapter and the previous one. He views Gutenberg's invention of moveable type as the fundamental driver of the whole notion of "childhood" in the West.[11]

Postman believes that during the Dark and Middle Ages, people made extremely little distinction between children and adults. Parental assistance was needed to keep infants and the young alive, but otherwise the responsibilities that parents feel today were largely unknown. With the exception of a tiny number of trained priests and scribes, no one was literate and no one went to school. Children gained skills and knowledge via participant observation, imitation, and oral transmission, and were absorbed by the adult world at around the age of seven.

Enter Gutenberg's invention in 1440. Set in motion were profound changes including that information on paper was no longer a secret. It was becoming affordable, it was turning up in multiple locations, and adults who were neither priests nor scribes were learning to decipher it.

Possible for the first time since the days of classical Greece and Rome was immersion by ordinary people in a non-social, wholly mental realm of knowledge, one that could be used to transmit skills and information to others. Gradually, a social gap appeared and widened between those who were literate and those who weren't. All young children were among those who were not literate; increasingly, they could no longer melt into the adult world if they didn't have rudimentary reading skills, for that adult world was expanding beyond custom and memory. Furthermore, writing and reading were solitary occupations, and writing preserved one's unique thoughts, so the concept of individualism was greatly strengthened.

Says Postman, "Childhood . . . could not have happened without the idea that each individual is important in himself, that a human mind and life in some fundamental sense transcend community. For as the idea of personal identity developed, it followed inexorably that it would be applied to the young as well. . . ."[12] Thus, parents began to sense that they bore previously unimagined responsibilities for the "development" of their children.

What paradigm, then, should adults *think with* when contemplating these newly recognized small individuals? Emerging out of the cacophony of ideas were two alternative paradigms.

One was championed by John Locke, who argued that infants are *tabula rasa* and unformed, thus needing to learn from adults how to be literate, self-controlled, reasonable, and capable of contributing to society. Locke's view will later be labeled "Practical."

The other paradigm was popularized by Rousseau, who said that it's not the unformed child who needs assistance but rather adults and their corrupting civilization. Adults, in fact, should be imitating and learning from the children. Rousseau's view will later be labeled "Romantic." (For additional insights, see Tables A.2 and A.3 in the Appendix.)

MUSINGS AND SPECULATIONS

In the United States, one often sees yellow, diamond-shaped signs displayed inside car windows that announce "Baby on board." The deep motivation for the display of these signs is the assumption that an infant is the most precious (pure and potential-rich) cargo that any car could possibly carry. There's a direct line between Rousseau's 18th century ideas and these little signs.

WHY CHAPTER 5 IS IMPORTANT

We've just explored the origins of a belief about young children, the impact of which has reverberated down through the centuries to affect our current practices of parenting and schooling. That belief was, and is, that *young children are precious*, which in turn implies *delicate, fragile, and easily damaged.*

Therefore, our responsibility vis-à-vis children is not merely to protect them from environmental dangers. Our responsibilities include being very cautious about expecting mental, especially academic, efforts that are stressful or exhausting for them, or that might exceed their spontaneously attained level of ability—in today's parlance, their "readiness." These notions resonate with Aristotle's idea of a teleological "final cause." In chapter 10, we will see these ideas reëmerge as the definitive pronouncement of a widely influential 19th century philosopher.

At TheAptitudeMyth.info are the genealogical chart and "What to Remember" list for chapter 5.

NOTES

1. First sentence of *Émile, or On Education* (1762); translation by William H. Payne, *Rousseau's Émile, or Treatise on Education* (D. Appleton, 1918), 1.

2. The book that opened the debate about childhood is Philippe Ariès, *Centuries of Childhood: A Social History of Family Life* (Vintage, 1962); it was originally published in France in 1960 as *L'Enfant et la vie familiale sous l'ancien régime*. For other perspectives I relied on Colin Heywood, *A History of Childhood* (Polity, 2001), 9–40; Shulamith Shahar, *Childhood in the Middle Ages* (Routledge, 1990), 9–20 and 95–120; and John Cleverley and D. C. Phillips, *Visions of Childhood: Influential Models from Locke to Spock*, rev. ed. (Teachers College, 1986), 1–53.

3. Ariès, *ibid.*, 15–136.

4. My thinking about Rousseau and his impact has been influenced by Leo Damrosch's excellent biography, *Jean-Jacques Rousseau: Restless Genius* (Houghton Mifflin, 2005) as well as by Dorinda Outram, *Panorama of the Enlightenment* (Getty Publications, 2006), 92–101; Gerald L. Gutek, *A History of the Western Educational Experience*, 2nd ed. (Waveland, 1995), 164–67; Denis Lawton and Peter Gordon, *A History of Western Educational Ideas* (Woburn, 2002), 94–97; and Cleverley and Phillips, *op. cit.*, 34–36.

5. Translation by Payne, *op. cit.*

6. Jack Weatherford, *Indian Givers: The Continuing Impact of the Discovered Americas on the World* (Crown, 1988), 124. In Rousseau's operetta, Christopher Columbus arrived in the New World with a sword while singing to the Indians the refrain, "Lose your liberty!"

7. John Willinsky, *Learning to Divide the World: Education at Empire's End* (University of Minnesota Press, 1998), 110–11. Willinsky says Rousseau was influenced by contemporary accounts of native life in North America.

8. Rousseau was *not* arguing that adults should abdicate all responsibility for guiding children in worthy directions. David Halpin, *Romanticism and Education* (Continuum, 2007), 45, 48, 67.

9. William Carew Hazlitt, ed., *Essays of Montaigne: Volume I*, translated by Charles Cotton (Reeves and Turner, 1902), 190.

10. I am indebted to E. D. Hirsch, Jr., for calling attention to the misunderstandings generated by equating all kinds of growth. Hirsch, *The Knowledge Deficit* (Houghton Mifflin, 2006), 3–7.

11. Neil Postman, *The Disappearance of Childhood* (Random House, 1982), Part 1, "The Invention of Childhood."

12. *Ibid.*, 28 (Vintage Books paperback edition, 1994).

SIX

New Views of Authority in Societies and Schools

Over the long term of several centuries, individuals [began] to pull themselves away from the webs of community and [became] increasingly independent agents both legally and psychologically.

—Lynn Hunt[1]

We've seen that during the 16th, 17th, and 18th centuries, slow but ultimately paradigm-shifting transformations were occurring in the ways that reading, thinking Europeans thought of nature, human nature, and human children.[2] Yet the winds of change were encompassing far more.

In our quest to understand the origins of the assumptions that many Americans reach for today when discussing the learning of children in classrooms, it's necessary to take note of two more thought trends. One of these is romanticism, which we'll address in chapter 7. But first, let's explore the changing views of authority in society—and in schools.

THOUGHT LEADERS QUESTION THE BASIS OF AUTHORITY

During the 15th century, the vast majority of Europeans lived their entire lives in the unquestioned expectation that someone in authority would tell them what beliefs and values to hold and what behaviors to enact and avoid. Their subordination to the patriarchal figures of clan, community, church, and kingdom was substantial if not total.

Today we wonder whether those 15th century authority figures—village elders, kings, bishops, and the like—left people enough wiggle-room to lead meaningful lives. (In those days, people probably had a sense of place, of belonging, and of certitude that eludes many of us today.) In any case, most historians agree that, over the past 600 years, Western people's obedience to, reliance on, and unquestioned respect for authority has gradually declined.

It's not possible to say, of course, whether the decline in authority was driven by the ideas of leading thinkers, or whether the ideas of leading thinkers were driven by emerging currents of public attitudes and values. What can be said is that the growing availability of books enabled these new ways of thinking to spread farther and more rapidly than would have been possible before Gutenberg's invention. Thought leaders wrote the books.

Martin Luther and the Protestant movement he spawned helped to start these currents flowing during the 16th century when they challenged the pope's authority, rejected priests as God's deputies, and claimed that each individual could work out his own salvation.

Beginning in the 17th century, the basis of secular leaders' authority also began to be challenged. John Locke questioned the divine right of kings; in *Two Treatises on Government* (1690), he argued that every individual had "natural rights" and that monarchs, like everyone else, were party to a "social contract." During the 18th century, François Quesnay formulated the economic doctrine of *laissez-faire*; rejecting mercantilism, he denied that monarchs could regulate commerce to suit themselves. His supporters were known as "physiocrats"; many, like Thomas Jefferson, were agrarians who advocated that not only the commercial order but also the natural order of field and forest should operate without imposed constraints.

Jean-Jacques Rousseau, arguably the 18th century's most popular author, railed against inequities arising from inherited wealth and power in *The Social Contract* (1762). Rousseau saw power not as grounded in an immutable God-given framework but as the outcome of a conscious agreement in which a group of people *allowed* someone to exercise authority.

Across the Atlantic, colonial leaders dared to declare that "all men are created equal" and to back up that by force of arms in 1776. Only 13 years later in France, a monarch lost his throne, then his head, after a similar declaration was made: "Men are born free and equal in rights. Social distinctions may be based only on considerations of the common good."[3]

CHANGES IN THE TEXTURE OF EUROPEANS' DAILY LIVES

Between the 15th and 18th centuries, the mindsets and assumptions by which Europeans lived their day-to-day lives were evolving. People in the 15th century were inextricably enmeshed in their in-groups of clan, community, and church. As Lynn Hunt points out in *Inventing Human Rights* (2007),[4] within each in-group, the social, psychological, and even bodily boundaries between members were indistinct and inconsequential. Members were engaged with one another on a daily basis and viewed each other as deeply and irreversibly similar. Our modern ideal of personal autonomy was absent.

Also absent was our modern Western assumption that *self* is the property of a single individual. Back then, *self* was the property of one's primary group. Such groups usually were dominated by a paternalistic authority figure who commanded deference; he (rarely she) enabled the group *to actually function as, and be perceived as, a unit* in thought, word, and deed.

At the start of the 15th century, authority figures wielded power through inheritance and usually with the sense that their place at the top of the heap had sacred sanction. Whatever the deep origin of these mindsets and assumptions might have been, almost everyone in clan, community, church, and kingdom accepted them as "the way things are." People were capable of hating authority figures who were cruel, but it was rare for anyone to argue that this accepted way of attaining in-group unity was, in a moral or practical sense, wrong.

By the end of the 18th century, a great deal had changed. People were coming to view themselves as separate and distinct. The boundaries between members of the same in-group had begun to matter. This was the flowering time of self-awareness and individualism, which had first appeared (or perhaps reappeared) during the Renaissance. The concept of *self* was coming to be a property of each individual, and people were learning, slowly, to think of themselves as self-directing free agents. As Lynn Hunt brilliantly reconstructs, people also were learning to have empathy for one another, i.e., to mentally put themselves in another person's shoes.

Another mindset shift resonated with ideas coming from natural philosophers. The universe had been assumed to exist in a fixed, hierarchical Great Chain of Being, an Aristotelian notion that had supplied the conceptual base for the powers and assumed perfections of authoritarian rulers. The emerging view, driven by empiricists such as Galileo and Newton, was that *all* things were composed of similar elements and were governed by all-pervasive laws. As atoms replaced vague principles, and as quantitative thought replaced metaphysics, people began asking whether authoritarianism could be replaced by human societies viewed in egalitarian, participatory terms.[5]

Of course, people still were living out their lives side-by-side in clans, communities, and churches. So authority remained necessary, not so much for unity's sake but, as always, for "practical utility." People now sensed that each group member was autonomous, equal to the others in terms of basic humanity; in this context, inherited authority of the old patriarchal type no longer seemed appropriate.

Guided by Rousseau, Locke, Quesnay, Jefferson, and other thought leaders, Europeans began to view authority as, properly, the outcome of a carefully constructed agreement—a contract—among reasoning, consenting human beings. This point of view was a critical intellectual driver of both the American and French revolutions.

AUTHORITY IN CLASSROOMS ENTERS THE 18TH CENTURY DISCUSSION

The emerging shift in Western people's sensibilities about authority was not confined to clans, communities, churches, kingdoms, and commerce. It extended to other relationships and institutions—including schools.

Schools and their classrooms became a topic in the ongoing debate about authority because in them, during every school day, the relationship between an authority figure—the instructor—and his (rarely her) subordinate learners was being played out. Some people paid attention because their own children were among the learners. Some people paid attention because, consciously or subconsciously, they thought: If we're preparing this community's young people for life in an authority-by-contract society, perhaps we should think about revising the authority-by-patriarch classroom.

Let's pause for a moment and review the time-honored paradigm for the teacher's role (see chapter 1). It entails six expectations that community members have of teachers, three of which relate to authority: guidance, criticalness, directiveness. Like the 15th century social and political arrangements described above, these three expectations had emerged from the mists of time to become established as "the way things are done in classrooms." It was easy to assume that they enjoyed sacred sanction.

The teacher—the one who fulfilled these traditional expectations (and still does in some world regions)—was assumed by members of the community to be a legitimate authority within, and to some extent beyond, his classroom. The teacher was "*in* authority." Usually, he also was assumed to be "*an* authority," implying that he possessed superior wisdom or skill, or impeccable virtue, or personal charisma or heroism, or all of these.[6]

This is why teachers operating within the framework of the time-honored paradigm were—and still are—accorded deference *by ascription* (i.e., by attribution, meaning that a mindset is shared by everyone in the community). Teachers operating within this framework never needed to strive to earn learners' deference and respect; those came automatically. In the same way, there was little reason for anyone to worry about whether the teacher was likeable.

Thus, to our previous list of five realms of human activity directed by patriarchal figures—clan, community, church, kingdom, and commerce—we now may add a sixth: classroom.

By the end of the 18th century, the way people were thinking about teachers and schools had started to change. One of the factors underlying this change was the dawning recognition that everything worth knowing was *not* known already; therefore, the function of a classroom teacher needed to encompass more than the authoritative delivering of timeless, fixed Truths to the next generation (while, of course, simultaneously personifying virtue).

Equally responsible for this change was this: Those widely read thinkers on the ideal of a social contract were simultaneously devoting major publications to education. In 1690, John Locke's *Two Treatises on Government* appeared within months of his *Essay Concerning Human Understanding*; he soon followed those with *Thoughts Concerning Education*. And in 1762, Jean-Jacques Rousseau repeated the same amazing feat when his *Social Contract* appeared almost simultaneously with his *Émile, or On Education*.

Broadly construed, these and other thought leaders were saying: It is no longer appropriate for societal and political leaders to be accorded deference and obedience solely by ascription. Thus, it also is no longer appropriate for classroom leaders to be accorded deference and obedience solely by ascription. Perhaps authority is indispensible. If so, then it must exist in people's lives, including students' lives, with some kind of *rational justification* . . . instead of simply existing.

MUSINGS AND SPECULATIONS

I have found no reason to conclude that Europeans began to think of classroom teaching in these new ways *for the specific purpose of attaining better learning outcomes* in terms of mastery, quantity, or speed. Their motives were political, not pedagogical. Their belief in people's capacity for self-direction was appropriate for adults. That same belief, applied to young children in the context of classroom learning, was neither appropriate nor wise.

WHY CHAPTER 6 IS IMPORTANT

As classroom instructors came to receive less and less ascribed deference, the time-honored expectation that they provide explicit guidance and direction to their students began eroding. The new ideas about authority emerged very largely or entirely for political, *not pedagogical*, purposes. Applied pedagogically, these ideas came to be understood by many as meaning that classroom teachers ought to exhibit very little authoritarian behavior toward students.

At TheAptitudeMyth.info are the genealogical chart and "What to Remember" list for chapter 6.

NOTES

1. Lynn Hunt, *Inventing Human Rights: A History* (W.W. Norton, 2007), 29.
2. A fascinating treatment of the shifting role of authority in society is provided by Lynn Hunt, *ibid.*, 60–61 and 82–83. Also influential in shaping my thinking about Europe was R. S. Peters, *Authority, Responsibility, and Education*, 3rd ed. (Allen & Unwin, 1973), 13–32, 47–55, and 132–39; Gerald L. Gutek, *A*

History of the Western Educational Experience, 2nd ed. (Waveland, 1995), 140 and 163; Denis Lawton and Peter Gordon, *A History of Western Educational Ideas* (Woburn, 2002), 149 and 152; and Dorinda Outram, *Panorama of the Enlightenment* (Getty Publications, 2006), 213, 221–29, and 237.

3. Declaration of Human and Civic Rights of 26 August 1789, Article first. English translation acquired from the Conseil Constitutionnel (Constitutional Council of the French Republic).

4. Hunt, *ibid.*, 60–61 and 82–83.

5. For more insight, see Stephen T. Asma, *Against Fairness* (University of Chicago, 2013), 48–57.

6. Peters, *op. cit.*, 14–17. Peters elucidates this distinction further by noting that one's being "in authority" is community sanctioned and thus has a *de jure* quality, while one's being "an authority" is an individual property and thus has a *de facto* quality. The *de jure* quality is related to teachers' receiving deference by ascription.

SEVEN

New Ideals for Human Life and Learning

How can the bird that is born for joy
Sit in a cage and sing?

—William Blake[1]

The Enlightenment in Europe, also known to historians as "The Age of Reason," transformed many of the assumptions, verities, and patterns by which human beings had long lived their lives in that part of the world.[2] As the 18th century passed its midpoint, the trend among educated Europeans was toward *rational thought* (especially of the inductive variety), *natural law* (applicable to human affairs as well as to science), and *intentional planning and control* (promising a future that, in numerous ways, would be superior to the past).

It's not surprising that a reaction to these sweeping trends would emerge. That reaction soon came to be known as *romanticism*, said by Isaiah Berlin in *The Roots of Romanticism* (1999) to be "the greatest shift in the consciousness of the West that has occurred."

INTELLECTUAL STREAMS FEED A ROMANTIC FLOOD

Historians have struggled to develop a concise definition of romanticism; some say that it only makes sense to talk about a variety of *romanticisms*. And, indeed, there were multiple European strands contributing to this broad shift in consciousness. For example:

- From Germany came metaphysical *idealism*, an offshoot of Platonic "Realism" and thought trends such as:

    —Immanuel Kant's previously noted dictum that immaturity is the inability to apply one's intelligence without another's guidance.
    —Johann Herder's view that individuals need not be constrained by the culture and traditions of their societies, and that groups develop on a botanical (organic) model.
    —Friedrich von Schiller's notion that play-urge (*Spieltrieb*) is indispensable for children *and* adults because spontaneity inspires aesthetic education and even political liberation.
    —Johann von Goethe's belief that the only type of authority worthy of obedience and respect is that which arises inside the individual (not authority imposed externally).

- From France came a combination of the social *utopianism* that characterized the Revolution of 1789 and the *laissez faire* commercial principles of François Quesnay and the physiocrats; France also was closely identified with the peripatetic and prolific Jean-Jacques Rousseau.
- From Britain came classic *liberalism*, the notion that individuals should attain whatever their inner abilities make possible, which in turn requires freedom of thought, free trade, freedom of contract, and the government's doing little more than preserving property and social order.
- From America's New England states came *Transcendentalism*, a quasi-religious movement inspired by German idealism, said to have been "a way of perceiving the world centered on individual consciousness rather than external fact." One of its early proponents spoke of the mind as a "delicate germ, whose husk is the body," and of its needing to grow not from "external accretion" but from an "internal principle." Near the end of the movement, a disappointed proponent wrote that adherents had "deified their own conceptions."[3]
- From a pan-European group of artists, philosophers, writers, and poets came the literary trend known as *Romanticism* (with a capital R), important for our purposes because it envisioned flower-like unfolding and enhanced growth potential for each human being.

LITERARY ROMANTICISM'S LOVE AFFAIR WITH CHILDREN AND NATURE

Literary Romanticism rejected the structured, mechanistic way in which Nature had come to be conceived during the Enlightenment, whose apostles of Reason had expected the application of natural laws (i.e., science) to enable thoughtful humans to control their own destinies.

The Romantics held that nature must be accepted rather than analyzed. Nature is mysterious. Our human intellect is less important for our well-being than our feelings and emotions and, indeed, our souls. So, they said, let us avoid all thought of harnessing fixed patterns and laws for future gain. *Yes*, humans are perfectible. But their perfection will *not* come via the application of reason but rather through a process akin to spontaneous botanical (organic) growth.

Let's pause to note that some observers do not view the Enlightenment and Romanticism as polar opposites. For example, in *Romanticism and Education*, David Halpin refers to the:

> . . . false antitheses . . . between Romantic and Enlightenment sensibility—emotion versus reason; individualism versus society; subjectivity versus objectivity; material versus spiritual; mechanical versus organic; rebellion versus order.
>
> The truth of the matter is far more complex. . . . Romanticism inherits many of the priorities of Enlightenment thinking, whilst augmenting them with themes it underplays or ignores.[4]

Halpin quotes D. Heath and J. Boreham with approval: "The liberation of the inner man was as much the aim of the Romantics as the Enlightenment thinkers. . . . Romanticism was the continuation of the Enlightenment by other means."[5] Halpin adds that the Romantic emphasis arose in opposition to the evils of 19th century industrialization and urbanization.[6]

The Romantics focused on two idealized exemplars of human excellence: artists (especially writers and poets) and children. What artists and children were thought to have in common were three qualities: an open-minded simplicity and innocence, an absence of preconceived ideas and the limitations they inevitably bring, and an unconscious psychic harmony and wholeness. Thus unfettered, artists and children were assumed by the Literary Romantics to be utterly free to realize the heights of human potentiality and creativity.

Vast attention came to be lavished by Romantics on an idealized image of the child, especially the precious very young child. Dozens of quotes are available to demonstrate their reverence for early childhood. Here are a few examples, beginning with excerpts from the work of two famous Romantics, one a German, the other an American.

In his essay *On Simple and Sentimental Poetry* (1795), Friedrich von Schiller wrote:

> It follows that the child is to us like the representation of the ideal; not, indeed, of the ideal as we have realized it, but such as our destination admitted; and, consequently, it is not at all the idea of its indigence, of its hinderances [sic], that makes us experience emotion in the child's presence; it is, on the contrary, the idea of its pure and free force, of the integrity, the infinity of its being. This is the reason why, in the sight of every moral and sensible man, the child will always be a *sacred* thing. . . .[7]

This idea—that in the very young, one finds an unspoiled image of divinity that shows the way for the redemption of adults—is also captured in *Nature* (1836) by Ralph Waldo Emerson:[8]

> The sun illuminates only the eye of the man, but shines into the eye and the heart of the child. The lover of nature is he whose inward and outward senses are still truly adjusted to each other; who has retained the spirit of infancy even into the era of manhood. [Chapter I, "Nature," 7]

> A man is a god in ruins. When men are innocent, life shall be longer, and shall pass into the immortal, as gently as we awake from dreams. Infancy is the perpetual Messiah, which comes into the arms of fallen men, and pleads with them to return to paradise. [Chapter VIII, "Prospects," 69]

If you're recalling the central thrust of Jean-Jacques Rousseau's *Émile* (1762), then you're joining historians and literary scholars in recognizing Rousseau as the 18th century intellectual whose work was a harbinger of these Romantics' 19th century educational views.

Some scholars believe, however, that leading 19th century Romantics *exceeded* Rousseau in their reverence for the young ("a child will be a *sacred* object") and in the radical nature of their prescriptions about what, therefore, to do. Because our task is to comprehend the origins of how many Americans today think of children, we must explore this feature of the Romantic mindset.

Let's explore the origins of the word so revered by the Romantics: "nature." It comes from the Latin *natura*, meaning "birth, constitution, character of things"; its verb form was *nasci*, "to be born." According to the *Oxford English Dictionary*, "nature" refers grandly to all elements of the physical universe, and it refers as well to "the essential qualities or properties of a thing; the inherent and inseparable combination of properties essentially pertaining to anything and giving it its fundamental character."[9]

Given the etymology of "nature," we can understand how the idea of "birth" became closely associated with the idea of "given" in terms of a human being's inherent guiding and limiting factors. E. D. Hirsch, Jr., who is not only a well-known commentator on American education but also an intellectual historian focusing on 19th century Romanticism, observes that "natural" became a term of honor in the United States, which elevated it to the status formerly occupied by "divine law." He quotes Wordsworth—"...Nature never did betray / the heart that loved her..."[10] —and adds, "To be natural was automatically to be good, whether in life or in learning."[11]

THREE LITERARY ROMANTICS IN THEIR OWN WORDS

Samuel Taylor Coleridge

Coleridge (1772–1834) is the author of well-known poems such as "The Rime of the Ancient Mariner," "Frost at Midnight," and "Kubla Khan." A native of Britain, he had spent time in Germany studying Immanuel Kant's philosophy. Coleridge believed that the human capacity for imagination (or "fancy") was critically important; he associated imagination with childhood's affinity with Nature and its innocence of adult concerns.

These ideas surface in Coleridge's poetry, but they're easier to grasp in his prose. Coleridge passionately believed that "the method of nature," acting on young children in unstructured ways, yields results that are superior to anything that could occur in a classroom. He believed that a *laissez faire* process "stores the mind with all the material for [later] use," implying that, when childhood ends, individuals possess inside themselves everything that's worth knowing:

> In the infancy and childhood of individuals . . . the first knowledges are acquired promiscuously. —Say rather that the plan is not formed by the selection of objects presented to the notice of the pupils; but by the impulses and dispositions suited to their age, by the limits of their comprehension, and the volatile and desultory activity of their attention, and by the relative predominance or the earlier development of one or more faculties over the rest. This is the happy delirium, the healthful fever of the physical, moral, and intellectual being, —nature's kind and providential gift to childhood.
>
> In the best sense of the words, it is the light-headedness and light-heartedness of human life! There is indeed, "method in't" but it is the method of nature which thus stores the mind with all the material for after use, promiscuously indeed and as it might seem without purpose, which she supplies a gay and motley chaos of facts, and forms, and thousand-fold experiences, the origin of which lies beyond the memory, traceless as life itself, and finally passing into a part of our life more rapidly than would have been compatible with distinct consciousness. . . . [12]

As the British scholar William Walsh observed in *The Use of Imagination: Educational Thought and the Literary Mind* (1959), Coleridge's view of children ". . . included candour which has not yet come to acquiescence in the routine corruption of the adult world, single-mindedness untainted by the hypocrisy of conventional valuation, spontaneity undrilled into the stock response, and a virtue of intense, fierce honesty." Early 19th century readers who were deeply influenced by Coleridge's views most likely would become advocates of preserving precious human capacities, such as imagination, beyond one's childhood years.

William Wordsworth

A friend of Coleridge, Wordsworth (1770–1850) is the author of still-celebrated poems such as "I Wandered Lonely as a Cloud" and "The World Is Too Much with Us." He had visited France twice in the 1790s and was an unabashed supporter of the 1789 French Revolution. He believed that wisdom could only be gained by those who, in many ways, remained childlike throughout life. "The Child is the father of the Man," is a Wordsworth phrase, from his lovely poem, "My Heart Leaps Up When I Behold."[13] Now consider these lines from Wordsworth's "Ode: Intimations of Immortality from Recollections of Early Childhood" (1807):

> Our birth is but a sleep and a forgetting:
> The Soul that rises with us, our life's Star,
>   Hath had elsewhere its setting,

> And cometh from afar:
> Not in entire forgetfulness,
> And not in utter nakedness,
> But trailing clouds of glory do we come
> From God, who is our home:
> Heaven lies about us in our infancy!
> Shades of the prison-house begin to close
> Upon the growing Boy,
> But he beholds the light, and whence it flows,
> He sees it in his joy;
> The Youth, who daily farther from the east
> Must travel, still is Nature's Priest,
> And by the vision splendid
> Is on his way attended;
> At length the Man perceives it die away,
> And fade into the light of common day.
> [Stanza V, 59–77][14]

From Wordsworth's personal point of view, his defining work probably was "The Prelude," subtitled "Growth of a Poet's Mind." Focused on the vitality and lasting impact of childhood experiences, its Fifth Book is entitled "Books." Here we find the inevitable companion to the Romantics' deification of childhood's wonderfully spontaneous imagination and organic self-development: an openly expressed suspicion that time spent on bookish study is largely or entirely wasted. In these lines, Wordsworth expresses "sadness" for those who merely pursue academic "palms":

> . . . I sometimes grieve for thee, O Man,
> Earth's paramount Creature! not so much for woes
> That thou endurest; heavy though that weight be,
> Cloud-like it mounts, or touched with light divine
> Doth melt away; but for those palms achieved
> Through length of time, by patient exercise
> Of study and hard thought; there, there, it is
> That sadness finds its fuel. Hitherto,
> In progress through this Verse, my mind hath looked
> Upon the speaking face of earth and heaven
> As her prime teacher, intercourse with man
> Established by the sovereign Intellect . . .
> [Book Fifth, 4–15][15]

So how *should* humans better spend their childhood years? "The Prelude" has an answer:

> May she long
> Behold a race of young ones like to those
> With whom I herded!—(easily, indeed,
> We might have fed upon a fatter soil
> Of arts and letters—but be that forgiven)—
> A race of real children; not too wise,
> Too learned, or too good; but wanton, fresh,
> And bandied up and down by love and hate;
> Not unresentful where self-justified;
> Fierce, moody, patient, venturous, modest, shy;
> Mad at their sports like withered leaves in winds . . .
> [Book Fifth, 406–16][16]

William Blake

For a view in verse of the evils of schooling, let's turn to the celebrated English poet William Blake (1757–1827), whose collection *Songs of Innocence* appeared in 1789. Within that collection is one of my favorites, "The School-Boy":

> I love to rise in a summer morn
>   When the birds sing on every tree;
> The distant huntsman winds his horn,
>   And the sky-lark sings with me.
>   O! what sweet company.
> But to go to school in a summer morn,
>   O! it drives all joy away;
> Under a cruel eye outworn,
>   The little ones spend the day
>   In sighing and dismay.
> Ah! then at time I drooping sit,
>   And spend many an anxious hour,
> Nor in my book can I take delight,
>   Nor sit in learning's bower,
>   Worn thro' with the dreary shower.
> How can the bird that is born for joy,
>   Sit in a cage and sing?
> How can a child, when fears annoy,
>   But droop his tender wing,
>   And forget his youthful spring?
> O father and mother, if buds are nipp'd
>   And blossoms blown away,
> And if the tender plants are stripp'd
>   Of their joy in the springing day,
>   By sorrow and care's dismay,
> How shall the summer arise in joy,
>   Or the summer fruits appear?
> Or how shall we gather what griefs destroy,
>   Or bless the mellowing year,
>   When the blasts of winter appear?[17]

THE ASSUMPTIONS, BELIEFS, AND IDEALS OF LITERARY ROMANTICISM

We could treat ourselves to more quotes from the European Romantic poets and American Transcendentalist authors of the late 18th and early 19th centuries, not to mention the words of contemporary pundits such as the philosopher Hegel, who called Romanticism "absolute inwardness." Instead, let's carefully review the beliefs and ideals of literary Romanticism, for they are exceptionally important for an understanding of our current American mindset:

- Young children are worthy models—mentally, emotionally, behaviorally, and spiritually—for the adult. They are precious. They should be imitated and regarded with reverence. This central tenet of literary Romanticism had an enduring impact, as we will see.
- The intellectual foundations of the Age of Reason—such as Descartes's systematic doubt, Bacon's observation-based inductive reasoning, and Newton's mechanization of just about everything—yield little of value for humankind. It's not that Reason is false or inadequate, but rather that it's misleading, for it gives its adher-

ents the false impression that they've attained precision and clarity about this world.[18] Contemporaries quipped that Reason "explains everything but understands nothing." Today we speak of "analysis paralysis."

- The idea that people should try to comprehend and control nature in order to exploit it for their comfort and material well-being is wrong in principle and dangerous in practice.
- Authority of all kinds—church, state, logical systems, classical aesthetics, good taste, *any* externally imposed structure or rule—is rejected. In Goethe's celebrated 1773 play *Götz von Berlichingen* a character says, "He alone is great and happy who fills his own station of independence, and has neither to command nor to obey."[19]
- Each individual's inner light illuminates the path to understanding, satisfaction, and Truth. Imagination, intuition, emotional feeling, "fancy," and "heart" contribute to that light. The meaning of *imagination* had shifted. Formerly it connoted a creative recombination of things remembered; for the Romantics, imagination transformed into *an instrument of insight superior to one's senses*. Watch for this specific notion to reappear in chapter 9.
- The most admirable beings and ideas come into existence in a manner analogous to the growth of a plant, i.e., not as a mechanical construction attaining a predetermined form but rather as the outcome of unpredictable, holistic, spontaneous, *organic* development.

Two insights about the Romantics' worldview emerge. The first is widely discussed. The second, virtually never recognized, is especially critical for our exploration of the roots of, and the implications of, the assumptions held by many Americans today about children and teaching:

1. *What is most valuable in anyone's being is inside him or her*. For the Romantics, there wasn't any question about this: Each individual's innate predispositions are capable of spontaneous, glorious unfolding, like that of a flower. This will occur if young people are in close communication with nature *and* remain innocent of adult preconceptions and society's strictures. Here's how Wordsworth begins "Influence of Natural Objects: In Calling Forth and Strengthening the Imagination in Boyhood and Early Youth" (1799):

   > Wisdom and Spirit of the universe! . . .
   >   thus from my first dawn
   > Of childhood didst thou intertwine for me
   > The passions that build up our human soul;
   > Not with the mean and vulgar works of Man;
   > But with high objects, with enduring things,
   > With life and nature; purifying thus
   > The elements of feeling and of thought . . .
   >   [lines 1 and 5–11][20]

2. *The organic principle is a passive principle*. The organic principle (also known as the botanical model) states that the most admirable beings come to be in a manner that's analogous to the growth of a plant, i.e., not externally planned and constructed by an agent but internally driven toward unpredictable, holistic, spontaneous development. From the point of view of any "I"—I the plant, I the animal, I the human—growth and development does not happen because I will it, I direct it, or I strive for it. It simply happens; it's beyond *anyone's* control. It happens when, internally and automatically, I become "ready."

Meanwhile, *I am passive* in terms of my awareness and intentionality. Note that this belief traces its lineage to Aristotle's teleological "final cause," the idea that each living thing has an inherent potential to attain its mature form; in the case of humans, this was thought to apply to both physical *and mental* development.

MUSINGS AND SPECULATIONS

A feature of Romantic thought was that innocent young children must be protected from corrupting influences. The dreaded influences came to be viewed as arising *from within the Europeans' own societies*. I believe that this assumption arose because the texture of daily social life was viewed as Not-Nature; recall the fascination of Rousseau and many others with "savages," who were viewed as aligned with Nature and therefore as Good.

WHY CHAPTER 7 IS IMPORTANT

The Romantics popularized many of the notions about the human mind, and about children and learning, that we encountered in chapters 2 through 6. One feature of the Romantics' message is critically significant for us. Their image of spontaneous growth and flowering, termed "botanical" and "organic," was applied to every aspect of human development. The application of this model to *mental* development casts it as inherently passive. That, in turn, implies that mental development *happens to* a child only when he or she is, internally and naturally, "ready." The child need not assume any volitional role in, or responsibility for, the process. Teachers and parents, too, must not impede this supposedly inexorable process.

At TheAptitudeMyth.info are the genealogical chart and "What to Remember" list for chapter 7.

NOTES

1. William Blake, "The School-Boy," *Songs of Innocence* (E. P. Dutton, 1912), 34–35.
2. This chapter is influenced by Tim Blanning, *The Pursuit of Glory: Europe 1648–1815* (Viking, 2007), 456–521; and by Judith Plotz, "The Perpetual Messiah: Romanticism, Childhood, and the Paradoxes of Human Development," in Barbara Finkelstein, ed., *Regulated Children/Liberated Children: Education in Psychohistorical Perspective* (Psychohistory Press, 1979), 63–95. Also in Finkelstein see Sterling Fishman, "The Double-Vision of Education in the Nineteenth Century: The Romantic and the Grotesque," 96–113. See also Colin Heywood, *A History of Childhood* (Polity, 2001), 19–27; Denis Lawton and Peter Gordon, *A History of Western Educational Ideas* (Woburn, 2002), 101–14; and Vernon L. Parrington, *Main Currents in American Thought, Volume II* (University of Oklahoma Press, 1987; original © 1927), xi–xviii and 317–20.
3. This thumbnail sketch of Transcendentalism is based on Philip F. Gura, *American Transcendentalism* (Hill and Wang, 2007). The first quote is Gura's own summary sentence (page 8). The second quote is attributed to Sampson Reed, *Observations on the Growth of the Mind* (Hilliard and Metcalf, 1826), 13. The final quote is attributed to Elisabeth Palmer Peabody, *Reminiscences of the Rev. William Ellery Channing, D.D.* (Roberts Brothers, 1880), 373; Peabody also described Transcendentalism as "egotheism."
4. David Halpin, *Romanticism and Education* (Continuum, 2007), 20–21.
5. Halpin cites D. Heath and J. Boreham, *Introducing Romanticism* (Icon, 1999), 11.
6. Halpin, *op. cit.*, 24.
7. Friedrich Schiller, *Complete Works of Friedrich Schiller. Aesthetical and Philosophical Essays,* vol. 8 (P.F. Collier, 1902), 273.
8. R. W. Emerson, *Nature* (James Munroe, 1849).
9. *Oxford English Dictionary* (Oxford University Press, 1971), Compact Edition, vol. I, 1900.
10. William Wordsworth, *The Complete Poetical Works of William Wordsworth* (Houghton Mifflin, 1904), 93.
11. E.D. Hirsch, Jr., *The Knowledge Deficit* (Houghton Mifflin, 2006), 3–7; quote, 6.

12. Quoted by Alice D. Snyder, ed., *Coleridge on Logic and Learning* (Folcroft, 1973), 105. The quote appears to be from "Logic" in *The Collected Works of Samuel Taylor Coleridge,* vol. 13 (Routledge & Kegan Paul, 1981), 8 (paragraph break added).

13. William Wordsworth, *The Complete Poetical Works of William Wordsworth, Vol. IV, 1801–1805* (Houghton Mifflin, 1919), 59.

14. Wordsworth (1904), *op. cit.,* 354.

15. *Ibid.,* 152.

16. *Ibid.,* 156–57.

17. Blake, *op. cit.*

18. Blanning, *op. cit.,* 521.

19. Brander Matthews, ed., *The Chief European Dramatists* (Houghton Mifflin, 1916), 598.

20. Wordsworth (1904), *op. cit.,* 110.

EIGHT

An Influential Educator
Reflects the Currents of His Time

Man, it is thou thyself, the inner consciousness of thy powers, which is the object of the education of nature.

—Johann Pestalozzi[1]

As we trace thought trends across centuries, we'd do well to observe how they came to bear on a humble Swiss teacher who eventually became a beacon for reform-minded Western educators.[2]

FROM OBSCURITY AND BANKRUPTCY TO PAN-WESTERN INFLUENCE

Born during the Enlightenment, Johann Heinrich Pestalozzi (1746–1827) lived in Switzerland throughout his life. At university he acquired a fascination with nature and gained a romanticized view of poor Swiss peasants. Upon leaving university, he turned to agriculture and, with his new wife, set up an experimental farm. He soon added a small school where, without conspicuous success, he educated the local pauper children. Eventually he lost the farm in bankruptcy.

A friend who owned a journal persuaded Pestalozzi to become a writer, which he did for 18 years. One of his writings, *The Evening Hours of a Hermit*, was a series of aphorisms, including:

> The powers of conferring blessings upon humanity are not a gift of art or of accident. They exist, with their fundamental principles, in the inmost nature of all men. Their development is the universal need of humanity.[3]

Pestalozzi was convinced that his school at Neuhof, which had been "permeated by the spirit of a well-ordered home," provided him with valuable ideas. Following Rousseau's model, he set out to write a novel conveying those ideas. *Leonard and Gertrude* (1781) tells the story of how a loving, resourceful housewife and mother, with the active support of an aristocratic, paternalistic landlord, brought about the sweeping transformation of a backward Swiss peasant village.

Widely read as a romantic novel by people with no interest in schools, *Leonard and Gertrude* won two awards and brought fame to its author. *How Gertrude Teaches Her Children* followed in 1801. Gertrude was portrayed as providing home schooling for her children, whom she trained through their senses, guiding their observation of nature and helping them learn how to contribute through work to the family's well-being. As summarized by Gerald L. Gutek, "Pestalozzi's thesis was that *knowledge of the natural patterns of development* would enlighten all ethical and political science and supply man with a solid educational base."[4]

When a revolutionary Helvetian Republic was proclaimed in Switzerland during 1798, the 52-year-old Pestalozzi quickly became involved as a professional educator and from then on headed a series of primary schools. These schools received visits by a constant stream of reform-minded educators from all across Europe and North America (this during an era when travel was arduous and slow). Amazingly, the Prussian government in 1808 sent 17 teachers to Pestalozzi's school—where they remained for more than three years!

Visitors included Friedrich Froebel, founder of the kindergarten movement, and Johann Herbart, who later developed a set of pedagogical principles. Pestalozzi's assistants also spread his gospel; one, Joseph Neef, wrote the first English-language book on teaching methodology.

PSYCHOLOGY ENTERS THE DISCUSSION ABOUT CHILDREN AND TEACHING

In a pamphlet he wrote during 1800, Pestalozzi made it clear that his basic purpose was to *psychologize education*. In the words of W. F. Connell, this phrase means that Pestalozzi was trying to *regulate instruction in accordance with a child's natural developmental pattern*, which in turn required the alignment of instruction with a psychological analysis of the nature and process of perception (on which rested, in Pestalozzi's view, the whole learning process). Pestalozzi promoted attempts to develop methods of teaching that would be *based upon a study of the child*,[5] an objective that will prominently reappear in chapters 10 and 14.

Pestalozzi's foundational criterion for educating young children was to create a "love environment" that would enable his charges to feel emotionally secure. He also developed a methodology known as "ABC of Anschauung," which organized classroom teaching into basic components and specified a step-by-step delivery process. In *How Gertrude Teaches Her Children*, Pestalozzi wrote that . . .

> I sought in all ways to bring the beginnings of spelling and counting to the greatest simplicity and into form, so that the child *with the strictest psychological order* might pass from the first step gradually to the second; and then without break, upon the foundation of the perfectly understood second step, might go on quickly and safely to the third and fourth.[6]

May we think of Johann Pestalozzi as having a global impact? Definitely! May we regard him as an innovator? Perhaps. May we honor him as an original thinker? No. Like most other educated Europeans, Pestalozzi flowed with the mindsets of his time, using them to consider how to educate young children. He was influenced by the empiricism of Locke and the sense realism of Comenius, developing a step-by-step instructional method using realia known as the "object lesson." He was influenced by the romanticism of Rousseau and the physiocratic economics of François Quesnay, both of whom looked to *nature* for their cues. Pestalozzi did likewise.

Pestalozzi had read *Émile* and, having applied it in raising his own son (named Jean-Jacques), he was aware of its practical shortcomings as well as its emotional appeal. But he agreed with Rousseau that it's not what the child *must* know to fit him for adulthood that's important, but rather what the child *can* know.[7] It's doubtful that Pestalozzi actually read the books of other Enlightenment thinkers, but he clearly was influenced by the climate of opinion they had fostered. His quest, then, was to develop a *natural* system of education based on a precise grasp of *human psychology* that would prove to be the pathway to human fulfillment.

PROTESTANT PERSPECTIVES—
CALVINISM AND PIETISM—ENTER THE DISCUSSION

Calvinism Posits Another "Given"

This is a good point to reflect on the religious climate throughout Europe during the second half of the 18th century. Religious establishment had long been a characteristic of European nations. Catholicism held sway in most of southern Europe; various forms of Protestantism dominated much of the north.

In Pestalozzi's own Swiss canton of Zürich, the Zwinglian-Calvinist church was established.[8] To the south, Geneva had once been the European and North American center of Calvinism, the Protestant sect founded by John Calvin (1509–1564). The Calvinists spread their doctrinal views to the Huguenots in France, the Reformed Church in The Netherlands, the Puritans in England and the American colonies, and especially the Presbyterians in Scotland. Though a theologian, John Calvin was interested in education, including practical secular education. His views had a strong impact on education in the American colonies (see chapter 11).

What interests us now is Calvin's close association with the doctrine of predestination, which had been debated as far back as Augustine and Aquinas. Predestination affirms that God has an eternal purpose including not only the creation of human beings but also their final destiny.

In Calvin's view, the key point of all Christian doctrine is "election in Christ"; he pointed to Ephesians 1:4, "even as he chose us in him before the foundation of the world, that we should be holy and blameless before him." Calvin interpreted this to mean that before time began (a) some individuals were chosen—"elected"—by Christ for salvation and (b) all other individuals were not chosen by Christ and thus destined for eternal damnation.

In his voluminous writings, Calvin said that Christian life does not have its foundation in any decision of the human will, nor in anyone's meritorious activity; it can be found only in the merciful love of God. This is significant because it's about something *granted at birth*. This very influential Protestant doctrine carried the unmistakable message that each individual is born with at least one highly significant "given" that simply cannot be changed by his or her willpower, decision, effort, activity, virtue, or behavior. Nor can anyone else change a "given," either.

Pietism Focuses on Inner Nature

The 18th century wasn't characterized only by religious establishment but also by one of the periodic "Great Awakenings."[9] Reform-Protestant sects appeared during this era, some of which remain today as substantial institutions—Amish, Baptists, Quakers, Brethren, Mennonites—plus others less familiar now, such as Millerites and Dunkers.

These denominations, collectively called "Pietist" or "Pietistic," were suspicious of formal, ritual observances and doctrinal debates (for example, they took no position on predestination). They called for and practiced a spontaneous "religion of the heart." Advocates emphasized salvation via personal religious experience; they focused on an individual's *genuine inner nature* instead of conformity to outer behavioral forms handed down from earthly authorities.

Pestalozzi himself had been educated in the Pietist tradition and remained identified with it throughout his life. We wouldn't be wrong to think of his approach to the education of young children as "instruction with heart." Gutek summarizes the influence of Pietism on Pestalozzi by saying that "Pestalozzi was a naturalistic Christian humanist who held that while the powers of human nature were God-given, *it was man's responsibility to cooperate with nature* and thus ensure his own self-improvement, or his own natural salvation."[10]

Here's what I believe to be a reasonably accurate summary of Pestalozzian thought: For each individual, God or Nature establishes, or "gives," a combination of potential capabilities and qualities. Unaided, each person can learn and develop to *some* extent but is not able to attain his or her full potential. However, the Pestalozzian instructional methods, which cooperate with each child's natural development style as revealed by psychology, can be instrumental in enabling each pupil to attain most or all of what God or Nature provided.

That image is attractive on the rhetorical and emotional levels, but it comes with a flaw: "Potential"—i.e., latent quality, ability, or power—is generally assumed to be finite. It implies "to a great extent." *But it also implies outer limits of attainment, and it implies only some courses of application but not others.* Discussions of potential rarely include references to limits. In *this* book's discussion, however, the limitations of "potential" will be addressed.

MUSINGS AND SPECULATIONS

When I think about "potential," which is a "given," I imagine a box—a large box, perhaps, but nonetheless a space bounded on all six sides. It is assumed to contain a finite quantity of an individual's abilities and powers; this assumption often rises into people's conscious awareness. But this metaphorical box also *rigidly limits and constrains the individual's abilities and powers*; these limitations of potential rarely enter people's awareness.

WHY CHAPTER 8 IS IMPORTANT

The importance of this chapter lies less in Pestalozzi's classroom methods, encapsulated by the phrase "instruction with heart," and more in his further dissemination of a paradigm that already had some credibility among educators and the educated public. This was the notion, termed by Pestalozzi "psychologizing instruction," that in order to improve teaching, first discover and understand the inner lives of children, *then devise methods and approaches that reflect and cater to their inner lives.* This belief will reappear as our story continues.

At TheAptitudeMyth.info are the genealogical chart and "What to Remember" list for chapter 8.

NOTES

1. From Pestalozzi's *The Evening Hours of a Hermit*, found in Henry Barnard, *Pestalozzi and His Educational System* (C. W. Bardeen, 1906), 723.
2. My overview of Pestalozzi is largely based on Gerald L. Gutek, *Pestalozzi and Education* (Random House, 1968). Also consulted has been W. F. Connell, "The Teacher in the Eighteenth and Nineteenth

Centuries," originally published in 1957 in *The Forum of Education* (16/2) and found in Margaret Gillett, ed., *Readings in the History of Education* (McGraw Hill, 1969), especially 145–48; and Gerald L. Gutek, *An Historical Introduction to American Education* (Crowell, 1970), 174–78.

3. Pestalozzi, *op.cit.*.

4. Gutek, *op. cit.*, 36–37 (italics added).

5. Connell, *op. cit.*, 146, 147 (italics added in both cases).

6. Johann Heinrich Pestalozzi, *How Gertrude Teaches Her Children*, Ebenezer Cooke, ed., L. E. Holland and F. C. Turner, translators (C. W. Bardeen, 1898), 53 (italics added). *Anschauung* has a variety of English translations, including "intuition," "observation," "sense-impression," and "opinion"; Gutek, 88. *Anschauungsunterricht* means "seeing teaching" according to Jack K. Campbell, *Colonel Francis W. Parker* (Teachers College, 1967), 70.

7. William Boyd and Edmund J. King, *The History of Western Education, 12th ed.* (Barnes & Noble Books, 1977), 325.

8. Details about Calvin come from Fritz Büsser, "John Calvin," an entry in *Collier's Encyclopedia* (Collier's, 1997), vol. 5, 186; and Hugh T. Kerr, "Predestination," *ibid.*, vol. 19, 315.

9. Gutek, *op. cit. Pestalozzi and Education*, 14–15.

10. *Ibid.*, 15 (italics added).

NINE

New Views and Ideals All Coalesce in One Man's Mind

In the three decades after the Civil War it was impossible to be active in any field of intellectual work without mastering Spencer.

—Richard Hofstadter[1]

In Western Europe during the late 18th and early 19th centuries, the romantic ideals and beliefs overviewed in the two previous chapters, and the new views of nature, human nature, childhood, and authority discussed in earlier chapters, were familiar to many educated people.[2] Among such people, these perspectives weren't merely familiar but were often discussed and debated.

One English family that actively pondered and disseminated such ideas, and had an interest in math and science as well, welcomed a new infant in 1820. This boy eventually would take these ideas, develop them in the context of Europeans' late 19th century mindset, apply them to child development, education, and classroom instruction, and disseminate them throughout and beyond Europe to an extent never previously equaled. This boy was Herbert Spencer.

A MAN WITH A PRODIGIOUSLY RESTLESS MIND

During the latter half of the 19th century (also known as the Victorian period), Spencer was almost certainly the most widely read and discussed philosopher in Europe, North America, and indeed the entire Western world. Spencer's contemporary, the philosopher Thomas Huxley, described Spencer as a "rope maker": People flocked to Spencer's books and lectures because he began with the "loose yarn" of familiar-sounding but seemingly unconnected ideas, then skillfully wove them into an intellectually satisfying "rope."

Historian Richard Hofstadter concludes that in the post-Civil War U.S., "Spencer [had] a public influence that transcended Darwin's," and goes on to observe that Spencer directed himself not only to professional thinkers but also to ordinary folks: the "homemade intellectual," the "cracker-barrel agnostic."[3]

In our quest for the origins of current western-contemporary paradigms about children and learning, we simply must pay careful attention to Herbert Spencer's ideas because, during Spencer's lifetime, millions paid careful attention to his ideas by reading his books and attending his lectures. Two reasons have been offered for his popularity:

- In relation to social and economic trends, Spencer's thought resonated perfectly with the rise of industrialism in England and the United States. Hofstadter says that Spencer's philosophy was "a system conceived in and dedicated to an age of steel and steam engines, competition, exploitation, and struggle." Hofstadter adds that expansion-minded American businessmen in particular welcomed "the expansive evolutionary optimism of the Spencerian system."[4]
- In relation to intellectual trends, Spencer's ideas spoke reassuringly to the many people who were mentally wrestling with the yawning gap that had opened between metaphysical and religious ideas on the one hand, and hard science on the other. Theirs was the first generation to grow up with beliefs derived from revealed religion[5] and the views of the Romantic poets while simultaneously witnessing the emergence of modern science, which promised an empirical explanation for just about everything. *Spencer specifically addressed this gap.*

Many of the scientific research areas and philosophical thought trends that had been current in Western Europe since the 15th century—including ideas traceable to pre-Christian Greek times and, specifically, Aristotelian perspectives—seemed to coalesce and funnel into Spencer's prodigiously restless mind. As the dust began to settle, Spencer—whose first job had been as a railway engineer—started writing books and publicly lecturing on first one topic, then another, then another, then another . . ., a rarely equaled intellectual *tour de force*.

The most widely purchased of Spencer's books was *Education*. It explained how children learn best and what types of classroom teaching are best. To fully grasp its prescriptions (the subject of chapter 10), we must first appreciate Spencer's worldview in the context of his times.

SPENCER'S VIEW OF EVOLUTIONARY DEVELOPMENT: HOMOGENEOUS-TO-HETEROGENEOUS

Spencer became a leading figure in an intellectual movement known as the "New Reformation" or "spiritualism," the object of which was to stake out a middle ground between orthodox Christianity (which was no longer satisfying due to scientific advances) and the most rigorous conception of science, that of the French positivist Auguste Comte (who denied the possibility of any purpose in the universe beyond cold, hard facts). The challenge for the New Reformation thinkers was to develop a way of viewing life and nature that respected science *and* resonated with the warm sensibilities expressed by Christianity at its best, and by the literary Romantics.

Spencer took up this challenge. As a young man, he had been deeply affected by the work of the father of modern embryology, German-Estonian Karl Ernst von Baer. In 1828, von Baer had stated a "biogenetic law" that, in the case of higher animals, an individual's early embryonic development passes through stages that are almost indistinguishable from the early embryonic stages of lower animals. Von Baer's "eureka moment" occurred when, finding in his laboratory the unlabeled embryo specimens of several disparate species, he—the world's expert—could not tell them apart! He concluded that across eons of time, lower animals had been the ancestors of higher animals. (You can see that von Baer's law was a precursor of evolutionary theory.)

An equally portentous outcome of von Baer's observation of embryos was his conclusion that specialized structures—lungs, brain, etc.—emerge by means of gradual changes in earlier, generalized structures or conditions. Put differently, the development of embryos proceeds from a condition of *homogeneity or simplicity* to one of *heterogeneity or complexity*.

If Herbert Spencer had a eureka moment, it occurred while he was studying von Baer's writings on homogeneous-to-heterogeneous embryonic development. We don't know if Spencer's "aha" came in a blinding flash or if he teased it out over time. What we do know is this: *For Spencer, "homogeneous-to-heterogeneous" became the template for everything of a developmental nature, including human and evolutionary development.*[6] In what he viewed as a universal developmental imperative, Spencer saw these connotations:

- Natural—Homogeneous-to-heterogeneous development is intrinsic to all living things.
- Interactional—Although intrinsic to all living things, development is not wholly driven by internal imperatives. It occurs through individuals' interactions with their environments.
- Gradual—This change process is extremely slow, proceeding at an evolutionary pace.
- Inexorable—Development happens! Humans cannot influence its course in any way.
- Unidirectional—All evolutionary development is invariably headed in a single direction.
- Teleological—The direction in which evolutionary development takes the human species is toward an ever more ordered, harmonious, and desirable world. It is *purposeful* and *proactive*, conveying us collectively toward a higher plane. Spencer's view was almost certainly inspired by Aristotle's teleological "final cause," posited as "that for the sake of which" a process of change and development occurs.

  Spencer's thinking differs from Darwin's view of evolution, in which development is *reactive* and *adaptive* in relation to changes and challenges in the environment. Darwin did *not* view natural selection[7] in teleological terms, i.e., in terms of proactively reaching for a higher plane or ideal state. *This is a key difference between Spencer and Darwin.*[8]

  Where observers differ is on whether Spencer believed that the course of teleological development was predetermined by some kind of Master Plan or Being,[9] or whether it spontaneously emerges and progresses toward an ideally ordered, harmonious world. In either case, however, humans are completely unable to foresee the final outcome.

- Uncompassionate—Inevitably, some individuals will suffer as teleological development unfolds because they are congenitally "unfit" for its direction. Other individuals, those fortunate to have been born "fit" for development's direction, ought not to take any action to ameliorate the suffering of the unfit. There's no point; the unfit are doomed.

  "Survival of the fittest," that famous phrase, was coined by Spencer, *not* Darwin; to Spencer, this phrase implied "demise of the unfit." In Spencer's worldview, the unfit cannot be helped to adapt. All individuals, fit and unfit, can attain the potential that they were "given" at birth, but no one is otherwise adaptable or capable of further development. So those who are fit should stand back out of the way and let the unfit die off.

  The distinction between Darwin and Spencer is this: Darwin said, "Organisms adapt." Spencer said, "Human organisms are given fixed characteristics and cannot adapt, not even with outside assistance." Spencer's view came to be known as Social Darwinism.

  During Spencer's heyday, his thinking greatly fortified and further disseminated the rigid view of children's "given" capabilities—one of the key thought trends that this book has been tracking from its emergence in pre-Christian Greece.

SPENCER'S "FIRST PRINCIPLES": INBORN, INTUITED, SCIENTIFICALLY ACCURATE TRUTHS

The embryologist Karl von Baer was not the only significant influence on Spencer's world view. Two others stand out: Henry L. Mansel, an Oxford philosopher of the Caledonian (Scottish) intuitionist school; and Francis W. Newman, author of two books widely read by intellectual Victorians, *Soul* and *Phases of Faith*. Like Spencer and other mid-Victorian intellectuals, Mansel and Newman were trying to establish a middle ground between the polar extremes of positivistic science on the one hand, and revealed Christianity and spiritualist mysticism on the other.

Living as they were during the heyday of literary Romanticism, Mansel and Newman's quest not surprisingly turned their thoughts to the human mind, and within that mind to *intuition and insight*, which both of them—and eventually Spencer—came to see as capable of bridging the polar extremes of science and spirit.

Francis Newman wrote that the "Infinite" exists in each individual's mind, an inborn, pan-human conception; therefore, he said, morality has an authentic basis independent of revealed religion. (The finding of a new basis for morality was significant because of the perception that science and other Enlightenment perspectives had undermined its traditional religious underpinnings.) For his part, Henry Mansel espoused a "philosophy of the relative" that placed Mind on the same level as Matter. That Mind and Matter were co-equal was said to be "common sense."

Emerging from Spencer's mind and pen was a set of perspectives based on "first principles." (*First Principles* also was the title of one of his major works, published in 1862 and revised several times.) For Spencer as well as his New Reformation and intuitionist colleagues, "first principles" was far more than a title given to a list of axioms. Spencer was convinced that *Truth could be found only within the mind* of each human being.

Where Should Humans Look to Discover Truth?

Thinkers within the Enlightenment's empirical tradition—those who favored evidence-based, inductive methods—had been saying that Truth was derived from scientific procedures such as observation of things and events *external* to the self. Spencer and his intuitionist colleagues now countered that Truth was derived from intuition, that is, from attending to something *internal* to the self, something "given." What is discovered from one's own inborn Truth was labeled "first principles" by Spencer. By whatever name—"Infinite" (Newman), "Mind" (Mansel), or "First Principles" (Spencer)—*this perspective must be recognized as belief-based and deductive.*

Herbert Spencer saw first principles as the long-sought bridge between scientific and metaphysical truths. Elaborating on this, he stated that *beliefs* link the individual with the natural universe; beliefs are the ultimate psychological facts. These facts are verifiable by each individual's instincts; rational or scientific verification is not required. Consequently, argued Spencer, the human mind serves as a scientific tool, able to detect falsehoods by looking inward.

Following Henry Mansel's notion that the psychological and material worlds are on the same level, *Spencer argued that thinking, by itself, is a valid means of scientific investigation.* Spencer wrote of "the irresistible evidence of our instincts," and held that instincts are never mistaken. He saw scientific progress as dependent on human insight.

Spencer was by no means ignorant of science; among his multiple and massive published works are *Principles of Psychology*, a two-volumed *Principles of Biology*, and a multivolumed *Principles of Sociology* . . . to name a few. He was no stranger to evidence-based techniques. But when Spencer wrote and lectured in a philosophical frame of mind, presenting himself as the bridge-builder between observational empiricism and romantic intuition, he made very clear that he relied on *deductive processes grounded in intuition* as the road to Truth.[10]

For the legions of late 19th century people who attended his lectures and devoured his books, Spencer erased the distinction between the subjective and objective worlds. *Cloaking himself in the mantle of "science," Spencer viewed each individual's introspective mind, acting alone, as a scientific tool capable of verifying "first principles," i.e., capable of verifying natural Truth.* His readers and listeners were encouraged to experience the world of spirit as anchored in reality.

THE RISE AND FALL OF HERBERT SPENCER

Within his lifetime, which extended into the early 20th century, Herbert Spencer went from being a railway engineer to reigning as one of the Western world's two or three most well-known intellectuals. Then his popularity sharply declined, and today his name is rarely recognized. Why?

Two overlapping and mutually supportive explanations have been advanced to account for Spencer's magnetism during his heyday. One concerns his style, the other his content.

In terms of *style*, the way in which Spencer presents his case is remarkably convincing. For example, 19th century educational historian Gabriel Compayré has observed that, "The air of breadth and candor with which [Spencer] sets out is eminently prepossessing, and the reader is almost obliged to assume that he is being led to foregone conclusions."[11] Then there's his *content*, his process of advancing an argument. Keeping in mind that Spencer was a widely traveled public speaker, I turn to our contemporary, Kieran Egan, for this explanation:

> Part of Spencer's success in stimulating a revolution in educational theory if not in practice was due to his rhetorical strategies. Apart from his own conviction, and his presenting learning as some kind of *binary moral choice* between the traditional, passive, forced, and vicious, and the progressive, active, effortless, and pleasurable, he constantly interspersed his arguments with attractive and plausible images of the new methods at work. In contrast with an image of frustrated and unhappy children toiling indoors over dull textbooks, consider this typical example of Spencer's descriptions of his proposed methods in practice: "Every botanist who has had children with him in the woods and lanes must have noticed how eagerly they joined in his pursuits . . . [and] overwhelmed him with questions." Who could be against . . . such scenes of eager learning?[12]

In spite of his ability to communicate and the public's hunger for a message of just the sort he was bearing, Spencer began falling out of favor even before he died. Four reasons for his decline have been advanced: intellectual, political, moral, and educational.

Intellectual

Spencer fell out of favor among intellectuals in two quite different ways. The first occurred because Spencer's philosophy sustained a serious blow from the findings of German theoretical physicist Rudolf Clausius, who introduced the concept of "entropy." Entropy usually is defined as a measure of disorder or randomness: The greater the measure of entropy in a physical or biological system, the more uniformly distributed throughout that system is undifferentiated randomness. In short, the more homogeneous it is.

Clausius gave us the second law of thermodynamics, which says that natural process-es all occur in such a way that the measure of entropy in a system is increased to a maximum. (The maximum is a state in which all matter has a uniform temperature and no energy exists.)

Spencer had staked his reputation on the principle that homogeneous-to-heterogene-ous development is intrinsic and inexorable. According to Clausius, Spencer was exactly wrong! Clausius said that heterogeneous-to-homogeneous is the direction of all things. Consequently, intellectuals had no option but to seriously doubt the validity of Spencer's entire world view.

A different feature of Spencerian thought came under attack in the United States during the latter years of the 19th century. We've seen that Spencer's developmental imperative included characteristics such as inexorable, unidirectional, and teleological; in short, his was a philosophy of inevitability. Inevitability, in turn, implies that no further effort is needed: *que será será*.

But *que será será* did not go down well with the Americans. In their portion of the world, resourceful pioneers and cowboys were taming the West, rails were being laid coast to coast, business was expanding apace, ports were teeming with hopeful immi-grants, and reformers were preparing to ameliorate ugly urban conditions. Spencer had cast human beings as powerless in the face of predetermined events. For Americans, there could hardly have been a worse fit.[13]

Political

Similar to the stance of the Libertarian Party in the United States today, political liberalism in mid-Victorian Britain was strongly *laissez faire*, arguing that government should involve itself in citizens' activities as little as possible. Spencer, a liberal, believed that the need for government would diminish as evolutionary development led humans into an ever more harmonious world.

But the trend was toward *more* state involvement and control in order to improve conditions that led to human suffering. Contemporaries referred to "meliorism." In Brit-ain, the Liberal Party split into classical and reform wings; the reformers gained ascen-dancy after 1906. In the United States, advocates found their appealing spokesperson, Theodore Roosevelt, in the White House after 1901. Spencer remained true to his hands-off philosophy and was left ever farther behind.

Moral

Being identified with the "out" political persuasion, by itself, might not have under-mined Spencer's towering reputation; but his stance on a moral issue did. Progressives in the United States and reformers in Britain hoped to alleviate human suffering directly by attacking its causes. Spencer disagreed. Consistent with his view of the uncompassionate developmental imperative, he never abandoned his dictum, "survival of the fittest," and loudly favored abandoning "the incapables" to their miserable fate. This made Spencer seem personally repugnant to a great many people.

Educational

Remaining consistent with his developmental imperative also lost Spencer the respect of many educators. He opposed state-supported education at the time when progressives and reformers were crusading to expand it. His belief that some groups had advanced along the developmental path much farther than others led Spencer to think of certain ethnic and national groups as among "the incapables." So he was strongly against education for the lower classes. In the United States in particular, where educators were trying to cope with the burgeoning influx of immigrant children (see chapter 12), Spencer's racism was received as worse than useless.

But in spite of his rapidly declining stature in the estimation of the general public on two continents, Spencer's ideas about how children learn best and what kind of classroom teaching is best remained astonishingly influential. Teachers, educators, and others actively interested in schooling gradually, almost imperceptibly, graduated from merely thinking *about* Spencer's educational ideals to thinking *with* his educational ideals.

In the introduction to this book, it is posited that a significant proportion of the American population shares characteristic value propositions about children and teaching:

- Children learn best when encouraged to perform wholly within their natural inclinations.
- Classroom teaching is best when guided first and foremost by attention to the children.

These two interrelated paradigms are traceable to Spencer more than to any other single source. But as Spencer began to fall out of favor, his paternity of these ideals came to be forgotten.

MUSINGS AND SPECULATIONS

One wonders whether Spencer was conscious of the fact that, while he was writing volume after volume on scientific topics that *appeared* to be evidence-based and dependent on inductive reasoning, he was simultaneously entertaining his captivated public with philosophical notions that were belief-based and dependent on deduction. I've found no answer to this question.

WHY CHAPTER 9 IS IMPORTANT

No historical figure has done more than Spencer to supply the value statements that many Americans reach for when they think about education. This chapter helps us fathom "where Spencer was coming from." That place was his deep conviction that each person's "givens" rigidly limit and circumscribe what he or she will be able to do and attain, regardless of any external guidance or support, regardless of any internal intention or commitment. Chapter 9 has prepared us for chapter 10, which takes a detailed look at Spencer's views on education.

At TheAptitudeMyth.info are the genealogical chart and "What to Remember" list for chapter 9.

NOTES

1. Richard Hofstadter, *Social Darwinism in American Thought*, rev. ed. (George Brazillier, 1959) chapter 2, "The Vogue of Spencer," 33.

2. This chapter relies primarily on Mark Francis, *Herbert Spencer and the Invention of Modern Life* (Cornell, 2007), 9, 112–14, 121, 154, 165, 185, 217, 254, 331, 336; and also on Gabriel Compayré, *Herbert Spencer and Scientific Education* (1907; University Press of the Pacific, 2002), 51–66; Kieran Egan, *Getting It Wrong from the Beginning* (Yale University Press, 2002), 11–114; and Hofstadter, *ibid.* See also Gerald L. Gutek, *A History of the Western Educational Experience*, 2nd ed. (Waveland, 1995), 300–10; and John Clever-

ley and D. C. Phillips, *Visions of Childhood: Influential Models from Locke to Spock*, rev. ed. (Teachers College, 1986), 44–47.

3. Hofstadter, *op. cit.*, 31–32, 33.

4. *Ibid.*, 35, 44.

5. "Revealed religion" is often used to denote any religion that claims its origin to be one or more events in which a supreme being directly communicated with humans, "revealing" eternal Truths to them.

6. For an alternative view of how Spencer arrived at his template, see Hofstadter, *op. cit.*, 35–40.

7. Natural selection begins with the physical and physiological variations that increase adaptability at the individual and species levels, spread throughout the entire species, and lead eventually to the emergence of new species.

8. "All the well-known pre-Darwinian evolutionary theories . . . had taken evolution to be a goal-directed process. For many men the abolition of that teleological kind of evolution was the . . . least palatable of Darwin's suggestions." Thomas S. Kuhn, *The Structure of Scientific Revolutions*, 3rd ed. (University of Chicago, 1996), 171–72.

9. Spencer did allow for the existence of an "Unknown," a mysterious presiding intelligence.

10. Thomas Huxley once quipped that ". . . Spencer's idea of a tragedy is a deduction killed by a fact!" Robert L. Carneiro, "Herbert Spencer as an Anthropologist," *Journal of Libertarian Studies*, vol. V, no. 2 (Spring 1981), 190.

11. Gabriel Compayré, *The History of Pedagogy* (D. C. Heath, 1894; University Press of Hawaii, 2002), 568 [¶ 667].

12. Kieran Egan, *Getting It Wrong from the Beginning* (Yale University Press, 2002), 45–46; italics added. Egan cites *The Works of Herbert Spencer*, published in Osnabrück, Germany, in 1890 (vol. 16, page 86).

13. The popular 19th century psychologist, William James, claimed in publications and lectures that Spencer ignored humans' willful efforts to improve their environment. Using *ad hominem* attacks, James described Spencer as "fatally lacking in geniality, humor, picturesqueness, and poetry," and as possessing a "dry school-master temperament." Hofstadter, *op. cit.*, 123–34.

TEN

Basic Guidelines for the Western-Contemporary Paradigm

Go where you will, and before long there come under your notice cases of children or youths, of either sex, more or less injured by undue study.

—Herbert Spencer[1]

Slightly more than 200 pages in length, Herbert Spencer's *Education: Intellectual, Moral, and Physical* was published in 1860, just as Spencer's star was ascending.[2] Barely noticed by his elite philosophical peers, it enjoyed multiple reprintings and numerous translations. In the post-Civil War United States, it was a huge best-seller, read by myriad citizens and most professionals involved in crafting the new system of state-supported schools. No other publication had greater impact on how people in the West thought about the "shoulds" of teaching and learning.

A RINGING DECLARATION ABOUT CHILDREN, LEARNING, TEACHING, AND PARENTING

Spencer's *Education* is a collection of four short essays. The first and longest of the four, "What Knowledge Is of Most Worth?," elaborately attempts to persuade the reader that, in pursuit of both "complete living" and mental discipline, science is the knowledge of most worth. Within this first essay lies a revealing declaration of the western-contemporary paradigm (this term is mine not Spencer's), three pages in length. The first half reads as follows:

> Grant that the phenomena of intelligence conform to laws; grant that the evolution of intelligence in a child also conforms to laws, and it follows inevitably that education can be rightly guided only by a knowledge of these laws. To suppose that you can properly regulate this process of forming and accumulating ideas, without understanding the nature of the process, is absurd. How widely, then, must teaching as it is differ from teaching as it should be; when hardly any parents, and but few tutors, know anything about psychology.
>
> As might be expected, the [current educational] system is grievously at fault, alike in matter and in manner. While the right class of facts is withheld, the wrong class is forcibly administered in the wrong way and in the wrong order. With that common limited idea of education which confines it to knowledge gained from books, parents thrust primers into the hands of their little ones years too soon, to their great injury. Not recognizing the truth that the function of books is . . . a means of seeing through other men what you

71

cannot see for yourself—[people] are eager to give second-hand facts in place of first-hand facts....

Not perceiving the enormous value of that spontaneous education which goes on in early years—not perceiving that a child's restless observation, instead of being ignored or checked, should be diligently ministered to, and made as accurate and complete as possible [—] they insist on occupying the eyes and thoughts with things that are, for the time being, incomprehensible and repugnant.

Possessed by a superstition which worships the symbols of knowledge instead of the knowledge itself, they do not see that only when his acquaintance with the objects and processes of the household, the streets, and the fields is becoming tolerably exhaustive—only then should a child be introduced to the new sources of information which books supply: and this, not only because immediate cognition is of far greater value than mediate cognition, but also because the words contained in books can be rightly interpreted into ideas, only in proportion to the antecedent experience of things.[3]

Particularly noteworthy in the above declaration are the following three features.

The Rigidity of Patterns Bestowed at Birth

Note first that Spencer references "laws" of intelligence and learning. Spencer is saying: Nature does its thing according to inexorable patterns; these aren't necessarily obvious but can be discerned through observation (the role of science). So if we humans want to obtain beneficial outcomes, then *we must conform to nature's patterns*; any deviation will inevitably result in failure and physical or mental injury.

In Spencer's view—and this is a central point—human beings must not stray from the patterns with which they were bestowed at birth. If they do so, they will not only fail but also injure themselves. Personal motivation and determination simply don't matter because—as noted in chapter 9—*human flexibility, adaptability, and resilience are not possible.*

The Primacy of Psychology When Making Educational Choices

Spencer states that the laws of intelligence and learning are susceptible to being investigated and understood; that's the role of psychology. Spencer knew that psychology was just beginning to come into its own (he never claimed that it already had everything figured out). But he assumed that he knew enough psychology to denounce the "established system [of education as] grievously at fault, alike in matter and in manner." His *Education* has no admiration at all for 19th century educational practices—the entire curriculum *and* the prevailing instructional style.

The key point here, however, concerns what Spencer passionately advocates for education's future—a future in the mold fashioned by Johann Pestalozzi. Spencer advocates *curriculum and classroom practices directly driven by the emerging science of psychology*, which he believes will eventually provide ever more clearly a window into the inexorable laws of intelligence and learning that, in turn, have always shaped and driven children.

Parents and Teachers as "Domestic Servants" to Each Child's Master Program

Spencer speaks of "the enormous value of that spontaneous education which goes on in early years" as each child explores "the household, the streets, and the fields." He contrasts this natural process with the prevailing one in which "second-hand facts" are "thrust" on children through books.

This brings us to a decisive juncture in our grasp of Spencer's prescription. Virtually everyone will agree that, during the earliest days of a child's life, it is pointless to expect her to learn from books. And many would agree that, at *some* point in the future as the child develops, expecting her to learn from books becomes, if not absolutely necessary, then at least reasonable. If Spencer were arguing that the time in the future when books become appropriate *should occur later* rather than earlier, then most of us would reply: "So *when* do you think this best occurs?"

But Spencer's position is not about *when*. He's *not* advocating that we turn children loose to spontaneously explore household, streets, and fields, and he's *not* advocating that we let exploration go on and on without end, and forget the books. What Spencer *is* stating is starkly unique: that each "child's restless observation . . . *should be diligently ministered to*, and made as accurate and complete as possible."

In other words, Spencer's principal prescription for education is this: *Although children may well be restless and spontaneous, it's nonetheless of critical importance that parents and teachers constantly perform an active role by insuring that the correct new experiences, in the correct order, are placed before them.* Spencer's metaphor was that parents and teachers are "domestic servants" to the unique master program of development inherent in each child.

How is a parent or teacher to know what, exactly, is correct? According to Spencer, the laws —i.e., the generalizations—of intelligence and learning, revealed by the science of psychology, will provide the answers. It's incumbent on parents and teachers to know those laws, to know which stimuli each child's mind requires at each stage of development, and on that basis to deliberately guide that child's intellect to the now-appropriate "food." *Each parent and teacher must follow these laws and guidelines in the course of actively guiding the child day-by-day through an ordered sequence of selected experiences.*

If you think that Spencer regards daily law-driven guidance, 24/7, as a beautiful, warmly inspiring ideal, you would be wrong. He warns that one ignores these laws at his peril:

> . . . Here are the indisputable facts: that the development of children in mind and body rigorously obeys certain laws; that unless these laws are in some degree conformed to by parents, death is inevitable; that unless they are in a great degree conformed to, there must result serious physical and mental defects; and that only when they are completely conformed to can a perfect maturity be reached.[4]

ARISTOTLE, SPENCER, AND THE BIOLOGICAL MODEL OF HUMAN MENTAL ACTIVITY

Let's reacquaint ourselves with the origin of this way of thinking about children's learning.[5] Is it Spencer's unique contribution? No. The original source was Aristotle.[6]

Recall that in chapter 2 we found that Aristotle "corrected" what he saw as a flaw in Plato's notion of the "Forms." Because Plato had conceived of the Forms as fixed, perfect, and existing in a separate world, Aristotle objected that they could not account for change and growth of all kinds, which Aristotle called "movement." Aristotle concluded that far from being separate from matter, form[7] is *embodied in* matter. A thing's essence is its form; what it's made of is matter. In the case of humans, the form is the soul (*psychê*, or life); the matter is flesh.

Then, elaborating the four causes of movement, Aristotle posited a "final cause," the goal or end (in Greek, *telos*) of the entire process. Readers of Aristotle down through 2,000 years—their number was legion and their influence, including via Catholic Church leaders, was massive—internalized the belief that all processes are *teleological*, i.e., that each one has as its aim the completion of a purposeful action or attainment of a final state of being.

That means that human's internal processes are guided by one's *innately provided* disposition to reach full maturity, to attain one's "given" essence or form—"if there is no impediment."[8] (One way in which Aristotle's influence survives today is in the modern notion of "readiness.")

Aristotle's view of growth and development works reasonably well in the case of humans' physiological bodies. But Spencer follows Aristotle in applying this narrative to human *mental* activity from birth to maturity. Spencer says that, like the body, the mind has an innately "given" disposition to reach full maturity, *and we as parents, teachers, and caretakers of children must carefully support that inexorable process and be very sure that we introduce no impediment.*

By the time influential people throughout the West had finished reading Spencer's "What Knowledge Is of Most Worth?," they had learned or reinforced a strong tendency to conceive of the human mental activity from birth to maturity using the terms "grow" and "develop."[9] To this day, it's automatic for most Americans of Western European descent to *think with* derivatives of "grow" and "develop" when *thinking about* the minds of children and life-long learning adults.

But "grow" and "develop" properly refer to the process of biological and physiological maturing. They liken the mind's activity to that of a child's increasing in stature, or of a plant's flowering and bearing fruit. *We have accepted into daily use an analogy that envisions growth and development up to a point, an innately predetermined point, after which it ceases.*

But is the biological analogy of innate development—which applies to the body of flesh, bones, blood, and organs (including the brain)—equally applicable to the activity of the mind from birth to maturity? What if that analogy is inaccurate? What if it's flatly wrong?

HERBERT SPENCER'S PRESCRIPTIONS FOR THE CLASSROOM TEACHING OF CHILDREN

Let's turn now to Spencer's second essay, "Intellectual Education," which contains detailed prescriptions for how classroom teaching should be conceived and practiced. Returning to the indispensable role of parents and teachers in supplying, for the child's mind as well as for her body, the conditions for daily growth, Spencer prefaces his discussion of methods by noting that they must "be made to harmonize in character and arrangement with the [mind's] faculties in their mode and order of unfolding."[10] Agreeing that the emerging field of "rational psychology" as yet lacks the full picture of mental unfolding, he makes "empirical approximations towards a perfect scheme" by setting forth seven guiding principles:[11]

1. Proceed from the simple to the complex.
2. Proceed from the indefinite to the definite.
3. Proceed from the concrete to the abstract.
4. Proceed from the empirical to the rational.
5. Follow the same course as the genesis of knowledge in the [human] race.
6. Encourage self-development and discovery.
7. Ask, "Does what we're doing create a pleasurable excitement in the pupils?"

Principles 1–4: General Prescriptions

In setting out his first four principles, Spencer took four perspectives on a single thing: the homogeneous-to-heterogeneous template for all things developmental that he had gleaned from Karl Ernst von Baer.[12] So let's begin by establishing the characteristics of knowledge that Spencer viewed as homogeneous.

Spencer applies "homogeneous" to knowledge or information received through one's five senses, evidently because it's acquired through direct personal experience. Spencer viewed information received thus as "simple," "indefinite," "concrete," and "empirical." He also said information received thus is "first-hand knowledge" and "immediate cognition," meaning that awareness of the information passes immediately into one's brain, i.e., without mediation by anyone or anything. For example, not included in "first-hand knowledge" are reading books and listening to verbal descriptions or analyses, both of which come into one's brain after the mediation or intervention of a third party: parent, teacher, author, speaker, and so forth.

Ask yourself: "If *I* were seeking a term applicable to information gained via *my* five senses, would 'homogeneous' be one of the best terms I'd come up with?"

The distinction that Spencer makes is this: Unlike information that comes into one's brain "directly" via her five senses, all other information comes via *someone else's* brain in the form of "intellectualized representations" such as symbols, generalizations, classifications, rules such as grammars, etc. He says that information received via someone else is "second-hand knowledge" and "mediate cognition," and labels it as "complex," "definite," "abstract," and "rational." All information received in this mediated way is categorized as "heterogeneous."

Ask yourself: "If *I* were seeking a term applicable to information that I gained via someone else's brain, is 'heterogeneous' one of the best terms I'd settle on?"

Let's address the first four principles in turn. Spencer advocates that one should "Proceed . . ."

1. "From the simple to the complex." Ask yourself: Is all information that I receive via my own five senses simple? Is all information that I receive via the mediation of another complex?
2. "From the indefinite to the definite." Ask yourself: Is all information I receive via my own five senses indefinite? Is all information that I receive via the mediation of another definite?
3. "From the concrete to the abstract." My view is that, in this case, Spencer's construction more or less approximates our day-to-day reality.
4. "From the empirical to the rational." By definition, information received via anyone's five senses is "empirical." Whether information received from others is "rational" is questionable!

Principle 5: Follow the Race's Genesis of Knowledge [13]

We turn now to Spencer's fifth guiding principle: "Follow the same course as the genesis of knowledge in the [human] race." With this recommendation, Spencer was lending his growing authority to an intellectual craze that was beginning to sweep mid-19th century Europe and the United States.

Recall chapter 9's story about von Baer's "eureka moment": He had found in his laboratory the unlabeled embryo specimens of disparate species that he couldn't tell apart. The explanation that came to be believed by many about the similarity of embryos was that, during prenatal development, an animal traverses all stages of development through which its distant ancestors formerly evolved. For example, the growing embryo of a cow in the womb was said to pass through the stages of fish, amphibian, and reptile until, in the final months before being born, it finally attained the attributes of a cow (von Baer himself said this explanation was impossible).

This "theory"—in truth, a hypothesis—had a mythopoetic appeal and gained a follow-ing. It was called "recapitulation" or "parallelism." One of its key proponents, German biologist Ernst Haeckel (1834–1919), coined the trademark phrase, "Ontogeny recapit-ulates phylogeny," short for "Ontogeny is a brief and rapid recapitulation of phylogeny." Meaning: What happens to an embryo in the womb (ontogeny) repeats or parallels the evolutionary development of all living creatures over eons of time (phylogeny). Haeckel said this was a "fundamental biogenetic law."

The Fateful Giant Leap of Recapitulation Thinking

At some point, *recapitulation thinking took a giant leap from the prenatal realm into the postnatal realm.* More precisely, the general notion that *physiological* development follows a certain path *prior to* birth came to be applied to human *mental* development *following* birth.[14]

The new thinking said that, as they grow, infants and children pass through all the stages of *cultural* development that humans passed through during past millennia. As this belief became popular, it came to be called "racial recapitulation theory"—"race" mean-ing "human race"—and in Europe (especially Germany), it came to be known as the "culture-epoch theory."[15]

Spencer was not the originator of recapitulation theory (he believed it came from Auguste Comte).[16] Nor can he be credited with the giant leap of this developmental hypothesis from the prenatal realm to the postnatal. But Spencer responded warmly to that leap, for he was committed to finding *one* principle underlying *all* natural processes. Recapitulation effortlessly fit into his von Baer-inspired notion that development pro-ceeds from homogeneity to heterogeneity.

The Powerful Impact of the Recapitulation Hypothesis

This much is certain: "Racial recapitulation theory" became, across half a century, widely popular among educated people in Europe and the United States. Prominent scientists and political figures—including no less than Friedrich Engels—spoke publicly or wrote in favor of it. Book after book explained its reality—one argued that a proof of recapitulation is that some young children walk on all fours instead of crawling using their knees—and described its processes and implications. For instance, Frederick Starr, an anthropologist, wrote that, "Every person who passes through a normal development represents the culture stages of man; the child at first is a savage, later he becomes a barbarian, still later it is possible that he may become a civilized being."[17]

From the point of view of Spencer and others, the savage and the child have much in common, being simpler and less complex antecedents of their mature counterparts, civil-ized adults. According to this view, each individual's personal experience is unique. The mechanism by which each one's experience comes to pass is guided by patterns grounded in the collective development over eons of time of *all* of one's ancestors, gained through biological (hereditary) transmission. These patterns, shared by all, are important for the development of each individual.

Stripped to essentials, this view says: Human beings have a "universal mind," grounded in the trajectory of cultural development of all foregoing human beings. It is inherited biologically by each infant. It deeply impacts the whole nature of each infant, including his or her intellect. *It dictates the order in which each infant's intellect is to master various kinds of knowledge*—an order identical to that in which all ancestral human beings mastered knowledge. To the extent that a child departs from his ancestor's order or pattern of mastery, problems will arise.

Spencer's Reasoning Finally Becomes Clear

We can now grasp Spencer's prescription for education: that it is critical for parents and teachers to actively and constantly insure that the correct new experiences, *in the correct order*, are brought to each child's attention. "... success is to be achieved only by rendering our measures subservient to that spontaneous unfolding which all minds go through in their progress to maturity."[18]

Therefore, warned Spencer, parents and teachers must know the natural laws and deliberately follow them, 24/7, in guiding the child through an ordered sequence of selected experiences. If *and only if* these laws are completely conformed to can the child reach perfect maturity.

Many people took the Spencer-proclaimed message of recapitulation very seriously. After all, this wasn't merely fascinating stuff. This was a clarion call to action on behalf of all children.

Principles 6–7: What Children Should Do in Classrooms

Spencer's 6th and 7th principles counsel that children should be very largely self-taught, i.e., they should discover for themselves as much as possible. When self-teaching occurs in classrooms, he says, children will be happy.

Spencer again reveals himself to resonate harmoniously with some of the major thinkers who had preceded him (Rousseau comes to mind) and with some of his contemporaries. For example, in support of child self-development he quotes the American Horace Mann: "... unfortunately education amongst us at present consists too much in *telling*, not in *training*. . . ."[19]

More interesting is that Spencer's view of discovery learning is heavily conditioned by his insistence that it will work if, *and only if*, "... the subjects be put before [the pupil] in right order and right form. . . ."[20] Ironically, Spencer appears unaware that he is undermining his own claims when he notes that the superiority of discovery learning is "... proved by the marked success of self-made men,"[21] who (it would seem) probably could *not* have had the benefit of having subjects deliberately put before them in right order and right form by conscientious caretakers.

It's worth pausing here to quote another classic example of Spencerian prose found in his discussion of the excellence of self-development, contrasted black-versus-white with the counterproductive practices of classrooms (in this excerpt, the child is referred to as "it"):

> We drag it away from the facts in which it is interested, and which it is actively assimilating of itself; we put before it facts far too complex for it to understand, and therefore distasteful to it; finding that it will not voluntarily acquire these facts, we thrust them into its mind by force of threats and punishment; by thus denying the knowledge it craves, and cramming it with knowledge it cannot digest, we produce a morbid state of its faculties, and a consequent disgust for knowledge in general; and when, [as a consequence of this damage that we've caused] the child can understand nothing without explanation, and becomes a mere passive recipient of our instruction, we infer that education must necessarily be carried on thus.
>
> Having by our method induced helplessness, we straightway make the helplessness a reason for our method. . . .[22]

This passage can leave the impression that it's bad to put a long series of materials in front of a child, and good to allow the child to spontaneously find exploration-worthy materials here, there, or anywhere. No. Spencer held that his scheme would work *if, and only if,* subject matter is introduced to each child in a uniquely correct order and form, which in turn places an enormous, exacting, and ultimately impossible burden on parents and teachers.

Spencer's final principle urges teachers to ask themselves whether or not what they're doing induces ". . . a pleasurable excitement in the pupils."[23] He begins by positing the axiom that ". . . a child's intellectual instincts are more trustworthy than our reasonings." (This was a comfortable idea for Spencer's contemporaries, having been popularized by the literary Romantics.) Then he adds that, "under normal conditions, healthful action is pleasurable, while action which gives pain is not healthful." He concludes that young pupils' on-the-spot emotional gratification is the final court of appeal when it comes to judging the effectiveness of classroom teaching styles.

So certain is Spencer that his previous six principles are what's best for, and therefore what's pleasurable for, all children that he advises that the ". . . requirements that knowledge shall be self-mastered, and pleasureably mastered, *become the tests by which we may judge* whether the dictates of abstract psychology are being fulfilled"; and that those dictates "must correspond with the stages of evolution in [each pupil's] faculties,"[24] a direct reference to recapitulation.

The Unnumbered 8th Principle: The Terrible Toll of Mental Overstrain

Not numbered by Spencer among his seven principles, but discussed by him across the final 22 pages of *Education*, is a topic that is "perhaps more urgently demanding consideration than any of the foregoing."[25] Were this Spencer's 8th principle, it would be:

8. Avoid mental overstrain at all costs, and especially in girls.

We must attend to this 8th principle because it adds value to our efforts to reveal the origins of the western-contemporary paradigm. For here again we recognize Spencer not as an original thinker but rather as what we might call a popular packager, taking thought trends that had been gathering strength across many centuries and popularizing them.

For example, in chapter 5, we were introduced to a thought trend that we've been following ever since: The younger the human the better he or she is, so that newborns are miraculously pure and totally innocent (if also ignorant). We revisited this line of thought in chapter 7, where we found the literary Romantics rhapsodizing about infants and young children—innocent, pure, close to Nature, an image of the divine, and therefore precious, fragile, and in need of protection.

Similarly, we've watched as another thought trend emerged and grew: speculations about what human beings are "given." Chapter 2 revealed this trend as originating in ancient Greece. In chapter 8, we saw that even though Johann Pestalozzi and John Calvin had polar opposite views of human life and learning, they did share a single assumption—that each individual is born with certain "givens" determined by God or Nature.

The Grave Danger of Excess Mental Application

Along comes Herbert Spencer in the mid-19th century. He absorbs these growing thought trends and goes public with an indictment of too much school work because of the grave dangers it poses to children's health:

> . . . among the educated classes [of] the younger adults and those who are verging on maturity are [many who are] neither so well grown nor so strong as their seniors. . . . Omitting from the comparison the labouring classes, we have noticed a majority of cases in which the children do not reach the stature of their parents. . . . Yet we who think much about our bodily welfare . . . and have the greater benefit of medical knowledge; —we are continually breaking down under our work. . . .

What is the meaning of this? [He lists a few possible causes.] But there has been yet another detrimental influence at work, perhaps more potent than any of the others: we mean—excess of mental application. . . .

Go where you will, and before long there come under your notice cases of children, or youths, of either sex, more or less injured by undue study. Here, to recover from a state of debility thus produced, a year's rustication has been found necessary. There, you find a chronic congestion of the brain, that has already lasted many months, and threatens to last much longer. . . . And, again, the insistence is that of a youth who has already had once to desist from his studies, and who, since he has returned to them, is frequently taken out of his class in a fainting fit. . . . Nor have we by any means exhausted the list.[26]

Spencer continues in this manner for several pages, naming the cause as "the merciless school-drill to which many children are subjected,"[27] and offering as evidence an overview of how 24 hours are spent in an average English middle-class girls' school, after which he provides details of the daily round at a training college for young men. What he describes *is* onerous.

Spencer then addresses the beauty-destroying impact of study on young women:

On women the effects of this forcing system are, if possible, even more injurious than on men. . . . In the pale, angular, flat-chested young ladies, so abundant in London drawing-rooms, we see the effect of merciless application, unrelieved by youthful sports. . . . Mammas anxious to make their daughters attractive, could scarcely choose a course more fatal than this, which sacrifices the body to the mind. . . . Men care comparatively little for erudition in women; but very much for physical beauty, and good nature, and sound sense. [Here he elaborates at length.] . . . it is folly to persist in a system which undermines a girl's constitution that it may overload her memory. . . . By subjecting their daughters to this high-pressure system, parents frequently ruin their prospects in life. Not only do they inflict on them enfeebled health, with all its pains and disabilities and gloom; but very often they actually doom them to celibacy.[28]

Spencer Reaffirms that "Givens" Are Rigidly Limiting

Most significant is Spencer's explanation of the reason why a high and sustained quantity of mental effort is—according to him—dreadfully debilitating for the physical body of infants, children, and youth:

. . . as in the fœtus the entire vitality is expended in the direction of growth, [likewise] in the infant, the expenditure of vitality in growth is so great as to leave extremely little for either physical or mental action; so throughout childhood and youth growth is the dominant requirement to which all others must be subordinated: a requirement which dictates the giving of much and the taking away of little—a requirement which, therefore, restricts the exertion of body and mind to a degree proportionate to the rapidity of growth—a requirement which permits the mental and physical activities to increase only as fast as the rate of growth diminishes.[29]

In this passage we see at work a now-familiar hidden assumption. The overt emphasis is on the superb potentials that "givens" confer. But hidden within that, as within a Trojan Horse, is the assumption that any "given" comes with limitations and restrictions.

In the case we're considering now, Spencer refers to the welcome vitality bestowed on the fœtus, the infant, the child, and the youth. But Spencer treats as a generally accepted fact this notion: *Each individual's vitality exists in fixed and finite quantity.* If a larger portion is allocated to physiological growth—there's much of *this* during childhood—then smaller portions are left over for physical activity—there's also much of *this* during childhood—and mental effort. *Quad erat demonstrandum*: To avoid terrible consequences, mental effort must be curtailed.

A few pages before the passage quoted above, Spencer is clear about the fixed quantity:

> Let it never be forgotten that the amount of vital energy which the body at any moment possesses is limited; and that, being limited, it is impossible to get from it more than a fixed quantity of results.[30]

MUSINGS AND SPECULATIONS

I have never decided which of Spencer's two key beliefs about children has had the most enduring impact. Is it that the young's fixed quantity of energy is needed for growth and activity, leaving extremely little for academics? Or is it that each young mind's fragile, rigid, spontaneously unfolding patterns require subservient compliance from parents and teachers?

WHY CHAPTER 10 IS IMPORTANT

No one's assertions about children or learning have had more impact than those of Spencer. Key components were (a) that young people are fragile, inflexible, and have a limited and fixed quantity of energy and (b) that their "given" developmental patterns *must* be catered to by all. These ideas were not original. As Thomas Huxley noted, Spencer began with the "loose yarn" of familiar but seemingly disparate ideas, then skillfully wove them into a satisfying "rope."

At TheAptitudeMyth.info are the genealogical chart and "What to Remember" list for chapter 10.

NOTES

1. Herbert Spencer, *Education: Intellectual, Moral, Physical* (E. L. Kellogg, 1892), 208.
2. This chapter reviews Spencer's *Education: Intellectual, Moral, and Physical* (1860). It's still in print, published in 2002 by the University Press of the Pacific, which reprinted the 1905 edition.
3. *Ibid.*, (1892), 38–39 (all three paragraph breaks added).
4. *Ibid.*, 42.
5. I'm indebted to Kieran Egan for this insight. Egan, *Getting It Wrong from the Beginning* (Yale University Press, 2002), 42, 69, 76, 80–82.
6. Spencer does not reference Aristotle, but Aristotle's influence on the Western mindset was all-pervasive.
7. The word "form" now is not capitalized because Aristotle did not conceive of it as an otherworldly ideal.
8. Aristotle, *Physics*, Book II, chapter 8 (full discussion and citation in chapter 2). Aristotle also uses the phrase "if nothing interferes." This word-choice encourages caretakers to be protective *but not proactive.*
9. I'm indebted to E. D. Hirsch, Jr., for this insight. Hirsch, *The Knowledge Deficit* (Houghton Mifflin, 2006), 3–7.
10. Spencer, *op. cit.* (1892), 88.
11. This set of seven principles is that discussed in the 1905 edition reprinted by University Press of Hawaii, *op. cit.*, beginning on page 87. Other editions have slightly different sets of principles.
12. Principles 1 through 4, as applied to instruction, also appear during the mid-16th century in the works of Judah Loew, Chief Rabbi of Prague, who is believed to have been a direct influence on John Amos Comenius (see chapter 4). Benjamin Kuras, *Restoring Comenius* (Publishing House Ideal, 2007), chapter 6. It's possible that Spencer was influenced by Comenius's works.
13. This section is influenced by John Cleverley and D. C. Phillips, *Visions of Childhood: Influential Models from Locke to Spock*, rev. ed. (Teachers College, 1986), 42–51. See also Stephen Jay Gould, *Ontogeny and Phylogeny* (Harvard University Press, 1977), 135–55; Lawrence A. Cremin, *The Transformation of the School: Progressivism in American Education, 1876–1957* (Alfred A. Knopf, 1961), 100–107; and Ernest Bel-

den, "A History of the Child Study Movement in the United States, 1870–1920, with Special Reference to Its Scientific and Educational Background," Ph.D. dissertation, University of California, Berkeley, 1965 (University Microfilms # 65-13,441).

14. "Romantic *Naturphilosophie* gained, by virtue of the triumph of Darwinism, a place within scientific psychology. Recapitulation theory passed from biology to psychology on the bridge of Naturphilosophie. If the embryo of higher organisms in its morphology recapitulates the lower forms of the species, why should not the same recapitulation occur in the postnatal psychic expressions? After all, were not psychic phenomena expressing biological forces?" Belden, *ibid.*, 111–12.

15. "Recapitulation" originated as a doctrine of human biological development focused on the emergence of one's characteristics in relation to those of the species ("race"). "Culture epochs" originated as a doctrine of curriculum that called for units of study to parallel alleged epochs of humankind during its advance toward civilization. Edward A. Krug, *The Shaping of the American High School, 1880–1920* (University. of Wisconsin Press, 1969), 113.

16. In "Intellectual Education" (chapter II of *Education*), Spencer writes (1892 edition, 122), "To M. Comte . . . society owes the enunciation of [parallelism]." But nearly a century before Comte's time, French philosopher Étienne Bonnot de Condillac (1715–1780) stated what came to be called racial recapitulation: ". . . the child must do over again, on his own account, 'that which the race has done.' He must be compelled to follow, step by step, in its long gropings, the slow progress made by the race." Gabriel Compayré, *The History of Pedagogy* (D. C. Heath, 1894), 313 [¶ 340]; Compayré is quoting and paraphrasing *Discours préliminaire sur la grammaire*, in Condillac's *Œuvres complètes*, Tome VI, 264.

17. Frederick Starr, *Some First Steps in Human Progress* (Chatauqua Assembly, 1901), 29.

18. Spencer (1892), *op. cit.*, 111.

19. *Ibid.*, 156; the Mann quote's origin is not identified.

20. *Ibid.*, 125.

21. *Ibid.*

22. *Ibid.*, 126 (paragraph break added).

23. *Ibid.*, 127; following quotes are also from 127.

24. *Ibid.*, 154, italics added.

25. *Ibid.*, 258.

26. *Ibid.*, 258–61.

27. *Ibid.*, 263.

28. *Ibid.*, 278–81. Nineteenth century fears about physical debilities and poor health have been replaced today by worries that hard study might result in a child's becoming a socially handicapped "nerd."

29. *Ibid.*, 281.

30. *Ibid.*, 268.

II

American Responses

Part Two explores how many Americans received, and began to apply, the ways of thinking about children, learning, parenting, and teaching that they were inheriting from their European forebears. Also explored is the unique "spin" that Americans gave those ways of thinking.

Chapter 11 explores how the early inhabitants of this nation slowly modified their views about how best to raise children; introduced are three value perspectives: the *Romantic*, the *Calvinist*, and the *Practical*. Chapter 12 focuses on the era between the Civil War and World War One, when a tsunami of immigrants arrived on America's shores, creating a crisis for educators. Chapter 13 revisits the period between the two wars, focusing on what thought leaders were saying about the mind; pushing onto center stage was a new science, psychology.

Chapters 14, 15, and 16 discuss an educational metamorphosis that occurred between 1875 and 1925. Chapter 14 probes further into how educators and civic leaders answered two questions: How much education for immigrant children? And to what end? Chapter 15 highlights the gain in credibility among Americans of ancient beliefs that Spencer had popularized and now were being further disseminated within the United States by two celebrity educators.

Finally, Chapter 16 explores a closely related belief also gaining wide credibility: that each individual has a single, inherited "general intelligence." This notion became widely accepted by the public as an outcome of the American mobilization for World War One. After the war, the *aptitude myth*—that each child's performance in school is strongly determined by a fixed, inborn "given"—became institutionalized as the Scholastic Aptitude Test.

ELEVEN

Evolving Notions of Child-Rearing in Pre-Civil War America

If a child exhibits any symptoms of [intellectual] precocity, it should be immediately taken from books and permitted . . . such amusements as will give rest to the mind and health and vigor to the body.

—S. B. Woodward[1]

I said Christianity, art, beauty, all are in the soul of the child, and the art of the teacher consists in drawing it out. . . .

—Amos Bronson Alcott[2]

We will now begin to explore what happened as the ideas and ideals of the Enlightenment and Romanticism slowly filtered into the New World. First we'll look at the mindset of the people living in the American Northeast. Then we'll explore the ways in which emerging thinking gradually transformed their ideas about child-rearing and school teaching.

THE CULTURE AND MINDSET OF COLONIAL AND POST-COLONIAL AMERICA

The scene across what we now refer to as the Northeast was extraordinarily different from what we sense and experience there now.[3] Many of us wouldn't have been able to physically survive there during the late 18th and early 19th centuries. And if we could be transported back in time to *that* Northeast for a survivable few days, we'd encounter much in the assumptions, values, habits of thought, and patterns of behavior of the inhabitants that would require serious getting-used-to.

Equally important, during the late 18th and early 19th centuries, the scene across the Northeast was significantly different from that of the centers of learning and high culture in Europe at the same time. Not even Philadelphia or Boston could match the cities of Europe where the growing number of people who were privileged to enjoy education and leisure time tended to congregate.

The majority of Europeans who decided to risk the arduous ocean passage to the New World during the 17th and earlier 18th centuries were hardly the continent's thought leaders. Most were repudiating Europe and its ways for a variety of reasons. Some risked coming to the New World because of economic distress, others because of religious conviction. Those who completed the passage tended to be people of limited means, little or no education, and simple tastes.

85

As Richard Hofstadter points out, the earliest immigrants were obliged in the New World to live a life of extreme self-reliance, of rough and ready habits of mind, of opportunism, and of quick decisions with little time for reflection. For most colonists, the circumstances of day-to-day life were not congenial to precision of thought, deliberation, abstraction, or theory-building.[4]

This is why the perspectives, values, and attitudes of Europe's Enlightenment did *not* take the Colonies by storm. Yes, political ideas grounded in Enlightenment thought did animate those leaders whom we now call "Founding Fathers." But those men were not typical colonists. They were among the very few who could genuinely find time for reading and reflection. The only others who could read and had access to books were men who occupied church pulpits.

VARIETIES OF PROTESTANTISM: CALVINISM, PIETISM, AND QUAKERISM

During the 18th century, Northern Europe had passed through a religious "Great Awakening" during which reform-minded Protestant sects appeared. These "Pietistic" denominations shared a suspicion of doctrinal debates and formal rituals such as were common within *both* the Catholic and Calvinist churches, plus a hunger for a spontaneous "religion of the heart" that anticipated salvation through the emotion-laden, transformative personal experience of being "saved." Along with Calvinists, members of Pietist sects were among the early immigrants to the Colonies.

The outlook of the Pietists has been termed "primitive," not in a pejorative way but to emphasize that one of their strongly claimed virtues was *simplicity*—of ordinance, of moral conduct, and of manner, speech, and dress—of a kind they associated with the earliest Christians. They came to the New World, in part, to attain such simplicity. One of their early leaders, John Cotton, wrote that greater simplicity gives "more evident witnesse to the truth of God," adding:

> The more learned and witty you bee, the more fit to act for Satan will you bee. . . . take off
> the fond doting . . . upon the learning of the Jesuites, and the glorie of the Episcopacy, and
> brave estate of the Prelates. I say bee not deceived with these pompes, and empty shewes,
> and false representations of a goodly condition. . . .[5]

Those who attended "primitive" churches were reminded often that the Devil did his dirty work in the guise of a high-born gentleman—sophisticated, suave, and accustomed to authority. Authority, in turn, was linked to extravagance, indolence, dilettantism, and deceit.

Significantly for us, *the Pietists also distrusted intellectualism and rationalism*. In their minds, all of that was anathema. Desirable for them was a quest for the spirit of primitive (i.e., earliest) Christianity, linked with the wisdom of intuition, believed to be God-given or "natural" —a point of view we've encountered in Enlightenment thinking and especially in Romanticism.

Also coming to the New World, though in fewer numbers, were members of Protestant denominations that were similarly inclined with respect to simplicity, but less suspicious of the fruits of mental labors and less oriented toward emotional responses; the best example is the Quakers. So during the decades prior to the American Revolution, three varieties of Protestantism were found in the Northeast: Quakers, Calvinists, and several denominations similar enough in mindset that they have been referred to collectively as one—the Pietists.

As Susan Jacoby reminds us,[6] the worldview of Pietism was attractive to many who inhabited the Colonies and, later, to frontier settlers. They were poorly educated if at all.

Given the risks of their day-to-day lives and the back-wrenching work they did to confront those risks, it's understandable that they were drawn to creeds and preachers who provided emotional solace and simple paths to salvation—with few intellectual demands. Jacoby adds that the same can be said of the slaves in the Southeast.[7] Intellectually demanding belief systems and complex liturgies, such as those of the Calvinists (and later, the Catholics) had difficulty competing.

THE VALUES AND PATTERNS OF AMERICAN PARENTING GRADUALLY EVOLVE

Calvinism Ascendant

Meanwhile in New England, the beliefs and values of John Calvin were experiencing a resurgence during the same era when the Founding Fathers were busy laying the groundwork for the new nation on the principles enunciated by Enlightenment philosophers.[8] These two views of life—tightly restrictive Calvinist and expansive Enlightenment—had arisen within the same cultural milieu, historical era, and broadly Christian tradition. They existed side by side, yet in most respects they were completely antithetical to each other.

With respect to children and child-rearing, it was the Calvinist perspective that for a long time dominated the values and activities of many parents and other caregivers, including teachers and educators, throughout the Northeast. Eventually its grip weakened. We need to be aware of this gradual mindset shift, for it directly addressed the question of how children learn best and, in turn, what kind of classroom teaching is best. (For additional insight, see Table A.1 in the Appendix.)

When we introduced John Calvin in chapter 8, we focused on his doctrine of predestination, with its message that everyone is born with at least one "given" over which the individual has no control or influence at all. We're revisiting Calvinism now because of its oft-expressed view of infants: that each was born sharing in the Original Sin of Adam and Eve and, by extension, in the common sins of all humanity. Infants were "by nature, sinners." They were "depraved."

These draconian beliefs had an impact on the daily lives of parents. They were responsible for insuring that their tiny fledgling being, relentlessly predisposed to evil, would be *quickly transformed by their rearing* to live a godly, moral life. Most Pietists shared such views, although often in ways that were less extreme in practice.

The obligation on parents was spiritual in nature: to save their child from God's final punishment of humanity for the sins of Adam and Eve. It was also social in nature: to save their community from the ravages of immoral inhabitants. Training their children to be Good was a moral imperative for parents, and was expected of them by other members of their community.

The source of correction and instruction to be applied by the parents was the Holy Bible. Its precepts had to be learned, not only thoroughly but also rapidly. Memorization of scripture passages, catechisms, and the like was a constant. The methods were didactic and prescriptive, the training strict. The expected outcome was to "break the will" of the child, meaning that the child's assumed inborn predisposition to be evil would be shattered through training, discipline, church-going, and other external pressures, unremittingly applied from the first months of life.

Calvinism in Decline

As we move into the first half of the 19th century, we observe in the Northeast an almost universally accepted obligation, the one described immediately above. We also observe that the "how" of attaining that goal gradually began to elicit a different response.

Very cautiously and hesitantly at first, a few people dared to question the orthodox view of the child's inherent depravity. That idea, in turn, led them to dare to question the efficacy of the harsh child-rearing methods associated with Calvinism. Caution invariably characterized the voicing of this counter-cultural view because questioning the doctrine of infant depravity was likely to be interpreted by others in the community as undermining the imperative that all children must be raised up to be moral, Christian adults.

Nevertheless, during the first decades of the 19th century, popular advice for the fledgling nation's parents began to shift, initially at a glacial pace, toward the notion that gentle guidance of children, including reliance on their own "sense impressions," *might* have advantages. Slowly, articles in popular magazines as well as entire books began to counsel mothers to give up harsh, didactic measures. A few passages are worth quoting.

- Lydia Sigourney's 1838 *Letters to Mothers* noted that the challenge of child nurture was ". . . how the harp might be so tuned as not to injure its tender and intricate harmony. . . ." Sigourney recommended that mothers ". . . feel with Rousseau that 'the greatest respect is due to children.'. . ." adding that without love, simplicity, and delicacy, and without the mother's recognizing that the child was incapable of conforming to adult standards, the child's potentialities as "an erring being" could triumph and ruin him.[9]
- Horace Bushnell's 1847 *Views of Christian Nurture* argued that proper nurture could counteract "tendencies" to depravity only if nurture began while wickedness was weakest (i.e., during infancy): ". . . depravity is best rectified when it is weakest, and before it is stiffened into habit."[10] He criticized attempts to quickly bring children to salvation.
- The Swedenborgian[11] magazine *The New Jerusalem* published an unattributed article during 1850 entitled "Errors of Education," which claimed that "at birth the child is . . . but an incipient receptacle of that thought and affection, the proper protection, nourishment, and exercise of which are capable of forming it into an angel."[12]
- An article by Paul Siogvolk in an 1852 *Knickerbocker* magazine entitled "The Rights of Children" worried that "we are sacrilegiously interfering with the ways of Providence in . . . arbitrarily mapping out the travels of an immortal soul" which is "a law unto itself" deserving appropriate freedom in the nursery.[13] [14]

ASSUMPTIONS ABOUT CHILDREN'S MENTAL FRAGILITY STRENGTHEN AND SPREAD

Another tendency was emerging in pre-Civil War Americans' assumptions: the notion that young children are extremely delicate, very easily damaged. This view did not originate in the New World. Values and ideals about parental responsibility had been evolving since the 16th century toward the preservation of children's miraculous purity and innocence for as long as possible. As described in chapter 5, prior to the Enlightenment in Europe there had been a gradual shift in the way educated people thought about children: The younger they are, the better they are. Rousseau stated this perspective clearly, and the literary Romantics further disseminated it.

The view of children as requiring constant protection and preservation evolved in the United States toward the notion that *children are mentally weak and easily exhausted*. Quoted above are these notions: *Letters to Mothers* cautioned against injuring the child's "tender and intricate harmony"; *The New Jerusalem* article called for protecting and nourishing the "incipient receptacle"; and the *Knickerbocker* article advised against "interfering with the ways of Providence."

An even earlier American voice to the same end was that of Thomas H. Gallaudet, recalled today as a teacher of the deaf; his book on the religious training of children, *The Child's Book on the Soul*, appeared in 1831. As paraphrased by Bernard Wishy, Gallaudet advised that, "Rather than overwhelm the child's mind or overtax 'tender emotions' with rote learning of ideas beyond his comprehension, the mother was . . . not to exceed the child's demonstrated ability at any stage of development."[15] [16] (This perspective antedated Spencer's *Education* by three decades.)

Significantly, Wishy also notes that during the 30 years prior to the Civil War, teachers were routinely expected to support parents in the inculcation of virtue while simultaneously dispensing knowledge; *yet teachers were increasingly discouraged from making demands on children*. Publications and talks by spokespersons for home, church, and school decried precociousness and the "forced feeding" of ideas as unnatural; at stake were general health, future growth, mental balance, and capacity for feeling and moral life.

The most eminent American school leader of this period, Horace Mann, referred in his *Fourth Annual Report* to the dangers of insanity if intellectual training began while the child's emotions were immature.[17] This theme went beyond mere *laissez faire*; it positively counseled caution to the point of diffidence in making intellectual demands on the young. Today, this perspective remains influential, in part, via the appealing concept of "readiness."

TWO ASSUMPTIONS ABOUT WHAT CHILDREN ARE INNATELY "GIVEN"

Let's return to the reasons why Americans in the Northeast gradually came to accept gentle child-rearing methods.[18] This shift required more than half a century to occur because, among other reasons, Protestants—including Calvinists and Pietists, if not necessarily Quakers—were obliged to do some nuanced thinking about their key underlying assumption: that children were born "in sin."

This assumption is actually *two* assumptions: (1) that all children are born with one or more "givens," and (2) that one of those innate "givens" is each child's inherent predisposition to evil. Only one of these needed to be modified to make way for gentler methods: the second one, about infant depravity. *The underlying assumption, that children have "givens," could remain intact.*

A long-accepted "given"—infant depravity, which required "breaking the will"—was looking less and less lovely to more and more Americans. Another "given" was needed to take its place. A substitute "given"—that children are inherently Good—was ready and waiting. We need not explore it in detail because we already have.

In chapter 5 we considered Enlightenment views, especially Rousseau's, that were the polar opposite of Calvin's. In chapter 7, where we addressed the perspective of the literary Romantics, we became familiar with lyrical views of children's nature that saw the little ones not only as inherently Good but also as having innate predispositions believed to be capable of glorious, spontaneous unfolding, like that of a flower. And in chapter 8, we were introduced to a widely influential educator, a life-long Pietist, who understood children very much in this fashion.

This substitute view resonated with the old Calvinist orthodoxy in that *both were grounded in the assumption of "givens."* Proponents of both views found common ground in the belief that each child had a soul and deserved an upbringing that recognized his or her "divine spark."[19]

The substitute view resonated in another way with the old orthodoxy. Calvinists, Pietists, and other religious traditionalists on the one hand, and the apostles of Romanticism on the other hand, all envisioned the child as programmed to carry out universal imperatives, *which in turn required thoughtful and deliberate upbringing by parents and instructing by teachers.* (We have seen Spencer, during the second half of this century, take this idea to unprecedented lengths.) The difference lay in the details of that upbringing, in the "how" of parenting and teaching.

But there weren't merely two competing perspectives on children and child-rearing in the United States prior to the Civil War. There were three.

"COMMON SCHOOLS," HORACE MANN, AND THE PRACTICAL PERSPECTIVE ON TEACHING

A Third Way

The two views we've been examining shared a focus on each child as unique. The third view arose out of concern about the child as a future member of local society and *as a potential contributor in practical ways to the welfare and strength of that society.*

The Americans who were drawn to this third view tended to be those who were preoccupied with the social, political, and economic challenges facing the young nation, and who believed that the most promising way to tackle those challenges would be to establish local schools that taught a practical, useful curriculum and were freely available to all children regardless of their parents' economic circumstances. Advocates spoke of "common schools."

The growing movement to make freely available schools a reality became known as the Common School Movement. The story of this quasi-religious movement and its success is fascinating in its own right . . . and beyond the scope of this discussion.[20] What will be useful is to acquaint ourselves briefly with the undisputed leader of the Common School Movement, Horace Mann. His life's work provides us with insights into the third view of children and child-rearing, and into the reasons for the gradual demise of the Calvinist perspective.

Horace Mann's Consuming Passion

Horace Mann (1796–1859) entered the world on a hardscrabble Massachusetts farm 20 years after the signing of the Declaration of Independence.[21] Subjected to an unforgiving Calvinist upbringing, young Horace abruptly turned against that way of life during the funeral of his 12-year-old brother, where the minister sternly warned other young people of the dangers of dying unconverted. Mann wrote that this minister . . .

> . . . expounded all the doctrines of total depravity, election, and reprobation, and not only the eternity, but the extremity, of hell-torments, unflinchingly and in their most terrible significance; while he rarely if ever descanted upon the joys of heaven, and never, to my recollection, upon the . . . happiness of a virtuous life.[22]

Revolted by Calvinism, Mann abandoned it. Admitted to Brown University, he studied law, which he viewed as the means by which society would redeem itself. Between 1827 and 1833, he represented Dedham, Massachusetts, in the state legislature, where he supported measures to ameliorate social conditions. One of those was a bill to create the State Board of Education.

Then, in 1837, Mann was invited to become the State Board's first secretary.

Mann ruminated over this invitation for six weeks. During this period he experienced two upsetting events. In the first, a malicious gang started a fire next to his hotel room; in the second, a riot between Catholics and Protestants raged for hours. Mann's response was characteristic of his general outlook: Proper training for *all* children would eliminate such scourges on society.

One reason Mann assumed that education could make a difference was that he had become enthusiastic about phrenology, a way of thinking about the mind's "faculties" that was widely accepted by physicians and luminaries such as Emerson and Whitman. Phrenology was grounded on the assumption that character and behavior can be modified, with desirable faculties expanded through training and exercise, and undesirable faculties inhibited through disuse.[23]

Education, concluded Mann, was a higher calling than law. Defending his decision, he wrote:

> Having found the present generation composed of materials almost unmalleable, I am about transferring my efforts to the next. Men are cast-iron; but children are wax. Strength expended upon the latter may be effectual, which would make no impression on the former.[24]

Mann now viewed education—tax-supported public education for all—as the way to improve human beings. He accepted the secretaryship, working for nearly 12 years with such furious commitment that, by all accounts, his health was severely impaired. His list of accomplishments is awesome. Along the way, he visited Prussia for six weeks to observe the gentle classroom methods of Pestalozzi; writing in high praise of them in his *Seventh Annual Report* (1843), he found himself in a protracted public conflict with a group of Calvinist-inspired principals demanding "stern virtue and inflexible justice."

Mann Advocates a Practical Perspective

Committed to using education to inculcate good character and citizenship, even good personal hygiene, Mann also pressed for the teaching of practical disciplines such as spelling, arithmetic, drawing, nature studies, surveying, and even physiology. Mann's opinion was that a school failed if it didn't prepare its pupils for the practical work of field, shop, forum, and desk. He wrote that schoolwork must not merely train skilled craftsmen but rather intelligent men who understand "the principles upon which their work proceeds" as well as its social, economic, and cultural implications.[25]

If Mann's ideals are reminding you of something, it's because his commitment to practical studies and his comparison of young children to impressionable wax are similar to views first enunciated by John Amos Comenius ("sense realism") and John Locke ("*tabula rasa*"). Those views, in turn, had as part of their foundation an inductive view of thinking about the natural world first enunciated by Francis Bacon and decisively strengthened by Isaac Newton.

All these ideas are associated with the third perspective on children and child-raising. It arises out of a vision of the child *as a future member of society and a potential contributor in practical and social ways to the welfare, strength, and improvement of that society.* (For additional insight, see Table A.3 in the Appendix.)

MUSINGS AND SPECULATIONS

I'm curious about the Pietists' child-rearing practices. From my investigations, and from my upbringing in a Pietist denomination (during the 1940s), here is my impression: In terms of desired outcomes, the Pietists almost certainly resonated with the Calvinists. But in terms of community-sanctioned methods, it's likely they were drawn to the Romantics—all the while worrying that this value-set might undermine their ability to bring up God-fearing children.

WHY CHAPTER 11 IS IMPORTANT

This chapter demonstrates that Calvinism and Romanticism—in spite of their differences in substance and spirit, and in spite of their disparate origins—share a similar foundational assumption. It is that each child's innate "givens" include universal imperatives, which in turn require teachers and parents to be cautious in their guidance, wary of contradicting any pre-programmed tendency.

This chapter also demonstrates that, even before the Civil War, the belief that children are mentally fragile and easily exhausted was gaining traction; thus, teachers began to be enjoined to sharply curtail the amount of academic demands made on them. This pre-Spencerian belief echoed ideals voiced by the Romantics and Rousseau, and originally by Aristotle.

At TheAptitudeMyth.info are the genealogical chart and "What to Remember" list for chapter 11. And in the Appendix of this book are Tables A.1, A.2, and A.3, which further clarify three of the four views of classroom teaching—the "Calvinist," the "Romantic," and the "Practical,"—by relating each to proponents' beliefs about the nature of children and how they learn.

NOTES

1. S. B. Woodward, "Treatment of Scholars," *North Carolina Journal of Education*, vol. 1 (July 1858). Quoted by Bernard Wishy, *The Child and the Republic* (University of Pennsylvania Press, 1968), 71.
2. A. B. Alcott, spoken at the 1872 meeting of the National Education Association. Quoted by Edgar B. Wesley, *NEA: The First Hundred Years* (Harper & Brothers, 1957), 169.
3. Sources for this section include Richard Hofstadter, *Anti-Intellectualism in American Life* (Alfred A. Knopf, 1970), especially 48–51; Charles L. Sanford, *The Quest for Paradise: Europe and the American Moral Imagination* (AMS Press, 1961), especially 105; Susan Jacoby, *The Age of American Unreason* (Pantheon Books, 2008), especially 38–47; and Bernard Wishy, *op. cit.*, especially 11–14.
4. Hofstadter, *ibid.*, 49–50.
5. John Cotton, *The Powring* [sic] *Out of the Seven Vials* (Printed for R. S. and are to be sold at Henry Overtons Shop in Popes-head Alley, 1642), the Second part of the Sixth Viall, 39–40; referred to by Sanford, *op. cit.*, 105.
6. Jacoby, *op. cit.*, 43–46.
7. Intellectuals, too, were susceptible to religious primitivism, which ". . . affected the thinking of many men too educated and cultivated to run with the frontier revivalists but sympathetic to their underlying distrust for civilized forms. It is visible in Transcendentalism—which sometimes set itself up as the evangelicalism of the highbrows." Hofstadter, *op. cit.*, 48 [see also note 8].
8. For this section I relied on Wishy, *op. cit.*, chapters 7 and 13; and Diane Ravitch, *Left Back: A Century of Failed School Reforms* (Simon & Schuster, 2000), chapter 2. Also useful were Lawrence A. Cremin, *The Transformation of the School: Progressivism in American Education, 1876-1957* (Alfred A. Knopf, 1961), Part I; Daniel T. Rodgers, "Socializing Middle-Class Children: Institutions, Fables, and Work Values in Nineteenth-Century America," in N. Ray Hiner and Joseph M. Hawes, *Growing Up in America: Children in Historical Perspective* (University of Illinois Press, 1985); Patricia Albjerg Graham, *Schooling in America: How the Public Schools Meet the Nation's Changing Needs* (Oxford University Press, 2005), chapter 1; Joel Spring, *The American School, 1642–1990*, 2nd ed. (Longman, 1990), 27–31; David Tyack and Elisabeth

Hansot, *Managers of Virtue: Public School Leadership in America, 1820–1980* (Basic Books, 1982), chapters 1, 2, 3, 6, 8, 9, and 10; William J. Reese, "The Origins of Progressive Education," *History of Education Quarterly*, vol. 41, no. 1 (Spring 2001), 2–24; Wesley, *op. cit.*, chapter 14; Sanford, *op. cit.*; Jacoby, *op. cit.*, especially 38–47; and Hofstadter, *op. cit.*, especially 48–51, 347–50.

9. Mrs. L. H. Sigourney, *Letters to Mothers* (Hudson and Skinner, 1838), 26, 22, 40. Referenced by Wishy, *op. cit.*, 21–22.

10. Horace Bushnell, *Views of Christian Nurture* (Edwin Hunt, 1847), 167. Referenced by Wishy, *op. cit.*, 22–23; Wishy reports that "'Weeding out' sin was the new metaphor."

11. Founded by Swedish scientist and philosopher Emanuel Swedenborg during the early 18th century, the Swedenborgian religion is one of the many varieties of Protestantism.

12. Wishy, *op. cit.*, 23; Wishy cites *The New Jerusalem* 23 (August, 1850), 296.

13. *Ibid.*, 23; Wishy cites *Knickerbocker* 39 (June 1852), 489–90.

14. Wishy notes that children's literature remained prescriptive: "The children were not themselves allowed to enjoy any significant freedom from moralism and homily in their books" even though "several of the more notable enlightened writers on nurture also wrote for children yet in a more 'conservative' style. . . ." *Ibid.*, 54–55.

15. Wishy, *op. cit.*, 30.

16. Gallaudet also provided a foretaste of child-centered parenting when he wrote, "If inquiries are made, or difficulties started, or doubts expressed, by the child, let them be treated with the greatest attention.—*They who would teach children well, must first learn a great deal from them.*" T. H. Gallaudet, *The Child's Book of the Soul, Part First* (Cooke, 1832), vii, italics in the original.

17. Wishy, *ibid.*, 70–72. This is only a sampling of the documentary evidence offered by Wishy.

18. Wishy's explanation for the gradual switch to gentleness is that American parents recognized that they were living in a society where offspring could easily leave home and make their own way in the world; gentle child-rearing came to be viewed as a way of insuring the life-long love of their offspring. Wishy, *ibid.*, 33; 77–78.

19. Wishy, *ibid.*, 109. Wishy puts "divine spark" in quotes but does not attribute it.

20. An excellent short treatment is Carl F. Kaestle, *Pillars of the Republic: Common Schools and American Society, 1780–1860* (Hill and Wang, 1983). S. Alexander Rippa, *Education in a Free Society: An American History*, 8th ed. (Longman, 1997), includes a chapter on "The Common School Movement." Spring, *op. cit.*, has a chapter entitled "The Ideology and Politics of the Common School." For another perspective, also see Tyack and Hansot, *op. cit.*

21. This view of the factors influencing Mann's thinking is based on Spring, *op cit.*, 83–93; Rippa, *op. cit.*, 93–98; and Merle Curti, *The Social Ideas of American Educators* (Littlefield, Adams, 1978), chapter 3.

22. Mary Peabody Mann ["His Wife"], *Life of Horace Mann* (Walker, Fuller, 1865), 13. Referenced by Spring, *ibid.*, 85.

23. This overview of phrenology relies on Lawrence A. Cremin, *op. cit.*, 12. Cremin says that phrenology provides "insights into the pedagogical reformism of the 1840s" in that it "reached for a naturalistic explanation of human behavior." As described by Cleverley and Phillips, *op. cit.*, 24–25, phrenology was related to faculty psychology; it claimed that there are some 40 distinct units or "faculties" of the mind—to name just four: inhabitativeness, firmness, acquisitiveness, and marvelousness—that are located in specific sites within the brain. The strength of each one could be determined by anatomical investigation because the stronger ones produced a tangible bump on the surface of the skull. (See also chapter 13.)

24. Mary Peabody Mann, *op. cit.*, 83. Referenced by Spring, *op. cit.*, 80–81, 83.

25. Curti, *op. cit.*, 103. Curti in turn cites several of Mann's papers and Annual Reports.

TWELVE

Emerging Social Currents in Post-Civil War America

It is obvious that the educational needs of the child in a district where the streets are well paved and clean, where the homes are spacious and surrounded by lawns and trees, where the language of the child's playfellows is pure, and where life in general is permeated with the ideals of America . . . are radically different from those of the child who lives in a foreign and tenement section.

—William H. Elson and Frank P. Bachman[1]

The 54 years between the surrender at Appomattox (1865) and the signing of the Treaty of Versailles (1919) was tumultuous and transformative for the American people.[2] We will review important occurrences during that period, then turn our attention to how society, and especially educators, responded to the presumed needs of the rapidly growing numbers of children.

RAPID SOCIAL CHANGES TRANSFORM THE CONTEXT AND CONCERNS OF SCHOOLS

The half-century between the Civil War and World War One is a fascinating period of American history. It probably strikes most readers of history as one of frenetic activity and growth of numerous kinds. An especially intriguing element of the story is the construction of the transcontinental railroad, an unparalleled feat of engineering and back-wrenching toil that, amazingly, was completed during the same decade in which the Civil War was fought.

The railroad story contains key elements of the entire story: It's about westward expansion, it's about the rapid growth of industrial capitalism, and it's about immigration (the railroad's western half was mostly constructed by Chinese laborers who, in spite of being widely judged as the best workers anyone had ever seen, were the objects of discrimination). If an indispensable element of the overall story is lacking from the railroad saga, it's about the burgeoning growth of cities—but of course some cities wildly expanded (Sacramento is one) *because of* the railroads.

Where we need to begin concentrating our attention is on the rapid increase of the population due to immigration, the changing national backgrounds of those immigrants, the crushing poverty of the great majority, their compression (along with migrant Americans from failed farms) into urban areas and, in response, the efforts of voluntary organizations as well as governmental agencies to deal effectively with the resultant bewildering changes.

Examination of some immigration statistics is revealing. Between 1861 and 1870, 87.8 percent of all immigrants came from northern and western Europe; only 1.4 percent came from southern and eastern Europe—33,628 to be exact. During 1901–1910, the ratios were 21.7 percent from northern and western Europe and 70.8 percent from southern and eastern Europe—6,225,981 of the latter.[3] The "new" immigrants began outnumbering the old during 1882.

The Senate Immigration Commission found in 1908 that in the larger American cities, an average of 58 percent of all schoolchildren had foreign-born parents. The percentages were even higher in some of the largest cities: 64 percent in Boston; 67 percent in Chicago; and 72 percent in New York. The number of nationalities enumerated by the Senate investigators was 60.[4]

Thus was created a highly visible, completely unprecedented social crisis for a nation that, even before the Civil War, had been well on its way to committing itself to the ideal of providing at least a rudimentary education for all children at public expense. Major cities were receiving tens of thousands of children every year, most of them the progeny of parents who could barely feed and clothe them and—worse from a teacher's perspective—unable to speak English.

Adding to the confusion was the widely acknowledged perception among many citizens that the "new" immigrants are *not people like us*. They don't behave like us, they aren't clean like us, most don't worship like us, in general their values are not like ours. . . . This is a threatening state of affairs . . . and it's getting worse because they just keep coming. *Something must be done!*

Doing something necessarily involved the educational establishment. "Establishment," however, is too grand a word. It's true that *some* progress had been made in attaining Horace Mann's objectives for common schools during the 1870s, 1880s, and 1890s. But a visit to almost any public school classroom during that era was an illusion-shattering experience.

A VISIT TO PUBLIC SCHOOLS AND CLASSROOMS DURING 1892

In 1892, someone actually did visit dozens of schools and hundreds of classrooms across 36 cities, then wrote extensively about what he had found. This story begins when the editor of a New York City monthly, *The Forum*, made a proposal to a 33-year-old pediatrician, Joseph Mayer Rice. Dr. Rice had become so interested in education that he'd devoted two years to studying pedagogy in Germany. The editor's proposal was that if Dr. Rice would examine schools across the American northeast and midwest, *The Forum* would provide financial support. Educational historian Lawrence Cremin continues Rice's story; excerpts:

> On behalf of *The Forum*, Rice was to prepare a firsthand appraisal of American public education. He was to visit classrooms, talk with teachers, attend school board meetings, and interview parents. He was to place "no reliance whatsoever" on reports by school officials; his goal was to render an objective assessment for the public. Rice . . . talked with some 1,200 teachers; he returned [with] notes crammed with statistics, illustrations, and judgments. The first article appeared in October [1892]. By the following June, Rice's name had become a byword—frequently an epithet—to schoolmen across the nation.
>
> Rice's story bore all the earmarks of the journalism destined to make "muckraking" a household word in America. In city after city, public apathy, political interference, corruption, and incompetence were conspiring to ruin the schools. A Chicago teacher, re-

hearsing her pupils in a "concert drill," harangued them with the command: "Don't stop to think, tell me what you know!" In Philadelphia the "ward bosses" controlled the appointment of teachers and principals; in Buffalo the city superintendent was the single supervising officer for 700 teachers. With alarming frequency the story was the same: political hacks hiring untrained teachers who blindly led their innocent charges in sing-song drill, rote repetition, and meaningless verbiage.[5]

We've now identified two ingredients of the social context of education between the two wars: first, immigration that vastly differed from anything previously experienced, and that settled in the larger cities; second, an educational establishment that was grievously flawed.

The third key contextual ingredient is the rapid rise of industrial capitalism (especially across the northeast and midwest) and, as a counterpoint, the growth of organized labor. We need not go into detail about the steps by which this came to pass, nor about the conspicuous excesses of very wealthy families during the late 19th and early 20th centuries, nor about the contentious and occasionally violent relationship between business owners and workers.

For our purposes, what's important is the relationship between the industrial capitalists and their supporters on the one hand, and the city, state, and university-based leaders of the American educational establishment on the other hand. Educational historians broadly concur that leading educators came to see things from the perspective of the owners of industry and the other members of the corporate elite. The outcome was that American public schools evolved into a "system to improve human capital as a means of economic growth."[6]

SOCIETY'S RESPONSE TO IMMIGRATION, INDUSTRIALIZATION, AND URBANIZATION

Educators Fall into Line Behind Industrialists

The challenge, simply stated, was how best to go about educating a veritable tsunami of children and youth whose cultural and linguistic traditions were deeply unfamiliar. To what extent should public school classrooms and personnel be used to "Americanize" the new arrivals? Besides "Americanization" skills and values (especially the learning of English), what should be taught to them?

While the cities were overflowing with immigrants, American industries and businesses were seriously in need of workers. The immigrants had the potential to solve the manpower problem. Industrialists and other capitalists agreed that immigrant youth needed education and training, so they had their own preferred response to the question, "What should be taught to them?" Their need was for *workers who had basic vocational skills and spoke a little English.*

What warrants scrutiny is not the fact that business leaders were looking out for their own interests. Rather, it's that virtually all leaders of the educational establishment fell into line behind the business leaders. As well, the educators began approaching their own challenges by applying the business leaders' efficiency-oriented mindset. Historian Merle Curti writes that . . .

> . . . the influence of business on the social outlook and on the policies of educators was largely indirect. Educators accepted, in general, the business man's outlook and consciously or unconsciously molded the school system to accord with the canons of a profit-making economic system. In contrasting educational methods with those of factories,

George H. Martin, secretary of the board of education in Boston, noted the crude, unscientific, and wasteful character of the former.

As early as 1911 the achievements of [Frederick W.] Taylor in scientific management were associated with the movement for efficiency in education. Efforts were made, by introducing specialized classes, tests, measurements, and new administrative methods, to reduce waste, speed up the rate of promotion, and increase the efficiency of the schools. In 1900 the president of the National Education Association, Oscar T. Corson, asserted that "the real educational leaders of the age whose influence will be permanent are those who have the business capacity to appreciate and comprehend the business problems which are always a part of the educational problem."[7]

Enter the Measurement of Mental Powers

Curti mentions "tests, measurements"; this requires our attention. At base, Taylor's scientific management was about measurement and comparisons; in a factory setting, these were applied to issues of volume of output during a defined length of time. As we will see in chapter 16, the investigations of psychologists including Edward L. Thorndike led to the belief that capacities of the human mind could be quantified, which led to the development of various procedures to measure and compare them.

"Whatever exists at all exists in some amount," Thorndike famously wrote in 1918. "Education is concerned with changes in human beings; a change is a difference between two conditions; each . . . known to us only by the products produced by it—things made, words spoken, acts performed, and the like. To measure any of these products means to define its amount in some way so that . . . this knowledge may be conveniently rcorded [sic] and used."[8]

Let's ask how that presumed knowledge was recorded and used. In a society dealing with (a) vast numbers of young people and (b) a need for workers, it wasn't long before someone decided that *both* challenges could be met through measurement. The plan was to measure the abilities, interests, and intelligence of the children, and on that basis to "sort" them into several groups that lumped together children with similar "probable destinies," i.e., life-long career paths. In other words, each pupil would be directed onto one of the paths of a "differentiated curriculum" *that would be appropriate for his or her predetermined future role in the national economy.*

The newly emerging tests were said to be "objective," which meant they were neither made nor scored by individual classroom teachers. They were praised as "rational" and "practical" and as promoting "efficiency," not only because they were becoming mechanized and standardized but also because they seemed to help handle the crush of students.

Note this as well: These tests were grounded in centuries-old, unquestioned assumptions about "givens"—in this case, the assumption that intelligence is innately predetermined and set for life, so the sooner we can aid its unbending dictates, the better for all concerned.

Critics of the Mental Measurement Trend

At least one turn-of-the-century educator opposed this trend. In 1915, William C. Bagley criticized the differentiated curriculum for students based on their mental measurements. Asking who was clamoring for this sea-change, he wrote:

> Not the "working people," one may be confident. *What they wish for their children is the opportunity that liberal education implies. . . .*[9] Hitherto in our national life we have proceeded on the assumption that no one has the omniscience to pick out the future hewers

of wood and drawers of water—at least not when the candidates for these tasks are to be selected at the tender age of twelve.[10]

More recently, historian Julia Wrigley made the same point after studying trends in Chicago's school district during the first half of the 20th century. Business leaders were demanding a differentiated curriculum emphasizing character development and vocational training. In marked contrast, organized labor was promoting increased education for working class children and a broad liberal education for all children.[11]

Historian Richard Hofstadter is sharply critical of the rush to measurement. He directs his critique at the educators who were eager to apply the researchers' findings in any way that promised a "scientific" solution to their problems. Commenting on educators who were committed to "democratic" values, Hofstadter observes that ". . . the supposed discovery of the mental limitations of the masses only encouraged a search for methods and content in education that would suit the needs of the intellectually mediocre or unmotivated."[12]

A REVIEW OF CRITICAL CHALLENGES AND SOCIETY'S RESPONSES

During the last few decades of the 19th century and the first two decades of the 20th, large American cities were being inundated with immigrant families, the great majority of whom were from nations and cultures that made them seem strange, even threatening. Industries and other large businesses were speedily expanding and sorely in need of workers.

The educational "establishment" was of questionable value to anyone. Yet it was these locally organized and governed educational units that were looked to more than any other institution as having, potentially, the means to ameliorate these unprecedented challenges.

Then "scientific" ways of measuring human abilities entered the picture. This made it easy to expect that the future economic role of children could be predicted, which led to the idea that young people should be "sorted" into groups and prepared for their inevitable adult roles.

Business leaders assumed that the great majority of youth so measured *would be found to possess quite modest capabilities and thus be fit for manual work (boys) or homemaking (girls), and would be directed into a suitable school curriculum delivered by suitable methods.*

Most local educational leaders as well as nationally prominent university professors came around to supporting the businessmen's solution. In fact, some school administrators came to the belief that what "scientific" measurement would reveal about local children was so obvious that it was unnecessary to actually do the measuring. For example, the superintendent and deputy superintendent of the Cleveland Public Schools expected differentiation to begin in the *first grade*. In 1910 they wrote the startling quote that opens this chapter.

What, in the minds of these leaders, was a suitable school curriculum for immigrant children? Details of curriculum changes are beyond the scope of this research[13] but, in general, those changes focused on intellectually non-demanding basic skills and vocation-oriented training. This was defended not only as valuable for the nation's economy *but also as "meeting the needs" of these youth*. But for youth deemed highly capable, the traditional curriculum would ready them for university and thus for adult lives as cultured citizens and community leaders.

These emerging social currents and the resulting trends in how people were conceiving of children and their education are significant for us as we try to understand our inheritance:

- The meaning of equal opportunity changed. The ideal of the common school was that an education of similar quality would bring *all* children, from whatever background, to an equivalent starting gate, at which point they would commence their productive adult lives. Then it would be *during their adult lives* that each one's interests, capabilities, and perseverance would take him or her on a uniquely appropriate economic and social path.

   That traditional ideal was replaced. "In the new way of thinking," writes Diane Ravitch, "equal opportunity meant that a banker's children would get a very different education from a coal miner's children, and all would be fitted to occupy the status of their parents."[14]

- Critical decisions about the trajectory of each child's life began being made by strangers who "sorted" them using impersonal instruments—or sometimes only their biases. The children's parents were not consulted, nor were they treated as credible if they expressed their wishes to decision makers. Some parents did express their wishes; only the labor movement listened.

- The process was enabled by a set of sweeping assumptions about the abilities of immigrant children, and about their expectations for, and interests in, the day-to-day school experience. These assumptions generalized that *all* of them were youth with a very limited capacity for, and very little interest in, learning traditional academic subjects in traditional ways.

- The inherited belief that each child possesses a set of immutable "givens" was strengthened among the general public while children increasingly were "sorted," metaphorically branded, and thus directed into permanent life trajectories on the basis of presumed knowledge of each one's aptitude and interests. *Little or no role was allowed or imagined for any child's new interests, willpower, or hard work and perseverance.*

Thus was portended a metamorphosis in the nature and purpose of American education.

MUSINGS AND SPECULATIONS

Perhaps we should remember, as we stand in historical judgment of those who made the decisions related in this chapter, that the challenges they encountered not only were vast, complex, and completely unprecedented, but also had an in-your-face quality that urgently demanded that *something* be done soon. Remember that, then as now, the findings of "science" seemed to be a safe basis on which to formulate public policy. If we had been in the shoes of those turn-of-the-century policy makers, what would we have done differently?

WHY CHAPTER 12 IS IMPORTANT

In this chapter we've observed the enormous influence among Americans of the value of *immediate practicality*, which is very closely related to *efficiency*. We also see another key American value, *democracy*, having its definition tweaked just enough to accommodate the attainment of immediate practicality and efficiency, as defined by the business community.

The central ideal of democracy held firm: Most Americans rejected any solution that would have denied schooling to immigrant children. But that ideal was adapted to insure that all the immigrant children, with extremely few exceptions, were sorted and tracked by educators in a way that would meet the immediate practical needs of the industrialists.

In chapter 12 we also see the methods of evidence-based empiricism called upon to support this change of values. For if the immigrant children's "givens" could be *scientifically* shown to be modest, then their schooling could guiltlessly be made intellectually easy in content and short in duration. This "met children's needs" and pleased the business people. Some parents voiced their displeasure, but only the labor movement paid attention to them.

Thus, the public's inherited assumptions about children's "given" aptitudes received strong institutional support. Possibilities offered by a child's interests and perseverance were ignored.

At TheAptitudeMyth.info are the genealogical chart and "What to Remember" list for chapter 12.

NOTES

1. William H. Elson and Frank P. Backman, "Different Courses for Elementary Schools," *Educational Review*, April 1910, 358. In Diane Ravitch, *Left Back: A Century of Failed School Reforms* (Simon & Schuster, 2000), 91.

2. This chapter relies largely on Joel Spring, *The American School 1642–1990* (Longman, 1990), chapter 7; Merle Curti, *The Social Ideas of American Educators* (Littlefield, Adams, 1978), chapter VI; and R. Freeman Butts and Lawrence A. Cremin, *A History of Education in American Culture* (Holt, Rinehart and Winston, 1953), chapter 9.

3. Butts and Cremin, *op. cit.*, 308, Table 4; their source is not cited.

4. Spring, *op. cit.*, 171; Spring credits David Tyack, *The One Best System* (Harvard, 1974), 230.

5. Lawrence A. Cremin, *The Transformation of the School: Progressivism in American Education, 1876–1957* (Alfred A. Knopf, 1961), 4–5. Cremin notes that "here and there Rice found encouraging departures from the depressing rule," most notably at Francis W. Parker's Cook County Normal School in Chicago. (See chapter 15.)

6. Spring, *op. cit.*, 153. Spring's chapter 7 reviews the interpretations of historians regarding the businessmen-educator alliance. All of the historians accept that such an alliance existed.

7. Curti, *op. cit.*, 230–31 (paragraph break added).

8. Edward L. Thorndike, "The Nature, Purposes, and General Methods of Measurement of Educational Products," in National Society for the Study of Education: *Seventeenth Yearbook* (Public School Publishing Company, 1918), Part II, 16.

9. The findings of my own doctoral dissertation support this contention. Cornelius Grove, "Cross-Cultural and Other Problems Affecting the Education of Immigrant Portuguese Students in a Program of Transitional Bilingual Education: A Descriptive Case Study"; Ed.D. dissertation (Teachers College, Columbia University, 1977), 258.

10. William C. Bagley, editorial, *School and Home Education*, March 1915, 238–41. In Ravitch, *op. cit.*, 93; italics added.

11. Julia Wrigley, *Class Politics and Public Schools: Chicago, 1900–1950* (Rutgers, 1982), 13. In Spring, *op. cit.*, 160–61.

12. Richard Hofstadter, *Anti-Intellectualism in American Life* (Alfred A. Knopf, 1970), 339.

13. Perceptive overviews include Ravitch, *op. cit.*, chapter 5; Butts and Cremin, *op. cit.*, chapter 12, especially 433–48; Hofstadter, *op. cit.*, chapter XIII; Cremin, *op. cit.*, chapter 8; and Herbert M. Kliebard, *The Struggle for the American Curriculum, 1893–1958*, 2nd ed. (Routledge, 1995).

14. Ravitch, *op. cit.*, 89–90.

THIRTEEN

Emerging Intellectual Currents in Post-Civil War America

The one causal factor which [a psychologist from Mars] would be sure was at work would be the intellect already existent. Those who have the most to begin with gain the most during the [school] year.

—Edward L. Thorndike[1]

In chapter 2, we looked at Greek thinking about human beings' capacity for consciousness. In chapter 4, we examined notions about these matters during the Renaissance of the 16th and 17th centuries, when awareness of each individual's uniqueness and potential autonomy was growing.

Now we're skipping forward to the second half of the 19th century,[2] when an avalanche of findings from scientists investigating the physical, biological, and social worlds became the impetus for renewed interest in human consciousness and individuality. Weighing into the intellectual fray were biologists, philosophers—and a new group of thinkers: psychologists.

Let's ponder for a moment the impact of Charles Darwin. His *Origin of the Species*, published in 1859, delivered a cataclysmic shock to conventional thinking about the place of humans in the cosmos. Those who needed a worldview characterized by fixedness and finality were profoundly unsettled by Darwin's message that all of nature is characterized by change, process, interaction, adaptation, and even extinction. Intellectual ferment engulfed the West.

During the half-century between the Civil War and World War One, three orientations to human consciousness emerged or were reaffirmed, each striving for acceptance among well-educated sectors of the populous. One was belief-based, viewing humans as a reflection of a spirit world. The second was evidence-based, grounded in the fact that humans are part of the biological world. The third also was evidence-based, seeing humans as inevitably social.

HUMANS AS REFLECTION OF A SPIRIT WORLD: FOUR BELIEF-BASED VIEWS OF CONSCIOUSNESS

A spiritual perspective underlay the way most Americans thought of people and their place in the natural order. This belief-based conception of humans is best understood in four manifestations: fundamentalist theology, liberal theology, philosophic idealism, and dualistic humanism.[3]

Fundamentalist Theology

Fundamentalism vociferously rejected evolutionary perspectives. It asserted that humans were qualitatively different from all other life forms and saw individuals as tainted by the "given" of Original Sin. To the question of which classroom teaching is best, the response of the fundamentalists was aligned with that of the Calvinists.

Liberal Theology

Liberals put great effort into finding ways in which Darwin's ideas could be reconciled with theological basics; their conclusion usually was that God or another supreme being utilized natural selection as his process of creation. The Unitarians went a step further by positing that ongoing evolutionary processes in the social realm would gradually sweep evil from the earth; Herbert Spencer was making a similar claim in Europe.

With their embrace of evolution as well as their warmth for the notions that humans are perfectible and God is benevolent, liberal Christians and Unitarians were attracted by child-centered approaches to teaching traceable to Rousseau and the Romantic poets.

Philosophic Idealism

Imported from Germany, idealism was alive in the United States during the first decades of the 19th century, when it flourished in New England as Transcendentalism.[4]

Not associated with any denomination or doctrinal stance, idealism claimed that the essence of the universe was spiritual or mental. The tangible world, including humans, was an expression of a universal mind or intelligence, which itself is not inert but rather evolving and progressively unfolding. The idea that a child's nature similarly needed to unfold and flower was appealing to the idealists and, like the liberals, they were drawn to child-centered approaches to instruction.

Idealism is also significant for our purposes because, as the 19th century was drawing to a close, it increasingly came under attack by Americans who were more and more enthralled by science and, as we shall soon see, had less and less use for any non-empirical philosophy.

Dualistic Humanism

This fourth view of humans as spiritual requires a more detailed explanation than the previous three because it included perspectives on consciousness, on education, and on teaching that, for a time, were both widespread and highly influential.

Aligned with the "classical humanism" of the Renaissance and the Pythagoras-inspired "rationalism" of René Descartes (see chapter 4), dualistic humanism was similar to philosophic idealism except that, for the dualistic humanists, a spiritual nature was the property *only* of human beings; everything else was viewed as material (hence, *dualistic humanism*).

These humanists were comfortable with scientific investigations and with the processes of evolution—so long as none of that was applied to the human mind. Human consciousness, together with the values, morals, knowledge, and esthetic sense that a human intellect can gain, were all categorized in a separate, higher, unchangeable realm having nothing to do with nature.

According to the proponents of dualistic humanism, the human intellect couldn't even be informed by observations of nature because, they said, learning does not occur by means of impressions on one's senses. Learning, as often conceived, did not fit at all into the mindset of the dualistic humanists. Their orientation was to a person's mental "faculties" and their objective was to train and "discipline" those faculties until they were developed to their highest potential.

In other words, their emphasis was not on gaining knowledge, nor on *learning about* the external world. Rather, it was on *learning how to manipulate concepts about* the external world. Sidestepping questions of knowledge acquisition and mastery, they went straight to the task of developing *mental process excellence*. For this philosophical perspective to work with students, it needed to have its own special curriculum and teaching style. It did: "faculty psychology."

Faculty Psychology

To understand that curriculum and style, we must attend to what the dualistic humanists meant by mental "faculties."[5] *Faculty psychology* had grown to become, during the latter half of the 19th century, the dominant variety of psychology taught in American universities. Similar to classical humanism, faculty psychology was a reaction against the rush to describe human nature and consciousness in the strictly materialistic terms of emerging science. Proponents drew attention to humans' spiritual qualities—to the soul, the self, and the mind.

Faculty psychologists referred queries about how the mind works not to empirical methods but rather to personal introspection. What one experiences inwardly was accepted as the primary, indeed the only, evidence for how the human mind functions. As we saw in chapter 9, Herbert Spencer in Europe was speaking similarly about the absolute authority of human introspection.

Faculty psychologists usually identified three mental "faculties": (1) intellect or reason, (2) feelings including desires, emotions, tastes, etc., and (3) will or volition, which spurs one to act.

The three faculties were *not* understood in Aristotelian fashion as the inexorable end of mental development. Rather, they were assumed to be poorly formed and in need of "training" or, more precisely, "mental discipline" (rarely was the need called "education" or "instruction"). Proper discipline was provided by intense study of classical humanist texts in Latin and Greek, plus mathematics. Study of the Bible (as a classical text) was sometimes included.

The Classical Perspective

Dualistic humanists and faculty psychologists were insisting on what had been known over centuries as "liberal" or "classical" studies. As set forth by Yale University president Jeremiah Day, the "commanding object" of a collegiate course should be:

> . . . to call into daily and vigorous exercise the faculties of the student. Those branches of study should be prescribed, and those modes of instruction adopted, which are best calculated to teach the art of fixing the attention, directing the train of thought, analyzing a subject proposed for investigation; following, with accurate discrimination, the course of argument; balancing nicely the evidence presented to the judgment; awakening, elevating, and controlling the imagination; arranging, with skill, the treasures which memory gathers; rousing and guiding the powers of genius. . . .[6]

It's important to note that President Day was speaking *not of knowledge mastery* but rather of the exercise and development of various mental powers. He believed (and later in his address, said clearly) that mental powers thus fully developed will subsequently enable one to perform well in any and all mental tasks such as are associated with any profession. This illustrates a key point: During this era, disciplining one's faculties by means of liberal studies was widely believed to transfer uniform mental excellence to *any* intellectual challenge that one might encounter subsequently in life. This belief had a name: "transfer of training." We'll revisit it shortly.

Here's a name for this constellation of prescriptions about teaching: the "Classical" Perspective. It joins the other three—"Calvinist," "Romantic," and "Practical"—introduced in chapter 11. (Additional insights into all four perspectives are found in the Appendix.)

What methods were employed by classical teachers? Educational historians R. Freeman Butts and Lawrence Cremin conclude[7] that didactic methods, buttressed by corporal punishment, prevailed. Common were Latin and Greek reading and study including sentence parsing and verb conjugation; extensive memorization of passages from Greek and Latin literature; practice of arithmetic; and lectures by professors. In short, there was much mental manipulation of symbols.

HUMANS AS GROUNDED IN THEIR BIOLOGY: AN EVIDENCE-BASED VIEW OF CONSCIOUSNESS

During the second half of the 19th century, an evidence-based biological view of humans was bursting into the awareness of educated Americans, driven largely by Darwin's *Origin of the Species*. This view held that not only the bodies of human beings but also every feature of their minds were the outcomes of eons of natural adaptation and development, and potentially were comprehensible by means of empirical methods. Minds were regarded as material, observable, tangible, even measurable. This view seemed deliberately calculated to provoke traditionalists such as the idealists, the humanists, the faculty psychologists, and especially the fundamentalists.

The Realists

One of the attacks on belief-based views came from within the ranks of philosophers. These "realists"[8] said that idealists and all others who thought of mankind as an extension of the spirit world were exactly wrong. Realists argued that *nothing* depends for its existence on being known by any conscious being, man or god. In effect, the realists pointed to biologists, physiologists, and other natural scientists and said, "*They* are getting it right."

The realists held that scientific observation and analysis were on their way to delivering verified, authoritative knowledge of all things natural and all laws—i.e., generalizations—governing or describing those things. The emerging knowledge was deemed worthy of transmission to learners, enabling them to adapt themselves more skillfully to the external world.

Significantly, historians Butts and Cremin note that, "Much of modern education rests implicitly upon such assumptions as these, although few [realists] carried their implications directly into the educational field."[9] Anyone enamored of philosophical realism would likely be drawn to the "Practical" perspective on children and teaching that traces its lineage from Francis Bacon through Comenius and Locke, and in the United States to Horace Mann. (Additional insights into all four perspectives are found in the Appendix.)

The Psychologists

A related attack on belief-based views came from other philosophers who, impressed by empirical methods and the growing body of scientific evidence gained thereby, came to regard the mind as a *process* that enabled humans to adapt ever more successfully to their environments. Consciousness and experience were identified with biological adaptation.

In 1890, a new book impacted the ongoing debate, being read by both academics and the well-educated: *Principles of Psychology*, by William James (1842–1910). James, the brother of novelist Henry James, went on to write many other well-received works such as *The Will to Believe* (1897), *The Varieties of Religious Experience* (1902), and *Pragmatism* (1907).

James declared that enough was known about physiology and evolutionary biology to permit psychology to become a science. A human is a biological creature whose intelligence responds adaptively to the environment, which is evidence of the plasticity of the central nervous system. Consciousness is active, functional, integrated, emotional, and most importantly *modifiable*. As a result of repetition of acts, it develops habits that subsequently drive observable behavior. It is not passive and it isn't split into separate "faculties." Thus, it *is* a fit subject for empirical study.

James's declaration encouraged the biologists, geneticists, physiologists, and the fledgling objective psychologists (i.e., non-introspective psychologists). Some objective psychologists, led by E. L. Thorndike, applied their findings about human consciousness to educational practice.

Objective Psychology and E. L. Thorndike

The goal of the objective psychologists was to use experimental and laboratory methods to study the mind and its functions such as adaptation and learning. Their idea that there were "connections" or "associations" in the mind between incoming stimuli and behavioral responses was not new. In chapter 4, for example, we quoted John Locke's view that if you want students to learn something permanently, you must ". . . settle [it] in them by an indispensable Practice. . . ."[10] Now was time for this facet of the mind to be studied by applying non-introspective, "objective" methods. Researchers on both sides of the Atlantic took up the challenge, none with greater vigor than Edward L. Thorndike (1874–1949).

In a veritable flood of publications, including his three volume *Educational Psychology* (1913–1914), Thorndike advanced by giant steps educators' grasp of the connection between a situation or stimulus ("S") and a behavioral response ("R"). He lent his authority to the already established belief that one's "givens" determine one's outcomes. He also undermined the notions of philosophical idealism about consciousness, mental "faculties," mental discipline, transfer of training—*and*, for good measure, the ages-old respect for the "liberal" or "classical" curriculum.

Let's look first at Thorndike's support for "givens" as deterministic. Writing in 1924, he asked rhetorically what would have been discovered by a "psychologist from Mars" (i.e., one unaware of current debates and prejudices) if he had carried out research to learn which factor made the most difference in humans' power to think. The Martian's conclusion:

> The one causal factor which he would be sure was at work would be the intellect already existent. Those who have the most to begin with gain the most during the year. Whatever studies they take will seem to produce large gains in intellect.[11]

This idea appealed to those responsible for doing *something* about all those immigrant children.

Regarding transfer of training, Thorndike claimed that there was no single curriculum or subject that people could study to *generally* improve their mind's functioning. Rather, "the intellectual value of studies should be determined largely by the special information, habits, interests, attitudes, and ideals which they demonstrably produce."[12] If students want to prepare for a certain career, they must study the specific subjects that lead directly to the needed skills.

One outcome of this perspective was that school and college administrators felt they finally could include in their curricula courses in the natural and social sciences, and technical skills. This change long had been vociferously opposed by all admirers of liberal and classical studies.

Thorndike's Work Criticized

Questioning the research of Thorndike and others, Richard Hofstadter writes that ". . . these experiments were pathetically inadequate; individually and collectively, they did not shed very much light on the grand question to which they were ultimately directed." The findings opened schoolhouse doors to those who had argued "that all pupils should in large measure get the kind of training originally conceived for the slow learner."

Referring to educators who were eager to loosen academic standards, Hofstadter observes that "without deliberate intent, [they] distorted experimental findings in the interests of their mission to reorganize the high schools to accommodate the masses. [But they] were simply ignoring all findings that did not substantiate their views."[13] [14]

HUMANS AS GROUNDED IN THEIR SOCIETY: AN EVIDENCE-BASED VIEW OF CONSCIOUSNESS

During the second half of the 19th century, another evidence-based view of humans also was gaining American adherents. It drew attention to the fact that, with virtually no exceptions, every human being is born, raised, and lives his or her entire life in social relationships with other human beings. Adherents said this must have significance for us as we ponder human nature, consciousness, behavior, and learning. They wondered, too, if evolutionary concepts could be applied to the understanding of human societies. Sociologists, social historians, and some philosophers began to look for ways in which evolution could be applied to their disciplines.

Herbert Spencer contributed to this effort with his 1850 *Social Statics* and 1877 *Principles of Sociology*. American thinkers who joined this trend each reached this conclusion: Interactions among humans from their first days of life are largely responsible for the high intelligence that humans have attained as well as for their capacity for adaptation to diverse environments.

George Herbert Mead's Social Perspective

One of the Americans, George Herbert Mead (1863–1931), argued that a newborn has neither a "mind" nor any conception of "self."[15] Self and mind emerge as the infant forms relationships with other humans, distinguishes between himself and them, and absorbs most (if not necessarily all) of their mindsets and values.

Fundamental to this process, said Mead, is that the child learns to understand and then skillfully employ not only the symbols of communication shared among those around him but also the unique constellation of *meanings* signified by those symbols. A human's mind is an amalgam of those symbolic learnings. A mind is active not only in that it enables the individual to adapt to the environment, but far more significantly in that a mind can proactively *adapt or rearrange the environment* in order to attain the needs and intentions of the individual.

Humans gained these abilities across millennia of social interactions. Modern humans' ability to modify and improve their circumstances applies to their physical environments *and to their social environments*. Mead went on to envision deliberate social action in order to bring about needed social reforms—and in so doing influenced a young colleague, John Dewey.[16]

William James's Individual Perspective

Whereas Mead saw mankind as social from the perspective of *society*, William James saw mankind as social from the perspective of the *individual*. James (to whom we were introduced earlier) said that the conscious mind is active, functional, and modifiable, and that as a result of repetition of acts (especially when humans are young) it develops habits that thereafter drive observable behavior. He viewed habits as a critical component in the day-to-day functioning of adults:

> Habit is thus the enormous fly-wheel of society, its most precious conservative agent. It alone is what keeps us all within the bounds of ordinance. . . . the man can by-and-by no more escape [his habits] than his coat-sleeve can suddenly fall into a new set of folds. On the whole, it is best he should not escape. It is well for the world that in most of us, by the age of thirty, the character has set like plaster, and will never soften again.[17]

Let's examine three features of James's doctrine of habit.[18] First, he saw *instincts* as the ground on which habits are formed in early life. An individual's instincts are inherited, and different individuals inherit different instincts in quality and quantity; thus, James posited critical controlling "givens" in each person's makeup that guided *and limited* his or her life possibilities.

Second, similarly to Mead, James focused on the capability of each mind to adapt in a plastic way to its environment *and to act upon that environment with purposeful intent* to rearrange it to suit individual and social needs. James's philosophy was (and is) known as pragmatism. He was an ardent critic of determinism and a strong proponent of free will and voluntarism.[19]

Third, James addressed himself to teachers in his well-received *Talks to Teachers*,[20] helping them grasp the biological basis of mental development, the usefulness of drawing on the child's own interests as the driver of learning progress, the value of guided activity in the formation of desirable habits, and the importance of teachers' focusing not on supposed "faculties" of a child's mind but on the whole child, the whole person who would soon take a place within society. He declared that "the teachers of this country . . . have its future in their hands."[21]

But James never viewed the schools, nor teachers, as agents of social change. Rather, James viewed teachers as the catalyst for producing better individuals.

JAMES ARGUES THAT THE LEARNER, NOT THE TEACHER, IS THE CRITICAL SUCCESS FACTOR

In *Doomed to Fail* (2004), classroom teacher Paul Zoch points out that James emphasized the importance of the self-willed mental activity of paying attention, regardless of whether the object of attention is fascinating or dull. A learner creates success or failure by managing his thoughts, argued James; success is the outcome of "turning the matter incessantly in his mind."[22]

> But, whether the attention come by grace of genius or by dint of will, the longer one does attend to a topic the more mastery of it one has. And the faculty of voluntarily bringing back a wandering attention, over and over again, is the very root of judgment, character, and will. No one is *compos sui* [in control of himself] if he have it not.[23]

A student's success, wrote James, depends on "the strength of his [own] desire and passion, the strength of the interest he takes in what is proposed."[24] In short, *academic excellence depends on the student's effort*; the teacher is a helper or assistant who makes the process more efficient.

James did not specifically propose a pedagogical approach, but his work obviously makes contributions to the practice of education as an application of psychology, contributions that are applicable to classroom teaching. This appears to be what James intended.[25] From James's point of view, though, the eagerness of some educators to apply his insights turned into a problem.

James's emphases on the individual learner, on the child's interests, on practical classroom activities, and on learning by doing were seized upon by educators in the tradition of Rousseau, Pestalozzi, and the Romantic poets. By the turn of the 20th century, however, that tradition was already drawing increasingly vocal criticism as "soft pedagogy." This upset James. He definitely did *not* identify with the Romantic perspective (see Table A.2 in the Appendix) and did not want to be on the receiving end of *that* criticism. He valued a certain amount of discipline and drill, and never advocated relying entirely on a child's own interests. "*Soft* pedagogics," he wrote:

> . . . have taken the place of the old steep and rocky path to learning. But from this lukewarm air the bracing oxygen of effort is left out. It is nonsense to suppose that every step in education *can* be interesting. The fighting impulse must often be appealed to. Make the pupil feel ashamed of being scared at fractions, of being "downed" by the law of falling bodies; rouse his pugnacity and pride, and he will rush at the difficult places with a sort of inner wrath at himself that is one of his best moral facilities. A victory scored under such conditions becomes a turning-point and crisis of his character. . . .
>
> I heard a lady say that she had taken her child to the kindergarten, "but he is so bright that he saw through it immediately." Too many school children "see" as immediately 'through' the namby-pamby attempts of the softer pedagogy to lubricate things for them, and make them interesting. Even they can enjoy abstractions, provided they be of the proper order; and it is a poor compliment to their rational appetite to think that anecdotes about little Tommies and little Jennies are the only kind of things their minds can digest.[26]

MUSINGS AND SPECULATIONS

Among teachers, educated citizens, and his fellow academics, William James's books were actually *read*. His views on "the old steep and rocky path to learning" were applauded by many teachers. Why didn't these views have more durability? I suspect his message was eclipsed by a more familiar point of view, the inherited one we've been tracing throughout this book. I also believe that other messengers were even more appealing, as we'll soon see in chapter 15.

WHY CHAPTER 13 IS IMPORTANT

Again we have witnessed evidence-based Empirical methods being called upon to support belief-based perspectives, the goal being to legitimate a public-policy objective that aligned with immediate practical needs. A prominent psychologist, E. L. Thorndike, ostensibly showed how that could be done. Meanwhile, another psychologist prominent in the minds of academics and the public, William James, was arguing against "attempts to lubricate things for students"—a view that commanded respect among teachers but soon became overwhelmed by contrary trends, as we shall soon see.

At TheAptitudeMyth.info are the genealogical chart and "What to Remember" list for chapter 13. And in the Appendix of this book is Table A.4, which further clarifies the fourth view of classroom teaching—the "Classical"—by relating it to proponents' beliefs about the nature of children and how they learn.

NOTES

1. E. L. Thorndike, "Mental Discipline in High School Studies," *Journal of Educational Psychology*, vol. 15, no. 1 (1924), 95; in Diane Ravitch, *Left Back* (Simon & Schuster, 2000), 66–67.

2. My principal source for this chapter has been R. Freeman Butts and Lawrence A. Cremin, *A History of Education in American Culture* (Holt, Rinehart, and Winston, 1953), especially chapter 10, "Reshaping the American Mind."

3. Butts and Cremin, *ibid.*, pp. 325–33.

4. Transcendentalism was based on the claim that humans can transcend the lower features of their natures. Grounded in German idealist philosophy and the British Romantic poetry, and a close cousin of liberal Christianity, Transcendentalism emphasized spirituality and self-cultivation in reaction against Enlightenment rationalism. See Philip F. Gura, *American Transcendentalism: A History* (Hill and Wang, 2007), especially 84–90.

5. This overview of faculty psychology draws on Butts and Cremin, *op. cit.*, 176–80, 183, 331.

6. "Original Papers in relation to a Course of Liberal Education," *American Journal of Science and Arts*, vol. 15, Art. VIII (Hezekiah Howe, 1829), 300–301 and 308–9. The words attributed to President Day are from an 1828 Yale faculty report.

7. Butts and Cremin, *op. cit.*, 122–24. They write that ". . . discipline was likely to be severe with heavy emphasis on corporal punishment . . . 'without respect to person.' The boys sat long hours on hard benches ['forms'] with little attention to comfort, relaxation, or play. Regulations spoke often of the punishments that should be meted out to fit the offenses of lying, cursing, swearing, quarreling, fighting, and playing cards or dice. Physical education, or music, or art, or science, or mathematics, or any subject that might appeal to the interests of seven- to fifteen-year-olds had no place in the curriculum, and methods of active involvement beyond memorizing seldom seemed to occur to teachers. There was little thought of child study, human psychology, or methods of teaching." 123–24.

8. Note that this 19th century brand of "realism" is utterly different from Plato's "Realism."

9. Butts and Cremin, *op. cit.*, 335–36; see also 342.

10. John Locke, *Some Thoughts Concerning Education* (Macmillan, 1902), §66, 39.

11. Thorndike, *op. cit.*, 98; in Ravitch, *op. cit.*, 66–67.

12. *Ibid.*, 98; quoted by Butts and Cremin, *op. cit.*, 338.

13. Richard Hofstadter, *Anti-Intellectualism in American Life* (Alfred A. Knopf, 1970), 349, 353. Hofstadter offers much more detail to support this conclusion about the people who wanted to loosen academic standards, concluding: "Their misuse of experimental evidence, in fact, constitutes a major scandal in the history of educational thought" (349).

14. Diane Ravitch notes that, "Thorndike had faith in the scientific value of measurement. . . . Only such a faith . . . could make possible the assumption that studies such as Latin and geometry had been decisively invalidated by laboratory experiments in which students memorized nonsense syllables or underlined meaningless letter combinations." Ravitch, *op. cit.*, 67. On 68–69, Ravitch draws on a dissertation by Pedro Orata, who found Thorndike's work misleading. Pedro Tamesis Orata, *The Theory of Identical Elements: Being a Critique of Thorndike's Theory of Identical Elements and a Re-interpretation of the Problem of Transfer of Training* (Ohio State University Press, 1928), 168–69, 171.

15. This paragraph relies heavily on Butts and Cremin, *op. cit.*, 340–41.

16. Dewey, Mead's colleague at the University of Chicago, carried forward the view of humans as social beings who can reconstruct environments and societies. See the Postscript to chapter 15.

17. William James, *The Principles of Psychology* (Henry Holt, 1890), vol. 1, 121. The full quote shows James to be very conservative in terms of a hereditary basis for established social stratification: "[Habit] alone is what keeps us all within the bounds of ordinance, *and saves the children of fortune from the envious uprisings of the poor.*"

18. This paragraph relies heavily on Merle Curti, *The Social Ideas of American Educators* (Littlefield, Adams, 1978), 445–51.

19. James's views were influential on John Dewey, who was drawn to the features of pragmatism that pointed to human beings' capacity to manipulate their environment, and to the importance of determining through actual practice what "works." Dewey once wrote in approval of James's ". . . fundamental idea of an open universe in which uncertainty, choice, hypotheses, novelties and possibilities are naturalized. . . ." Richard Hofstadter, *Social Darwinism in American Thought* (George Braziller, 1959), 123; this quote begins Hofstadter's chapter on pragmatism; the quote's provenance is not cited. For more on Dewey, see the Postscript to chapter 15.

20. William James, *Talks to Teachers on Psychology: and to Students on Some of Life's Ideals* (Henry Holt, 907); available from Nabu Public Domain Reprints.

21. *Ibid.*, 3.

22. James, *Principles, op. cit.*, 598.

23. *Ibid.*, 424.

24. James, *Talks, op. cit.*, 114.

25. This paragraph, especially the last three sentences, relies heavily on Curti, *op. cit.*, 450. Curti cites James's *Talks to Teachers*, 28, 54-55, 68–69, 111–12. The point about James's not wanting to be identified as child-centered is also made by Cremin: "In view of subsequent developments, it is interesting to note James's recurring concern with possible charges of 'softness' against his pedagogy." Lawrence Cremin, *The Transformation of the School: Progressivism in American Education, 1876–1957* (Alfred A. Knopf, 1961), 108, note 1.

26. James, *Talks, op. cit.*, 55, 151–52.

FOURTEEN

American Educational Metamorphosis, I: Socially Efficient Education

Here we come upon a new function for the teachers in our elementary schools. [They] ought to sort the pupils and sort them by their evident and probable destinies.
—Charles W. Eliot[1]

During the last quarter of the 19th century and the first quarter of the 20th, education in the United States underwent a metamorphosis.[2] The forms and functions of public education at the end of that 50-year period, during the "Roaring Twenties," bore little resemblance to what they had been at the beginning. During that time, education was reconceptualized and realigned, and its energies were redirected, in order to attain *social efficiency* and *child-centeredness*, and to institutionally support the ages-old belief in innately "given" and thus fixed mental aptitudes.

Although these trends were mutually supportive, they were not variations on a single theme. The oldest had roots dating back some 2,500 years: assumptions about innate "givens." Another surfaced some 600 years ago: the rhetorical and emotional attractiveness of child-centered classroom practices.

This chapter's topic, social efficiency, concerns society's response to challenges that arose after the Civil War: burgeoning school enrollments of immigrant children; growing respect for scientific thinking; and emerging social and political influence of practical-minded businessmen.

PUBLIC SECONDARY SCHOOLS DURING THE LAST DECADES OF THE 19TH CENTURY

For educators concerned about American secondary schools as the 19th century turned into the 20th, three statistics dominated:

- Less than 10 percent of youth aged 14–17 was attending school; this made it possible for critics to charge that high schools were "highly selective" and serving only "elite" families.
- Secondary school enrollments were rapidly growing; this made it possible for people to be preoccupied by the appearance of "the masses," meaning the children of "the laboring classes"; this, in turn, caused concern because many believed—and said openly—that those children were *not fit* to become future American leaders.[3]

- The dropout rate was astonishingly high; in most states, the high school *graduation* rate was in the vicinity of only 10 percent.[4]

School professionals were proud that the doors of secondary schools were open to all comers. The Common School Movement's democratic values were satisfied.

But the dropout rate was troubling. According to secondary school historian Edward Krug, school people did not seriously consider an economic explanation for dropping out, one that referenced family economics and dynamics. Rather, school leaders' discussions "tended to center on the suitability of existing high school programs. What was needed, argued many, was a more practical course of study, particularly for those who had to earn their living immediately after finishing high school," or who as girls were going to become housewives or teachers.[5]

In terms of the curriculum, the situation in secondary schools during the 1890s was far too complex to be discussed in detail.[6] A few generalizations can be stated: Most schools offered multiple curricular paths. Almost all had a "classical" path intended for students aiming for college admission; it included Greek (sharply declining enrollments), Latin (discussed below), higher math, and other challenging courses associated with the classical perspective. Some schools had a "Latin-Scientific" curriculum, strongly academic but not college prep. Other curricular paths were more practical, including both academic and non-academic courses; the latter included courses in manual (vocational) training, music, art, bookkeeping, and surveying.

Scholars concur that the secondary curriculum in the United States at that time was more diverse and flexible than was the secondary curriculum in Europe.[7] Because of that diversity, communities with adequate resources were beginning to establish separate secondary schools for different purposes, a practice that followed a pattern typical of Europe.[8]

When Academic Subjects Reigned, Enrollment Rose

It's important to note, however, that "academic" subjects—history, modern languages, and several sciences—were prominent in *all* curricular offerings and figured significantly in the expectations placed on *all* students. In the mind of the public, secondary schools were associated with academic work; that association was very largely appropriate if not entirely accurate.

Despite the public's association between high schools and academic work, and despite the fact that no student was compelled by state law to attend high school, enrollments of youth aged 14–17 rose steadily, both in percentage terms and in absolute terms. But only a small fraction of those youth planned to attend college. For example, the *Report* of the U.S. Commissioner of Education for 1899–1900 says that only 10.8 percent of students in public high schools was preparing for college; the *Report* for 1905 actually shows the percentage dropping to 9.5 percent.[9]

With those facts in mind, the picture regarding enrollments in Latin is significant. Latin was *not* required of all students—in fact, it was no longer required by all colleges— yet during the decade of 1890–1900, Latin enrollments nationwide *increased from 34.7 percent to 50.6 percent!* This fact keenly embarrassed those who had been doubting the abilities and interests of the children of "the masses," i.e., the children of immigrants and workers.[10]

Let's maintain perspective on all this by recalling that the very idea of a state-supported public secondary school, free to all who wish to attend regardless of their backgrounds or future plans, was a social and educational experiment entirely without precedent in world history.[11]

PUBLIC SECONDARY SCHOOLS DURING THE
FIRST DECADES OF THE 20TH CENTURY

One of the most significant developments in American education occurred when the ideal of education for all began to be extended from younger to older students, the visible outcome of which was rapid increases in public secondary school enrollments. The resulting demands and strains on secondary schools led to rapid changes in their culture and practices, and to changes in the way many educated Americans thought about the objectives of schooling.

Compulsory Attendance and a School's "Holding Power"

The reason why secondary school attendance grew rapidly after the turn of the century was that political leaders with a social reform agenda joined forces with trade unionists with a job-protection agenda to fight the evil of child labor.[12] They saw that a way to end child labor was to require all children to remain in school. By 1918, all states had compulsory attendance laws, enacted with the goal of protecting youth from exploitation, and requiring them to remain in school until at least age 16.

School leaders did not necessarily oppose the enactment of the attendance laws; in fact, in the 1918 NEA Report known as the *Cardinal Principles of Secondary Education* (discussed later in this chapter), it was recommended that "normal" children remain in school until age 18.

But the compulsory attendance laws became a game-changer for educators. Until these laws came into effect, the student population of high schools had been very largely self-selected. The students in school were there because they and/or their parents had sought their admission.

By the second decade of the 20th century, present in secondary school classrooms were more and more youth who wouldn't have been there if the state hadn't insisted on it. The belief arose that, therefore, changes were necessary in both curricular content and teaching methods.

As already noted, in most high schools around the turn of the century, "academic" subjects were prominent in *all* curricular offerings and figured in the expectations placed on *all* students. In spite of these facts, *school leaders began trying to come up with more and more courses that, presumably, would hold the interest of youth who weren't in school voluntarily.* And the most important performance criteria of a secondary school gradually came to be seen as its "holding power" in terms of maintaining ongoing attendance and discouraging dropping out.

Even more significant for our purposes, attention came to be focused not only on inventing new courses *but also on trying to eliminate or emasculate traditional academic courses*, which many viewed as threatening the holding power of a school and causing slow learning by some students.

If your mental image is that secondary educators noticed large numbers of uninterested, fractious students in the academic classes (or noticed that many of those students were often absent), and then began conjuring up easier, "fun" courses, you might be mistaken. For in the view of historian Richard Hofstadter, the actual sequence of events was exactly the reverse:

> The problem of numbers [in attendance] had hardly made its appearance before a movement began in professional education to exalt numbers over quality and the alleged demands of utility over intellectual development. Far from conceiving the mediocre, reluctant, or incapable student as an obstacle . . . in a school system devoted to educating the interested, the capable, and the gifted, *American educators entered upon a crusade to exalt*

the academically uninterested or ungifted child into a kind of culture-hero. They were not content to say that the realities of American social life had made it necessary to compromise with the ideal of education as the development of formal learning and intellectual capacity. Instead, they militantly proclaimed that such education was archaic and futile and that the noblest end of a truly democratic system of education was to meet the child's immediate interests by offering him a series of immediate utilities. [13]

Expressed differently, the ideal of "mastery" of subject matter was eclipsed by the ideal of "meeting the needs" of *all* students by applying a lowest-common-denominator approach.

Who Decides What Each Student Needs?

The apostles of social efficiency decided to reduce academic subjects by insisting that *every* subject prove its practical utility, i.e., its real-life value outside of the classroom in adults' work-a-day world. (During this era, the concept "functional" was popular in other facets of American life, including architecture, art, house furnishings, etc. [14])

Faced with this kind of demand, traditional subjects such as foreign languages, mathematics, history, English, and (surprisingly) science faired poorly, not the least because those who had set themselves up in judgment were committed skeptics. Two historians who examined this period three-quarters of a century later (1999), David L. Angus and Jeffrey E. Mirel, conclude that:

> . . . progressive reformers shared certain underlying principles and values, including their beliefs that 19th century high schools were "bastions of elite, college preparatory training"; that the high school could become "democratic" only by expanding its curriculum to include practical, vocational studies; that programs should be designed to meet the "needs" of students; and that professional educators, not lay boards of education, should decide how to group students and how to determine their "needs." [15]

Equally important, at least some of the reformers didn't stop at reducing the availability of academic subjects. They went even farther by reducing the opportunities for high school students to select the courses and programs in which they were interested.

One memorable story has been unearthed by historian Diane Ravitch: A professor at the University of Illinois reported in 1914 that the high school in Springfield, Massachusetts, offered to its pupils five curriculum track choices. (From among the five available curriculum tracks, each pupil chose one by marking and handing-in an "election card"; the pupils' decision making about this choice was not guided or supervised by any Springfield faculty member.) From the point of view of the professor in Illinois, it was unfortunate that:

> . . . the unsupervised pupil election cards showed that only one curriculum was actually provided in practice [i.e., actually delivered because most pupils chose it]. This curriculum was the "college preparatory," despite the fact that only 16 pupils out of a high-school enrollment of 883 went to any college. In other words, the pupils *elected* of their own choice to enroll in college preparatory courses, even though few intended to go to college. Professor Johnston could not understand this failure of supervision. More admirable to him was Newton, Massachusetts, where a progressive superintendent had installed fourteen district curricula, based on the pupils' "vocational needs and expectations." This example of "the most modern basis of curriculum building . . . automatically restricts *vicious habits of election* by students." [16]

In other words, the school authorities in Newton were acting as though they knew much more about each pupil's "givens" than did the pupil himself or his parents; therefore, the Newton authorities didn't need to take into account (beyond a pupil's alleged "givens") any other factor such as the pupil's curiosity or perseverance. Based on their "knowledge," they mandated each pupil's curriculum path—and almost certainly his or her lifelong career as well.

THE SHIFT IN EDUCATIONAL AUTHORITY
AROUND THE TURN OF THE CENTURY

Leadership of American public education first came into being during the middle third of the 19th century with the "educational evangelists," personified by Horace Mann, itinerant preachers who aroused citizens across the country to begin creating what became the "common school system."

Later, as school districts began being established, local school leaders—superintendents—came into prominence. The criteria used to select them relied very heavily on their demonstrated Christian uprightness and, often, on their mastery of the classical curriculum as well.[17] The selecting was done, of course, by locally elected lay school boards and committees.

The "Educational Trust"

As the 19th century neared its end, a new type of school leader at the local and state levels came into vogue. Known collectively at the time as "the educational trust," these men inched away from the Christian revivalist mentality without, of course, giving up their acknowledgment of Christian values. They also remained firm in their belief in moral absolutes.

But as the turn of the century approached, moral absolutes for them (as for many educated Americans) increasingly were expressed in terms of science as a worldview and as a process for making decisions. Steadily gaining in credibility was the objective and inductive rationality of science, as wielded by trained experts acting in bureaucratic institutions. Within this mindset, "science" referred to the systematic collection of factual data for the purpose of policy formation.

This "scientific management" was expected to give the "educational trust" the right to render decisions that affected the masses, and to put an end to armchair theorizing by mere laypeople. The result would be "social efficiency," an evolution brought about by conscious means.[18]

The University-Based Schools of Education

Simultaneously, another shift in American educational leadership came into view as the 19th century turned into the 20th. As schools of education were established within American universities, they began to eclipse both the teacher-training "normal schools" and the influence of local district superintendents.

The leading schools of education were those established at Columbia, where the school of education became known as Teachers College,[19] and at Harvard, Stanford, and Chicago. In all four cases, the schools of education came into being with a surprisingly large degree of autonomy from the larger universities of which each was a part. (At Columbia, it was said that 120th Street, which separates Teachers College from the main campus, was "the widest street in the world.")

The outcome was that the newly minted professors of education, isolated from the day-to-day milieu of academic scholars, did their work with little input from some of the leading thinkers of the era. Reform pedagogy had emerged largely as a protest against traditional academic subjects; it's hardly surprising that almost no sustained communication passed between the two groups.[20]

Note, too, that these schools of education, including many at state colleges, were established during the heady decades around the turn of the century when educational reformers were busy remaking the American educational landscape. Professors of education were convinced that they had a golden opportunity to redirect tradition-bound concepts and methods into pathways guided by modern science. So they dedicated themselves to convincing one and all of the futility of teaching academic subjects except to a few college-bound learners, and thus of the importance of replacing many if not all of the traditional subjects with practical studies.

Using watchwords such as "democracy," "differentiation," and "meeting individual needs," and with heavy reliance on their assumption that each individual had immutable "givens" and therefore "needs" that could be measured, the professors crusaded for a system in which non-college-bound high school students would be funneled into occupation-linked programs such as industrial education, manual training, commercial studies, domestic science, and agriculture.

These practices gradually became the working definition of "equality of opportunity."[21]

An Interpretation of the Shift in Authority

Here is an interpretation of the 50-year period under consideration:[22] The habit of moral absolutism fostered by Christianity was alive and well—and deeply ingrained in the minds of most Americans. As the educated public's commitment to organized Christianity began to waver, that habit gradually was transferred to science as both a worldview and a process for making practical decisions.

Consequently, the objective rationality of evidence-based science gradually supplanted the belief-based certainty of religion as the generally accepted way in which the few could make decisions affecting the many. Leaders who could reasonably cloak themselves in the authority of "science" were able to expropriate for themselves at least some of the public's acceptance of decisions affecting the many that the public had previously granted to moral Christian leaders.

In the realm of educational policy and practice, this tendency goes far in explaining why the authority and influence of God-fearing district superintendents was slowly eclipsed by that of the young professors of education. The latter had been learning about scientific methods and were determined, from their base in relatively isolated but highly respected university schools of education, to reform the allegedly archaic manner in which the nation had been going about educating its youth.

DOCUMENTING THE COURSE OF EDUCATIONAL REFORM: 25 YEARS OF NEA REPORTS

The National Education Association was the most prominent shared space of U.S. educators. The NEA's history during the 50 years under consideration[23] reveals formal reports that are indicative of social trends in the nation and a parallel metamorphosis among educators.

The Report of the Committee of Ten (1893)

Prompted by the rapidly rising tide of enrollments by youth aged 14–17 and concern about the appropriate role for the growing number of public secondary schools, the NEA during 1892 established a committee to study whether secondary schools should treat all students similarly, or whether they should make distinctions.

Chairing the committee was that generation's most prominent educator, Charles W. Eliot, president of Harvard University. Committee members included four other college presidents, a college professor, three high school principals, and the U.S. Commissioner of Education. These discussants were known then, and thereafter to history, as the "Committee of Ten."[24]

In 1893, the Committee of Ten's report stated that "The secondary schools . . . do not exist [solely] for the purpose of preparing boys and girls for colleges. . . . Their main function is to prepare for the duties of life that small proportion of all children . . . who show themselves able to profit by an education prolonged to the eighteenth year. . . ." Academic excellence for *all* students was the appropriate objective. ". . . Every subject which is taught at all . . .," declared the report, "should be taught in the same way and to the same extent to every pupil so long as he pursues it, no matter what the probable destination of the pupil may be. . . ."[25]

Many educators, especially those beginning to think of themselves as "progressives," were upset that the Committee of Ten supported an academic curriculum for all students, even those not college-bound. They argued that an academic education was too difficult for most students, and that students who were members of the laboring classes would become overeducated.

Choosing to ignore the curricular diversity that was, largely, the norm across the nation, and paying no attention to the tiny percentage of students preparing for college, the progressives portrayed high schools as elitist institutions that ignored the needs of the non-college-bound. They attacked the academic curriculum as though it were the classical curriculum, and they denounced the classical curriculum at a time when only 3 percent of students were studying Greek.[26]

Said one critic: "No builder thinks of laying the same foundation for a cottage as for a ten-story block."[27] Said the highly influential college president and apostle of childhood G. Stanley Hall: ". . . This principle does not apply to the great army of incapables . . . *for whose mental development heredity decrees a slow place and early arrest*, and for whom . . . both studies and methods must be different."[28] Hall on another occasion had branded the growth in Latin enrollments as "calamitous to the point of pathos."[29]

In spite of this ferment, the great majority of secondary schools did not eliminate the distinction between students whose objective was to attend college and those whose objectives were "practical" or "vocational" in nature.[30]

The Tipping Point (1908)

Fast forward 15 years to 1908. That year has been identified by some historians as the "tipping point" for two reasons.

The first is that Charles W. Eliot, the former chairman of the Committee of Ten, still president of Harvard University, and a consistent and visible supporter of a "liberal education" (i.e., common academic curriculum) for all students, changed his mind—in public. In a speech to the National Society for the Promotion of Industrial Education, he addressed the question of how to deal with students in their early teens, saying: "Here we come upon a new function for the teachers in our elementary schools. . . . [They] ought to sort the pupils and sort them by their evident and probable destinies."[31] Because *Charles W. Eliot* said this, it was huge!

The second reason 1908 is viewed as the tipping point is that at the NEA convention that year, a resolution was adopted saying that secondary schools should not be primarily "fitting schools" for colleges, and urging that secondary schools "be adapted to the general needs, both intellectual and industrial, of their students."[32] (As we have seen, high schools were far from being fitting schools for colleges.) This resolution was, at base, a signal that many educators remained contemptuous of the academic curriculum and, more significantly for our purposes, believed that the great majority of students could not, *should not*, take an academic curriculum.

The Report of the Committee of Nine (1911)

Another NEA committee, the Committee of Nine on the Articulation of High School and College, submitted a report in 1911 that is especially useful in revealing the mindset shift of many educators. The committee's chairman, Clarence Kingsley, was a former social worker and math instructor.[33] The other eight members included four high school principals, two university professors, one city superintendent, and one official of a state department.[34] Their report said that American public high schools are:

> . . . responsible for leading tens of thousands of boys and girls away from the pursuits for which they are adapted and in which they are needed, to other pursuits for which they are not adapted and in which they are not needed. By means of exclusively bookish curricula false ideals of culture are developed. A chasm is created between the producers of material wealth and the distributors and consumers thereof.[35]

This choice of words reveals the factors driving the thinking of American educators at the beginning of the 20th century. Note the double pairing of "adapted" and "needed":

- *Adapted* ("they are adapted," "they are not adapted") is anchored in an assumption whose origin and growing acceptance we have been tracing across 2,500 years—that there are innate "givens" over which the individual infant, child, and youth has no control. Of even greater significance is the associated assumption that we adults, we educators, we the leaders of society know what those "givens" are for each individual.

- *Needed* ("in which they are needed," "in which they are not needed") is the much more recently activated driver of the thinking of influential business leaders and educators, which emerged with arrival on American shores of waves of immigrants. How can schools, and society as a whole, efficiently deal with all these? The answer: Make sure they're assigned to where they are needed, which is very largely in menial occupations, which in turn requires that they receive schooling with extremely little intellectual content.

Let's be explicit about the educators' path of reasoning, which proceeds as follows:

> Because schooling begins early in life and involves exposure to one kind of learning before others can be commenced, it is necessary for us to "sort" children into ability groups while they're still in elementary school so that we can direct them onto the correct learning paths after elementary school.
>
> How should we sort them? We should sort them by their evident and probable destinies, that is, by their "givens" (in more recent parlance, by their "aptitudes"). Everybody recognizes the self-evident truth that different people, at birth, are endowed with different strengths and limitations. And now, thanks to modern science, we are enabled to assess with confidence the strengths and limitations of each individual child. So we can,

and should, sort and track children. The outcome of this assessing, sorting, and tracking is *socially efficient* education.

The Cardinal Principles of Secondary Education (1918)

Fast forward one more time, to 1917–1918. As the First World War was ending, two events signaled that the corner had been turned by American educational thought leaders. One was an enactment of the Congress of the United States, the Smith-Hughes Act, which became law during 1917. Supported by both labor and business leaders, this act provided federal funds for the hiring of teachers to instruct workplace skills. In so doing, it gave federal sanction and support to the notion that every kind of curriculum had an equal claim to be offered in the nation's secondary schools.

Almost 25 years after the Committee of Ten had submitted its report, the Commission on the Reorganization of Secondary Education, or CRSE, submitted to the NEA in 1918 a report with vastly different conclusions. The *Cardinal Principles of Secondary Education* is a seminal document in American educational history. Even before it was formally submitted, the U.S. Bureau of Education distributed 130,000 copies of the 32-page booklet. Richard Hofstadter notes wryly that some teacher-training institutions required their students to memorize portions of it, thus directly contradicting a key principle of the popular new instructional doctrines.[36]

The Cardinal Principles set forth seven objectives of secondary education: health; command of fundamental processes; worthy home-membership; vocation; citizenship; worthy use of leisure; and ethical character. Not mentioned was mastery of subject matter, nor development of intellectual capacity, nor awareness of a common cultural heritage.

Schools were urged to differentiate the curriculum beginning when pupils moved on from elementary school. A traditional academic curriculum available to all was not countenanced. Schools were encouraged to offer what students would need in adult life. What was important, the report said, was "the application of knowledge to the activities of life, rather than primarily in terms of the demands of any subject as a logically organized science."[37]

It's interesting to contrast the membership of the CRSE with that of the Committee of Ten twenty-five years earlier. The chair of the CRSE was Clarence Kingsley, who also had chaired the Committee of Nine; in 1918 he was the state supervisor of high schools in Massachusetts. Otherwise, the CRSE's membership was dominated by university professors of education.[38]

The *Cardinal Principles* is full of Progressive Era idealism. One passage notes that, "Among the means for developing attitudes and habits important in a democracy are the assignment of projects and problems to groups of pupils for cooperative solution and the socialized recitation whereby the class as a whole develops a sense of collective responsibility." And another passage calls for education to enable each young person "to find his place and use that place to shape both himself and society toward ever nobler ends."[39] Note that this lofty vision was stated during the same era when the Versailles Conference was busy "making the world safe for democracy."

MUSINGS AND SPECULATIONS

I believe that the majority of the public was conditioned to accept the authority of those who seemed to have good reason to tell them what to think. Traditionally, that role had fallen to those claiming the authority of revealed Christianity. That role was being transferred to those claiming the authority of objective science; this claim was made by the young reformers, largely found in the isolated schools of education. This is *not* to argue that lay citizens had superior ideas about educational policy that they feared to advance. Most people simply went along with the trend.

WHY CHAPTER 14 IS IMPORTANT

In this chapter we've seen at work the political, social, and moral power of the unexamined assumption. By "assumption" I mean an out-of-consciousness belief about how the world works. The operative assumption in this case was made by numerous educated, mainstream people; it told a story about the intellectual abilities that other people had been innately "given." Those other people were mostly recent immigrants from southern and eastern Europe.

Ignoring the possibility of environmental influences, the educated people's story alleged that those other people not only lacked innate capacity for academic studies but also lacked interest in those studies. Contrary evidence, such as rising academic enrollments and sharply increasing interest in Latin, was ignored. Almost no effort was made to probe the personal aspirations of the immigrants—even though it was well known that they had endured the arduous ocean passage to American cities in order to improve their lives and the lives of their children.

The other people looked and sounded *very* different from educated, mainstream community leaders. They lived in circumstances that were simply appalling. What else needed to be known?

The story's operative assumption—that immigrants lacked intelligence and interest in learning—undoubtedly applied to *some* of them, but as an all-inclusive generalization (i.e., stereotype), it was factually inaccurate, extremely prejudicial, and contrary to the desires of many of them.

What we have witnessed in this chapter is this: A public policy that had a determining and life-long impact on millions of less-advantaged Americans was adopted by many educated Americans via reasoning about innate "givens" that traced its lineage back 2,500 years to the speculations of Greek philosophers, and that was not evidence-based, but belief-based.

At TheAptitudeMyth.info are the genealogical chart and "What to Remember" list for chapter 14.

NOTES

1. Edward A. Krug, ed., *Charles W. Eliot and Popular Education* (Teachers College, 1961), 19–20.
2. The best discussion of this period is David Tyack and Elisabeth Hansot, *Managers of Virtue: Public School Leadership in America, 1820–1980* (Basic Books, 1982), chapters 8 through 12. Also useful are Diane Ravitch, *Left Back* (Simon & Schuster, 2000), chapters 1, 2, and 3; Edward A. Krug, *The Shaping of the American High School, 1880-1920* (University of Wisconsin, 1969), chapters 2 through 9; and Richard Hofstadter, *Anti-Intellectualism in American Life* (Knopf, 1970), Parts IV and V. Also consulted were Patricia Albjerg Graham, *Schooling America: How the Public Schools Meet the Nation's Changing Needs* (Oxford, 2005), chapters 1 and 2; Lawrence A. Cremin, *The Transformation of the School: Progressivism in American Education, 1876–1957* (Knopf, 1961), chapters 1 through 5; and Edgar B. Wesley, *NEA: The First Hundred Years* (Harper, 1957), especially Part II.
3. Krug, *op. cit.*, 175–76. Krug reports, for example, that James Earl Russell of Teachers College asked, ". . . how can we justify our practice of schooling the masses in precisely the same manner as we do those who are to be our leaders?" Krug cites James E. Russell, "The Trend in American Education," *Educational Review*, vol. XXXII (June 1906), 39.
4. *Ibid.*, 13–14, 175–76.
5. *Ibid.*, 14.

6. For a detailed overview and analysis, the best source is Krug, *op. cit.*, chapter 3, which includes tables. Some information here comes from Ravitch, *op. cit.*, chapter 3, especially 98–101.

7. Isaac L. Kandel, a scholar of international comparisons, wrote that the American high school had a "remarkable flexibility" of curriculum as compared with European secondary schools. Kandel, *The Dilemma of Democracy* (Harvard, 1934), 26–27; quoted by Ravitch, *op. cit.*, 48. Other scholars are similarly quoted by Ravitch.

8. L. Freeman Butts and Lawrence A. Cremin, *A History of Education in American Culture* (Holt, Rinehart and Winston, 1953), 419–20. They add that many U.S. educational leaders had received degrees in Germany, and knew that the *realschule* offered a practical education while the *gymnasium* offered the classical curriculum.

9. Krug, *op. cit.*, 289. Krug notes that the way the figures are reported is confusing. Using an alternative interpretation of the 1899–1900 *Report*, 30.3 percent of graduates were "prepared for college" in 1900. Krug cites U.S. Commissioner of Education, *Report 1899-1900*, II, 2122; and U.S. Commissioner, *Report 1905*, II, 816.

10. *Ibid.*, 176–77.

11. Germany did *not* offer public secondary education at state expense to all comers.

12. This and the immediately following paragraphs are based on information in Richard Hofstadter, *Anti-Intellectualism in American Life* (Knopf, 1970), 326–29.

13. *Ibid.*, 328; italics added.

14. Wesley, *op. cit.* (Harper, 1957), 201–2.

15. Ravitch, *op. cit.*, 54. Ravitch cites David L. Angus and Jeffrey E. Mirel, *The Failed Promise of the American High School, 1890–1995* (Teachers College, 1999), 13.

16. *Ibid.*, 101; second set of italics added. Ravitch cites Charles Hughes Johnston, "Curriculum Adjustments in Modern High Schools," *The School Review*, November 1914, 577–90. Additional examples of reformers' attacks are in Ravitch's *Left Back*, 93–95.

17. For a thorough and nuanced discussion of the values underlying school leadership, and of the backgrounds of typical local leaders, see David Tyack and Elisabeth Hansot, *Managers of Virtue: Public School Leadership in America, 1820–1980* (Basic Books, 1982).

18. *Ibid.*, 116, 119-20. Tyack and Hansot cite two other scholars: Jean Quandt, "Religion and Social Thought: The Secularization of Post-Millennialism," *American Quarterly*, vol. 25 (1973), 391; and Magali Sarfatti Larson, *The Rise of Professionalism: A Sociological Analysis* (University of California Press, 1977), 137.

19. Teachers College got its start as an alternative to the academic tradition. It was incorporated in 1880 as the Kitchen Garden Association to teach "the domestic industrial arts among the laboring classes," which meant that it trained girls to work in domestic service. In 1884, the institution became the Industrial Education Association, adding classes in carpentry and manual training in order to attract males. Teacher training was added to the curriculum in 1887. Ravitch, *op. cit.*, 52.

20. Ravitch, *op. cit.*, 52; Hofstadter, *op. cit.*, 383.

21. Ravitch, *ibid.*, 15, 26, 50–51, 57.

22. This interpretation is not unique; I am indebted to the eight scholars cited in footnote 2.

23. The best source for events and trends within the NEA is Edgar B. Wesley, *NEA: The First Hundred Years* (Harper, 1957), especially Part II, "Development of American Education."

24. Ravitch, *op. cit.*, 41–44.

25. National Education Association, *Report of the Committee on Secondary School Studies . . . 1892*, Document 205 (Government Printing Office, 1893), 17, 51. The report urged colleges to admit students who had not studied classical languages, and supported new "academic" [college-prep worthy] high school subjects such as history and the sciences. Ravitch, *op. cit.*, 41–43.

26. *Ibid.*, 54–55. Regarding Greek enrollments (*ibid.*, 49), Ravitch cites John F. Latimer, *What's Happened to Our High Schools?* (Public Affairs Press, 1958), 26.

27. W. R. Butler, "Should Preparatory and Non-Preparatory Pupils Receive Identical Treatment in the High School?" *Educational Review* (December, 1896), 479. On p. 480 Butler added that ". . . there is a strong feeling on the part of some of our best and most thoughtful citizens . . . that the higher education of girls is of doubtful utility to the race . . . and that, above everything, 'the future mothers of our race' should not be intellectually overworked."

28. Ravitch, *op. cit.*, 45; she cites G. S. Hall, *Adolescence*, vol. 2 (Appleton, 1904), 510 [italics added].

29. Krug, *op. cit.*, 177; Krug cites G. Stanley Hall, "How Far Is the Present High-School and Early College Training Adapted to the Nature and Needs of Adolescents?" *School Review* (December 1901), 656.

30. *Ibid.*, 89.

31. Ravitch, *op. cit.*, 86–87. Ravitch cites Edward A. Krug, ed., *Charles W. Eliot and Popular Education* (Teachers College, 1961), 19–20.

32. Hofstadter, *op. cit.*, 332–33. Hofstadter cites NEA, *Proceedings*, 1908, 39.

33. Krug, *op. cit.*, 265, 295: Ravitch, *op. cit.*, 123.

34. *Ibid.*, 296. Hofstadter, *op. cit.*, 333, reports a slightly different committee membership.

35. NEA, "Report of the Committee of Nine on the Articulation of High School and College," *Proceedings*, 1911, 559–61. Quoted by Hofstadter, *ibid.*, 334.

36. *Ibid.*, 335.

37. National Education Association, *Cardinal Principles of Secondary Education: A Report of the Commission on the Reorganization of Secondary Education, appointed by the National Education Association,* Bulletin No. 35 (Government Printing Office, 1918), 8.

38. Ravitch, *op. cit.,* 123.

39. NEA, *Cardinal Principles, op. cit.,* 9, 14.

FIFTEEN

American Educational Metamorphosis, II: Child-Centered Teaching

The guardians of the young should first of all strive to keep out of nature's way, and to prevent harm, and should merit the proud title of defenders of the happiness and rights of children. They . . . should be convinced that there is nothing else so worthy of love, reverence, and service as the body and soul of the growing child.

—G. Stanley Hall[1]

One of the key threads we've been following is the strengthening over centuries of the ideal that the child, not the content to be learned, should be the focus in any classroom.[2] G. Stanley Hall and Francis W. Parker were colorful, quirky advocates of this ideal around the turn of the century. We'll begin with Col. Parker, credited by John Dewey as the "father of progressive education"[3] and arguably the most memorable, even loveable, figure to represent the ideal of child-centeredness.

CHILD-CENTERED EDUCATION AND ITS GRANDFATHER FIGURE, COL. FRANCIS W. PARKER

"One hypothesis we can accept as true: the inherited organism of bone, muscle and brain determines exactly the limits or boundaries of the baby's development. Each nerve-fibre or convolution of the brain says, 'Thus far shalt thou go and no farther.' . . ."[4]

Thus spoke, and wrote, Francis Wayland Parker, commonly referred to as Col. Parker because of his service, at a young age, during the American Civil War; he took a bullet in the throat that left him with a raspy voice. Parker was a large, rotund, mustachioed man who looked like a no-nonsense Prussian general; during his years in Germany, a crowd of students once stood up when he entered the room because they mistook him for Chancellor Otto von Bismarck.

In spite of his size and appearance, and despite his years as a soldier, Parker loved children and apparently could establish rapport with a classroom full of them within five minutes.[5]

Col. Parker Experiences European Education First-Hand

Raised in near-poverty on a New Hampshire farm, Parker (1837–1902) was largely self-educated; he later said that "the best-taught school in a densely populated city can

125

never equal in educative value the life upon a good farm, intelligently managed."[6] He was a 21-year-old principal in Illinois when the Civil War began.

Military service actually had soured Parker on regimentation, discipline, drill, and all else that smacked of militarism, so when he became principal of a school in Ohio after the war, he abolished practices that he viewed as needlessly lock-step and harsh, such as learning drills.

In 1872, Parker inherited $5,000 from an aunt and headed for the University of Berlin. He spent more than two years there. In this way he is similar to other young American professionals who matured during the last third of the 19th century; studying in Germany was quite common.

Parker studied under "a direct pupil of Hegel"[7] and came to view all of history as a struggle between two ideals: the "thesis" was the rule of the many by the few and the "antithesis" was the ideal of society ruling itself. Parker thought the former resulted from an education of "limitation" based on "Quantity" teaching characterized by word-cramming, text memorizing, and corralling the mind within preset limits, all of which left learners unable to think for themselves.

The antithesis of Quantity education, said Parker, was made possible by an education of "freedom" based on "Quality" methods that encouraged "self-effort" and "original inference," and that were characterized by object lessons, investigation, and liberty to think and experiment.

Parker very likely became acquainted with the work of Pestalozzi as well as with that of Johann Friedrich Herbart and his disciples, who treated pedagogics as a science.[8] [9] At the university, Parker encountered not only hoary old methods such as the disputation (see chapter 3) but also the new seminar method, which stressed learner activity over that of the teacher.

Parker also became familiar with *Anschauungsunterricht*, literally "seeing teaching" (object teaching), and grasped that it required more than simply presenting a succession of objects to the child for sensory exploration. Parker became acquainted with kindergartens and is likely to have visited Frau Froebel, the widow of the revered founder of kindergartens, Friedrich Froebel.

Finally, Parker noted that Germany had compulsory education for all children, although the lower classes had separate schools—and the girls were isolated from the boys. Parker's pride in American common schools grew because Americans were achieving a superior democratic ideal.

The Quincy System Brings Visibility to Child-Centeredness

In 1875, Parker was hired as the superintendent of schools in Quincy, Massachusetts.[10] He professed himself appalled that five- and six-year-olds came to Quincy's schools after "vigorous development" in "Nature's great methods, object teaching, and play," only to find "imagination, curiosity, and love for mental and physical activity" destroyed by "dull, wearisome hours of listless activity upon hard benches," which made it impossible for the "little innocents" to love school.[11]

Within a few years, Parker's "Quincy System" had become a showcase of new methods and approaches. The old curriculum had been abandoned, and with it the spelling book, the reader, the grammar book, and the children's copybooks. Replacing those texts were magazines, newspapers, and materials developed by the teachers themselves. Learning the alphabet by rote was dropped; now the children were started on simple words and sentences. Arithmetic was approached via objects instead of rules; geography began with local field trips. Drawing was added to encourage both manual dexterity and individual expression. Conventional methods were introduced gradually after the children's abilities began to be demonstrated.

Ostensibly dismissive of the stream of admiring visitors to Quincy, Parker protested that there was nothing novel about his natural approach. "I am simply trying to apply well established principles of teaching, principles derived directly from the laws of the mind," he said. "The methods springing from them are found in the development of every child. They are used everywhere except in school. I have introduced no new principle. . . ."[12]

Far more could be written here about Francis W. Parker, his ideas, and his influence on turn-of-the-century education. Here's a capsule summary.

In 1880, Parker became head of the Cook County Normal School in Chicago, which he organized as "a model home, a complete community and embryonic democracy" where schoolwide assemblies and classroom activities were conducted with surprising informality, and where the Colonel assumed the posture of an amiable autocrat, benevolently paternalistic about children, faculty, and school. He was well loved by all.[13] A legend in his own time, Parker regaled teachers with his Talks on Pedagogics, first delivered at a Chautauqua Teachers' Retreat in 1891, and subsequently repeated in New York City, Minneapolis, and Chicago.[14]

My own view is that Parker was a popularizer who commanded attention because of his size, appearance, and ostensibly authoritarian demeanor, which were endearingly contrasted with his good nature and obvious love of, and quick rapport with, children of elementary school age. He apparently possessed indefatigable energy in putting forward his convictions about children and teaching, which he did verbally, in writing, and in the daily practices of the schools he led.

But Parker was not an original thinker. If he transformed child-centered education, it was only in nuance and respectability. For as we have seen in the foregoing chapters, child-centered ideals and practices had been developing for some 500 years; they would have been on the ascendance in the United States even without Parker's apostleship. In fact, contemporaneous with Parker was a movement—one is tempted to say a "craze"—that was focusing the attention of tens of thousands of educated Americans on little children: the child study movement.

THE CHILD STUDY MOVEMENT AND ITS CHAMPION, DR. G. STANLEY HALL

Recapitulation and Child-Study

Recall that in chapter 10, which explored Spencer's ideas, we encountered the doctrine of recapitulation. There you learned "Ontogeny recapitulates phylogeny," which meant that what happens to an embryo in the womb (ontogeny) repeats and parallels the evolutionary development of all living creatures over eons of time (phylogeny).

Very significantly for our purposes, the recapitulation hypothesis *took a leap from the prenatal realm into the postnatal realm.* The notion that development follows a certain path *prior to* birth came to be applied to human development *following* birth. It was claimed that as they grow, infants and children pass through the stages of *social and cultural* development that humans passed through during tens of thousands of past years.

These fanciful ideas, girded as always with claims of "scientific" sanction, drew wide attention. Their implicit—and probably explicit—train of reasoning went something like this:

If a child's growth and development occurs from within (in "organic" fashion) . . .

and if that process closely parallels the cultural development of human beings across eons of time (because cultural development is assumed to be biologically transmitted) . . .

and if one's goal is "natural education" as envisioned by Rousseau and later outlined in detail by Spencer (i.e., the correct experiences presented in the correct order) . . .

then we ought to learn more about these developmental processes by paying close, sustained attention to little children. After all, we have living children right here among us, but we can't go back in time to observe the social and cultural development of our species.[15]

And that's exactly what came to pass. Here, for once, is an important, education-related trend that appears to have gotten its start in the United States instead of in Europe.

Where child study first emerged in the United States isn't clear. What is clear is that, by 1880, child study was sufficiently well developed and widespread to become a key topic at the meeting of the education section of the American Social Science Association. The attendees drew up a broadside that asked parents to observe and record the behavior of their youngsters; they also supplied a "register" for the recording of observations regarding the infant's first smiling, recognizing mother, following a light with the eyes, speaking, and so forth.[16]

In essence, that's what child study was. If you practiced it actively, you literally got out your notebook and writing instrument, found a comfortable chair in the immediate vicinity of an infant, toddler, preschooler, or young school-age child, then watched, listened, and took notes for several hours. Perhaps you also took photographs (or wished you could). You did this month after month, maybe year after year, because your goal was not to capture a snapshot description but rather to painstakingly record every aspect of the child's developmental process over time.

Many who took on such a project recorded the development of their own infants, and in some cases published their findings. Examples are given by Stephen Jay Gould in *Ontogeny and Phylogeny* (1977). In one case, a British paleontologist named S. S. Buckman regarded his own babies as miniature apes and tried to identify physical and behavioral characteristics of a simian past. He believed that human babies pass first through a quadrupedal stage like that of distant animal ancestors, then entered an arboreal stage; as proof of this, he pointed out that young children could not straighten out their hands until they passed through the bough-grasping stage of their phylogenic past, sometime after the age of five or six.

Buckman relates how he examined not only his own children but also random village schoolchildren whom he stopped on the street, to whom he offered a prize to the one who could hold out his fingers the straightest. Presumably with earnestness and a straight face, this scientist reported his finding that "practically all but one showed a more or less definite curvature."[17]

Another example related by Gould was penned by Milicent W. Shinn in her 1900 book, *The Biography of a Baby*. Like many other child study devotees, Shinn was an educated woman. Because of social convention, women were obliged to stay home; some became eager for something to do that would stimulate their intellects. Shinn said this about her rationale:

> . . . there are curious resemblances between babies and monkeys, between boys and barbaric tribes. . . . The speculation that children in developing passed through stages similar to those the race had passed through . . . has become an accepted doctrine since embryology has shown how each individual before birth passes in successive stages through the lower forms of life. . . . If we can thoroughly decipher this ontogenic record, then what may we not hope to learn of the road by which we human beings came?[18]

We now know that embryology did no such thing, but it took more than half a century for that fact to become apparent. Meanwhile, the curiosity and commitment of Milicent Shinn, S. S. Buckman, and thousands of others on both sides of the Atlantic coalesced into a widely recognized but never formally organized interest group known as the "child study movement."

Besides thousands of observational studies of individual children and countless public lectures by roving authorities, the child study movement yielded a mass of statistical data about children—the validity and reliability of which were questioned from the moment they began appearing—gathered by dozens of questionnaires. The author and interpreter of almost all of those questionnaires, and the highly visible standard-bearer of the child study movement, was the turn-of-the-century psychologist, educator, college president, and (by all accounts) supremely gifted public speaker, G. Stanley Hall (1846–1924).[19]

Dr. Hall Fortifies the Assumption of "Givens"

Like Parker, G. Stanley Hall as a young man spent a few years in Germany studying at the feet of leading scholars. Then, under William James, he earned the first American Ph.D. in psychology. Known as "Darwin of the Mind," Hall served for a time as president of Clark University and was long the editor of the educational journal *Pedagogical Seminary* (now the *Journal of Genetic Psychology*).

In addition to dozens of articles and books on a wide range of topics, Hall authored a two-volume treatise, *Adolescence*, published in 1904.[20] Although he was a controversial figure,[21] there's no argument that Hall lent inspiration and credibility to the child study movement.

Much has been written about child study and G. Stanley Hall. We need not delve into all that because the point is this: During the half century beginning in the 1870s, an enormous number of parents, teachers, and others in the United States (and in Europe) undertook to learn about certain allegedly inherited tendencies of human beings by patiently, painstakingly, and persistently observing and recording the activities and growth trajectories of infants and children.

Whatever else might be said about the child study movement, it certainly represented a huge outpouring of adult attention on the characteristics of individual children. This was bound to have consequences for the course of American teaching and parenting.

Child study and recapitulation "theory" were intricately intertwined.[22] One reason for this link is that Hall had been captivated by Darwin's thesis at a young age—he was 13 years old in 1859—and devoted much of his career (as a "genetic psychologist") to reconciling biological evolution and human mental life. He came to accept, and to persistently champion, the twin ideas (a) that the human mind and body evolved in parallel over eons of time through a series of stages from savagery to civilization and (b) that each individual "recapitulates" in his or her growth and development the biological, social, psychological, and emotional evolution of our species.

Child study drew the attention of educated citizens to recapitulation, a heredity doctrine that claimed to explain virtually everything about each child.[23] *The child's day-to-day environment—home, community, playground, church, school, etc.—was viewed as explaining just about nothing.* For parents, teachers, and educational policy makers, the message was hard to miss.

THE MESSAGE: PASSIVITY IN THE FACE OF ASSUMED INBORN INEQUALITY

The eminent Dr. Hall's message of recapitulation and the grandfatherly Col. Parker's message of child-centeredness united to support the belief that *humans are inherently unequal*; it's nature's way.[24] All children have a right to be educated, but only to the limit of their "given" abilities. Dr. Hall and his followers upheld "individualization" as key for the new education. They called for classroom approaches to be continually adjusted to each child's combination of age, gender, socioeconomic background, and vocational expectation, all of which in turn were alleged to yield decisive data regarding that child's mental capacity, including its rigidly set outer limits.

What, then, should teachers do? Adapt and go with the flow. Don't trouble yourself to do anything special for your apparently dull pupils. That's the way they emerged from the womb.

What, then, should *parents* do? Accept nature's roll of the dice, and don't question decisions of your local school authorities regarding your child's curriculum path and, consequently, his or her future occupation. The experts know what's best.

Let Nature Take Her Course

The first section of this chapter began with a Col. Parker quote: ". . . the inherited organism of bone, muscle and brain determines exactly the limits or boundaries of the baby's development. . . . The brain says, 'Thus far shalt thou go and no farther.' . . ."

Below are two quotes that exemplify the widely disseminated opinion of G. Stanley Hall. All three quotes represent a perspective on children and learning with a 2,500-year-old genealogy; it's the perspective we've been tracing since chapter 2, the one with these four big ideas:

1. from Aristotle: an imagined "final cause" that promises certain attainment of one's predetermined mental capacity "if there is no impediment";
2. from Rousseau: "negative education" with its admiration for the savages of Nature uncorrupted by civilization;
3. from the literary Romantics: deep reverence for the "organic principle" with its internally driven growth that's beyond *anyone's* control;
4. from Spencer: "survival of the fittest" with its stricture against doing anything to assist those whom Nature made unalterably less fit.

That is the antique paradigm animating Dr. Hall when he wrote that one should not pity:

> . . . the undervitalized poor . . . , moribund sick, defectives and criminals, because by aiding them to survive it interferes with the process of wholesome natural selection by which all that is best has hitherto been developed. . . . Pity has its highest office then in removing the handicaps from those most able to help man to higher levels . . . in ushering in the kingdom of the superman . . . so that the plateau of the best half of the race will be high, so that the summits of human possibility may be easier attained.[25]

Hall believed that the growing child needs, *very deeply* needs, to pass through all the various stages of evolution on his or her way to adulthood, so it's critical for their caretakers to "keep out of nature's way." Arguing that city youths should be allowed to act out savage rites, he wrote:

> The child revels in savagery, and if its tribal, predatory, hunting, fishing, fighting, roving, idle, playing proclivities could be indulged in the country and under conditions that now, alas! seem hopelessly ideal, they could conceivably be so organized and directed as to be far more truly humanistic and liberal than all the best modern school can provide.[26]

Most important for our purposes is that the strong influence of recapitulation on the child study movement meant that *many tens of thousands of educated citizens all across the United States came into sustained contact with the unquestioned assumption that each child is strongly influenced by "givens" over which he or she has no control.* As we've seen throughout this book, this was not at all a new idea. At the hands of Hall and other child study enthusiasts, this assumption became even more firmly rooted in the American mindset.

Let Pedocentric *Schooling Reign*

Very early in the new century, Hall wrote "The Ideal School as Based on Child Study," published in an influential journal. In it, he used Latin terminology to draw a distinction between two types of school: The traditional school in the Western world, he said, had been *scholiocentric*[27]; the coming new type of school would be *pedocentric*.

As phrased by Lawrence Cremin in his review of Hall's impact, "The former . . . fitted the child to the school" whereas the latter, "fitted the school to the child."[28] Drawing on the Romantic poets, which along with Darwinism were influential in the development of young Stanley's worldview,[29] and resonating with Aristotle's belief in effort-free mental development "if there is no impediment" as well as with that famous first sentence of Rousseau's *Émile*, Hall wrote:

> The guardians of the young should first strive to keep out of nature's way, and to prevent harm, and should merit the proud title of defenders of the happiness and rights of children. They should feel profoundly that childhood, as it comes fresh from the hands of God, is not corrupt . . .; they should be convinced that there is nothing else so worthy of love, reverence, and service as the body and soul of the growing child.[30]

Calling the trend toward *pedocentric* education "truly Copernican," Cremin writes that:

> . . . it subtly shifted *the burden of proof in the educational situation,* and in so doing, the meaning of equal opportunity as well. Formerly, when the content and purposes of the school had been fairly well defined and commonly accepted, the burden of proof was on the student: he was told to perform up to standard or get out. Educational opportunity was the right of all who might profit from schooling to enjoy its benefits. Now, the "given" of the equation was no longer the school with its well-defined content and purposes, but the children with their particular backgrounds and needs. And educational opportunity had become the right of all who attended school to receive *something* of meaning and value.[31]

OTHER FACTORS STRENGTHENING THE SHIFT TOWARD CHILD-CENTERED TEACHING

Individuals embody and hasten social and cultural trends that arise due to multiple forces and factors. Col. Parker and Dr. Hall are fine examples of that type of personal influence. But there were fundamental social and cultural reasons for the shift toward child-centered teaching.[32]

As recounted by historian Patricia Albjerg Graham,[33] during the final decades of the 19th century and the early decades of the 20th century educators at the state and local levels were preoccupied by challenges arising due to the unprecedented increase in immigrant enrollments.

"Assimilation" is the word Graham uses to refer to this period, which she portrays as a time when public schools were serving the needs of the nation by offering a curriculum of assimilation for democratic citizenship. The characteristics of this curriculum were that (a) it emphasized virtue over knowledge, (b) it was identical for all children, native and immigrant, (c) it subordinated the needs of the children to the needs of society, and (d) it was delivered authoritatively and with the expectation that all children would adapt to it.[34]

As previously noted, in response to the problem of legions of immigrant children, adults sorted them based on assumed innate "givens" and assigned them to career-limiting curricular tracks. Testing yielded "scientific" evidence[35] that almost all had, *at best*, modest aptitudes. It's fortunate that consideration was never given to any solution that would have withheld schooling from those with modest aptitudes. There needed to be *some* type of opportunity for them.

This need, says Graham, was one of the factors that led to vocational education, also known as "manual training." She reviews the history of manual training, which was not the same as technical instruction for a specific trade. Manual training was about motor skills associated with common tools; it was thought to contribute to the development of intellectual capability.

Graham makes the significant point that *the advocates of child-centered education such as Col. Parker believed strongly that manual activity was useful for all children in all aptitude groups*. These educators, who were just beginning to be called "progressives," referred to this type of classroom activity as "active learning."[36]

Children who had been sorted into the higher groups—mostly those from well-educated, affluent families in upscale neighborhoods—were put together in the same classrooms and often in the same schools, including emerging private schools that were trumpeting the fact that they were "progressive" and "child-centered." These schools quickly became characterized by "individualized instruction," "active learning," and renunciation of the traditional curriculum.

On the other hand, the children sorted into the lower groups found themselves increasingly thrown together in classrooms and schools doing "manual training" and other mentally undemanding, non-academic work.[37] Writes Graham:

> Prescient school men recognized that the focus was shifting . . . to one defined by informed, ambitious, and often affluent parents seeking a more supportive school environment for their children, and by newly articulate professors of education. . . . Hence, the educators made a transition from assimilation, something the nation needed, to adjustment, something the children needed.
>
> The change in emphasis was dramatic: from the poor to the rich; from the immigrant to the native born; . . . from the disciplinary subjects of English, mathematics, and science to the arts of music, painting, and dance.
>
> The children whose needs emerged as paramount where those who came from middle- and upper-class families who believed the schools were too rigid in their curriculum, pedagogy, and administration, and who took action to assure that their children would have a superior education. . . . For children from families with strong academic and cultural resources and with gifted and imaginative teachers, these schools were marvelous. . . .[38]

An Italian immigrant mother in Greenwich Village offered this assessment:

> The program of ["The Little Red School House"] is suited to the children of well-to-do homes, not to our children. We send our children to school for what we cannot give them ourselves, grammar and drill. The Fifth Avenue children learn to speak well in their homes. We do not send our children to school for group activity; they get plenty of that in the street. But the Fifth Avenue children are lonely; I can see how group experiences is [sic] an important form of education to them.[39]

MUSINGS AND SPECULATIONS

This chapter has featured two educational celebrities, but not because they were innovators. A key purpose of this book is to show that when we think *about* education, we think *with* concepts that have deep roots—as deep as the ancient Greeks. Hall and Parker gained a following because, in vibrant ways, they made explicit a set of assumptions and beliefs that had long been gaining credibility in American culture, and that they shared with the majority of Americans. I believe that Parker, Hall, and their willing listeners can be thought of as corks bobbing on the waves, carried forward by the sweeping tide of historical trends.

WHY CHAPTER 15 IS IMPORTANT

In this chapter, we can see how the "satisfying rope" that Herbert Spencer wove of seemingly unconnected but familiar beliefs finally became established in the mindset of many Americans as "the way we ought to be doing things with children and in classrooms." Thus, the principal value propositions of the time-honored paradigm (see chapter 1) were gradually eclipsed, in the minds of many Americans, by those of the western-contemporary paradigm.

Also significant in this chapter is the continuing story of the influence among Americans of the recapitulation hypothesis, spurred by their home-grown child study movement. Both of these perspectives were grounded in the assumption that each child's future is determined by "givens."

It's important to keep in mind that, as the 19th century turned into the 20th, many well-educated Americans accepted as literal truth, and were guided in their own activities and decisions, by the perspectives of recapitulation and child-study. This book argues that those perspectives were informed at the deepest level by a 2,500-year-old mindset, a mythopoetic set of beliefs that imagines a child's development as needing to follow a predetermined pathway toward the attainment of an ideal form that, likewise, is predetermined.

In that deterministic view, *parents, teachers, and child all play a merely passive role.*[40]

This chapter argues that one reason why these faux-scientific notions about child development came to be accepted as "modern" in the United States was that they were being advocated by, among others, two charming, loquacious celebrity-educators who cloaked themselves in the authority of science: Col. Francis W. Parker and Dr. G. Stanley Hall.

At TheAptitudeMyth.info are the genealogical chart and "What to Remember" list for chapter 15.

POSTSCRIPT: DID JOHN DEWEY JOIN THE SHIFT
TOWARD CHILD-CENTERED TEACHING?

The foregoing chapters have had almost nothing to say about the eminent American philosopher and educator John Dewey (1859–1952), an apparent oversight that some readers will find strange.[41] It's not an oversight. The research on which this book is based never revealed Dewey as being focused on the questions that this book was written to answer.

American thought leaders such as Francis W. Parker, G. Stanley Hall, and Edward L. Thorndike were well known by Dewey, personally and professionally; together, they all inhabited an era in which interest groups of every type were clamoring for school reform of one kind or another. John Dewey definitely was one of those thinking reformist thoughts! After Dewey's visibility increased in 1896 upon the opening of his little Laboratory School at the University of Chicago, other reformers hoped to claim him as a supporter, especially those already being called progressive educators.

The key to understanding why this book rarely mentions John Dewey is that, similarly, this book rarely mentions progressive educators. For, to make a critical distinction, this book is not about the origins and spread of progressive ideals for education. Rather, this book is about the origins and spread of assumptions held by many Americans about the power of inborn traits.

Progressive educators, and their supporters among parents, politicians, and concerned citizens, willingly participated in the aptitude myth. But (a) progressive ideals for education encompassed far more than the assumption that aptitude determines all, and (b) Dewey, so far as I can discover, did *not* participate in that assumption. If he did, he had nothing to say about it.

And John Dewey had a great deal to say. As a producer of articles and books on various facets of education, he had a highly thoughtful and productive career. And that's merely his career as an educational visionary. Dewey was also, and probably even more so, a general philosopher. When he left Chicago in 1904 to accept a post at Columbia University, he also left behind his Laboratory School and joined Columbia's Department of Philosophy on the main campus, not its school of education, Teachers College, across 120th Street.

John Dewey was an unparalleled visionary regarding the education of young children, conceiving of nuanced possibilities beyond anything that emanated from the likes of Francis W. Parker and G. Stanley Hall. It's as though Dewey were thinking, if not living, on a higher plane.

Dewey wrote and spoke largely in conceptual generalizations, infrequently stating specific do's and dont's of teaching methods. He used terms that encouraged those eager for his *imprimatur* to claim his authority when Dewey had meant something not merely different but also profound. For example, he advocated addressing "occupations" in primary school classrooms, which was eagerly seized upon by the advocates of vocational education. [42]

Finally, Dewey wrote in a style that, if not impenetrable, was nonetheless found by many, then and now, to be difficult to grasp with a feeling of certainty. Lawrence Cremin, speaking of "the semieducated among [Dewey's] proponents and detractors alike," comments that, "The difficulty is [that] too many who quoted him did not read on, if, indeed, they read him at all." [43]

Misinterpretation of Dewey was egregious in the case of some smitten by child-centeredness, a corollary of which was that all choices of curriculum and methods must be driven by children's interests instead of being "externally imposed" by adults. Dewey was opposed to this line of thought—so strongly opposed, in fact, that in his 1928 inaugural address as the first honorary president of the Progressive Education Association, he went out of his way to criticize it. [44]

On another occasion, Dewey apparently said that the studied avoidance of guidance practiced in some progressive schools was "really stupid." [45] Dewey also disagreed with other goals on the progressive educators' agenda, although in still other ways he did share their perspectives. [46]

Progressive educators who, around the time of World War One, were looking for something in Dewey's *oeuvre* that would bolster their preferred approach to children would likely gravitate to *Schools of To-morrow* (1915). Co-authored by John Dewey and his daughter, Evelyn, and first published in 1915, this volume seems intended for classroom teachers and interested citizens. Included are numerous photographs from progressive classrooms and schoolyards.[47]

In chapter 1 of *Schools of To-morrow*, "Education as Natural Development," Rousseau's *Émile* is quoted at great length and with the reverence due holy writ. Subsequent chapters address progressive principles—"Play," "Freedom and Individuality," "Education Through Industry," etc.—while admiringly portraying day-to-day activities in progressive classrooms.

Schools of To-morrow provided a good opportunity for Dewey to demonstrate allegiance to the idea that each child's inborn "givens" determine the direction and the extent of his or her achievement in school. *But Dewey didn't seize that opportunity.* To the contrary, all children of whatever background are treated as extremely similar to one another and, if the conditions are right, similarly capable of learning a great deal.

For example, consider this passage on page 139: "Give a child freedom to find out what he can and can not do, *both in the way of what is physically possible and what his neighbors will stand for,* and he will not waste much time on impossibilities but will bend his energies to the possibilities" [italics added]. The limits on a child's learning efforts, says Dewey, are found *in the environment*: what's physically possible, what's socially tolerable. If Dewey thinks limits are imposed *from within*, he's missing an opportunity to say so.

Contrary to the Romantic view of children, Dewey believed that appropriate schooling could bring children to intellectually master the modern world. In a passage reminiscent of William James's criticism (see chapter 13) of "the namby-pamby attempts of the softer pedagogy to lubricate things for [children]," Dewey opposed those who would sugarcoat classroom content. He wrote that, "[The child] soon learns to turn from everything which is not artificially surrounded with diverting circumstances. The spoiled child who does only what he likes is the inevitable outcome of the theory of interest in education."[48]

At TheAptitudeMyth.info, in the "What to Remember" portion of chapter 11's entries, there appear three tables that interrelate proponents' expectations about classroom teaching and their views about the nature of children. In the table for the Romantic Perspective, Dewey is not listed as a historical thought leader. Dewey *is* listed as a thought leader of the Practical Perspective.

Historian Lawrence Cremin agrees: "Dewey's formulations must be seen as essentially continuous with Horace Mann's. . . . Like Mann, Dewey recognized that education is a matter of individual growth and development; but like Mann too, his emphasis was ever on the social, the common, the public aspects of experience."[49]

Did Dewey share progressive educators' views on child-centered teaching? No.

NOTES

1. G. Stanley Hall, "The Ideal School as Based on Child Study," *The Forum*, XXXII (September, 1901), 24–25.

2. For this chapter I relied most heavily on Diane Ravitch, *Left Back* (Simon & Schuster, 2000), chapters 1, 2, and 3; Edgar B. Wesley, *NEA: The First Hundred Years* (Harper, 1957), chapters 14 and 17; Richard Hofstadter, *Anti-Intellectualism in American Life* (Knopf, 1970), Parts IV and V; David Tyack and Elisabeth Hansot, *Managers of Virtue: Public School Leadership in America, 1820-1980* (Basic Books, 1982), chapters 9 and 10; and Patricia Albjerg Graham, *Schooling America: How the Public Schools Meet the Nation's Changing Needs* (Oxford, 2005), chapter 1. Also consulted were Edward A. Krug, *The Shaping of the American High School, 1880–1920* (University of Wisconsin, 1969), chapter 5; Lawrence A. Cremin, *The Transformation of the School: Progressivism in American Education, 1876–1957* (Knopf, 1961), chapters 4, 5, and 6; S. Alexander Rippa, *Education in a Free Society: An American History*, 8th ed., Longman, 1997), chapters 6, 7, and 8; Joel Spring, *The American School, 1642–1990* (Longman, 1990), chapter 7; and William J. Reese, "The Origins of Progressive Education," *History of Education Quarterly*, vol. 41, no. 1 (Spring 2001), 1–24.

3. Cremin, *op. cit.*, 129. Dewey sent his own children to Parker's school in Chicago.

4. Francis Wayland Parker, *Talks on Pedagogics: An Outline of the Theory of Concentration* (E. L. Kellogg, 1894), 4.

5. The best source for Parker is Jack K. Campbell, *Colonel Francis W. Parker: The Children's Crusader* (Teachers College, 1967). Shorter treatments include Merle Curti, *The Social Ideas of American Educators* (Littlefield, Adams, 1978), chapter XI; Cremin, *op. cit.*, chapter 5; Rippa, *op. cit.*, chapter 7; and Wesley, *op. cit.*, chapter 4.

6. Curti, *op. cit.*, 376. Curti in turn cites *Elementary School Teacher*, vol. II (June 1902), 720–23.

7. Campbell, *op. cit.*, chapter VI. Campbell cites *Talks on Pedagogics, op. cit.*; and Col. F. W. Parker, "The Conflict of the Two Ideals," Parker Scrapbooks, 1884, Archives, Harper Library, University of Chicago.

8. *Ibid.*, 70.

9. Herbart, a figure in late-19th century European and American education, focused on the social and moral goals of education but is remembered for his approach to the instructional process, known as "associationism," which advised teachers to present new ideas in a way that associated them with ideas already within the learners' experience. (Curiously, historians seem not to note how strongly this resonates with Spencer's demand that both teachers and parents present children with the correct new experiences in the correct order.) Discussions of Herbart appear in most educational histories; I have relied on R. Freeman Butts and Lawrence A. Cremin, *A History of Education in American Culture* (Holt, Rinehart and Winston, 1953), 381–82.

10. Cremin, *Transformation, op. cit.*, 129–30.

11. Campbell, *op. cit.*, 79. Campbell cites superintendent Parker's *Annual Report, School Committee, Town of Quincy, 1875–1876*, 117, 123–24.

12. Cremin, *Transformation, op. cit.*, 130. Cremin in turn cites *Report of the School Committee of the Town of Quincy for the School Year 1878–1879*, 15. Parker's statements resonated strongly with Spencer's ideas (chapter 9); educational historians seem not to make this connection.

13. *Ibid.*, 132.

14. Parker's *Talks on Pedagogics* can be purchased today from Bibliolife at Bibliolife.com/store.

15. The link between recapitulation and culture-epoch theory on the one hand, and child study on the other hand, is well made by Ernest Belden, "A History of the Child Study Movement in the United States, 1870–1920," Ph.D. dissertation, University of California—Berkeley, 1965 (University Microfilms #65-13,441), 105–10. My "train-of-reasoning" reconstruction is only loosely based on Belden; it's much more my own construction.

16. *Journal of Social Science, Containing the Transactions of the American Association*, No. XV, February 1882. Saratoga Papers of 1881, Part II (A. Williams Co., 1882), 50–51.

17. S. S. Buckman, *Proceedings of the Cotteswold Naturalists' Field Club*, vol. XIII, Part II (John Bellows, 1899), 99.

18. Milicent Washburn Schinn, *The Biography of a Baby* (Houghton, Mifflin, 1900), 6–8.

19. For a full-length Hall biography, see Dorothy Ross, *G. Stanley Hall: The Psychologist as Prophet* (University of Chicago Press, 1972). A good short treatment is chapter XII in Merle Curti, *The Social Ideas of American Educators* (Littlefield, Adams, 1978). See also Stephen Jay Gould, *op. cit.*, 135–55.

20. The full title is *Adolescence: Its Psychology and Its Relations to Physiology, Anthropology, Sociology, Sex, Crime, Religion and Education* (Appleton, 1904).

21. In a biographical memoir, Edward Thorndike wrote that G. S. Hall had been "interested in philosophy, psychology, education, and religion in every one of their aspects which did not involve detailed experimentation, intricate quantitative treatment of results, or rigor and subtlety of analysis." Krug, *op. cit.*, 109.

22. This paragraph relies heavily on S. Alexander Rippa, *Education in a Free Society: An American History*, 8th ed. (Longman, 1997), 182.

23. This paragraph relies substantially on Dorothy Ross, *op. cit.*, 311.

24. *Ibid.*

25. F. H. Sanders and G. S. Hall, "Pity," *The American Journal of Psychology*, vol. XI, October 1899 (Clark University, 1899–1900), 590–91. Educational historians fail to note how thoroughly a statement such as this resonates with Herbert Spencer's views.

26. Hall, *Adolescence, op.cit.*, Vol. I, x.

27. *Scholio* derives from the same Greek and Latin root as "school"; its precise root is *scholium* (plural, *scholia*), denoting an explanatory note or comment added to another text in order to illustrate or amplify. This footnote is a *scholium*. *Compact Edition of the Oxford English Dictionary* (Oxford University Press, 1971), vol. II, 2665; *Random House Dictionary of the English Language*, 2nd ed., Unabridged (Random House, 1987), 1715.

28. Cremin, *op. cit.*, 103.

29. "Of the various influences which affected the outlook of G. Stanley Hall perhaps none was so important as the spirit of romanticism, which . . . was a dominant current of thought during Hall's young manhood. It was in the air. He could not have escaped it if he would." Curti, *op. cit.*, 403.

30. Hall, "The Ideal School . . .," *op. cit.*, 24–25. Lawrence Cremin notes that, back in 1895, the NEA's Committee of Fifteen observed that "Modern education emphasizes the opinion that the child, not the

subject of study, is the guide to the teacher's efforts." Cremin, *Transformation, op. cit.*, 103, note 1. Cremin references National Educational Association, "Report of the Committee of Fifteen . . . ," *Addresses and Proceedings* (American Book Company, 1895), 24.

31. Cremin, *Transformation, op. cit.*, 104 (italics added).

32. Many historians observe that the shift toward child-centered teaching occurred more in the cerebral realm of "oughts" and expectations, less in the day-to-day realm of classroom practice. An entire book has been written, in part, to make this point; see Larry Cuban, *How Teachers Taught: Constancy and Change in American Classrooms* (Teachers College, 1993).

33. Patricia Albjerg Graham, *Schooling America: How the Public Schools Meet the Nation's Changing Needs* (Oxford, 2005). Graham's first chapter is "Assimilation: 1900–1920" and her second chapter is "Adjustment: 1920–1954." I am drawing primarily on Graham's first chapter.

34. *Ibid.*, 9–10, 16–18, 24–25.

35. "The prestige of science was colossal. The man in the street and the woman in the kitchen, confronted on every hand with new machines and devices which they owed to the laboratory, were ready to believe that science could accomplish almost anything. . . ." Frederick Lewis Allen, *Only Yesterday* (Harper and Row, 1964), 164. Quoted by Paul Zoch, *Doomed to Fail* (Ivan R. Dee, 2004), 25.

36. Graham *op. cit.*, 38–43; Butts and Cremin, *op. cit.*, 382–83.

37. Graham, *ibid.*, 51–52.

38. *Ibid.*, 52–53, 55.

39. Caroline Ware, *Greenwich Village: A Comment on American Civilization in the Post-War Years* (Houghton Mifflin, 1935), no page. Quoted by Graham, *ibid.*, 62.

40. For a highly informed and intelligent discussion of the ancient, metaphysical view of children's development, and of a Darwin-inspired modern alternative, see Brent Davis, *Inventions of Teaching: A Genealogy* (Lawrence Erlbaum, 2004), chapter 2, "Western Worldviews: The Metaphysical [vs.] The Physical."

41. This Postscript relies primarily on Herbert M. Kliebard, *The Struggle for the American Curriculum* (Routledge, 1995), chapters 2 and 3; and Lawrence A. Cremin, *The Transformation of the School: Progressivism in American Education, 1876–1957* (Alfred A. Knopf, 1961), chapter 5. I also consulted Merle Curti, *The Social Ideals of American Educators* (Littlefield, Adam, 1978), chapter XV; and Richard Hofstadter, *Anti-Intellectualism in American Life* (Alfred A. Knopf, 1970), chapter XIV.

42. Herbert Kliebard explains: "Dewey urged that we [focus on] the characteristic activities in which the individual or society engages and the ability of those individuals to achieve command of their environment. . . . 'This simplified social life,' he hoped, 'should reproduce in miniature, the activities fundamental to life as a whole, and thus enable the child . . . to become gradually acquainted with the structure, materials, and modes of operation of the larger community. . . .'" Kliebard, *op. cit.*, 60–61. Kliebard cites the Dewey quote as from "The University School," *University [of Chicago] Record*, vol. 1, 417–19.

43. Cremin, *op. cit.*, 238. Cremin's view is that, "[Dewey's] arguments are, in the last analysis, comprehensible."

44. Excerpts from this portion of Dewey's inaugural speech may be read in Kliebard, *op. cit.*, 165–66. Also see Cremin, *op. cit.*, 249.

45. Reported by Hofstadter, *op. cit.*, 374, note 8. In this note, Hofstadter cites specific passages in both *The Child and the Curriculum* (1902) and *Democracy and Education* (1916) in which Dewey is critical of extreme child-centeredness. But the "really stupid" remark is identified only as occurring during 1926.

46. Kliebard, *op. cit.*, portrays Dewey as keeping the progressive educators at arms length; see his chapters 2 and 3. Cremin, *op. cit.*, views Dewey more as sharing a community of interest with the progressives; see his chapter 4, section VI.

47. Originally published by E. P. Dutton in 1915, *Schools of To-morrow* was republished in 2003 by the University Press of the Pacific. Its ninth chapter, "Industry and Educational Readjustment," is an insightful review of the fundamental and changing purposes of education.

48. The first sentence displays Dewey's obfuscating prose. Restated, it might read, "[The child] soon learns to turn towards everything surrounded by diverting circumstances." John Dewey, "Interest in Relation to Training of the Will," *Second Supplement to the Herbart Yearbook for 1895*, Rev. Ed. (National Herbart Society, 1899), 8. Quoted in Kliebard, *op. cit.*, 47. John Dewey, "Interest in Relation to Training of the Will," *Second Supplement to the Herbart Yearbook for 1895*, rev. ed. (National Herbart Society, 1899), 8. Quoted in Kliebard, *op. cit.*, 47.

49. Cremin, *op. cit.*, 126.

SIXTEEN

American Educational Metamorphosis, III: A "Given" Joins the Establishment

> G [general intelligence] is in the normal course of events determined innately; a person can no more be trained to have it in higher degree than he can be trained to be taller.
> —Charles Spearman[1]

The research for this book was driven by curiosity about the fact that many people in the West today are guided by two assumptions:[2] (a) that there is in actual existence an ultimate reality not perceivable by our senses, and (b) that each human is born with a set of fixed mental "givens" that, largely or entirely, channel and restrict his or her ability to learn.[3] The writing of this book has been about satisfying the latter curiosity, especially about why many Americans think *with* such "givens" when they're thinking *about* children's mental development and learning.

This chapter ends the story about when and where the idea of "givens" originated and how it was passed down to us across some 2,500 years. But it doesn't end because the idea of "givens" withers and dies in our own scientifically sophisticated era. Quite the opposite. The story ends because, during the 1920s, the notion of innate "givens" finally attained the ultimate credibility. It became enshrined in an institutionalized, ritualized practice that annually impacts hundreds of thousands of American children and families: the administration of the Scholastic Aptitude Test.

EUROPEAN ANTECEDENTS: EARLY THINKING ABOUT GENERAL INTELLIGENCE

Galton, Spearman, and the "g" Factor

Let's return to 19th century Britain one final time. It was there, during the adult lives of Darwin and Spencer, that sustained interest in "general intelligence" arose.[4] Sir Francis Galton (1822–1911) is usually credited as the originator of this interest. A cousin of Darwin, Galton had a lifelong preoccupation with counting, measuring, and statistics. He was also a world traveler and explorer who had "a love affair with Africa."[5]

Impressed by his cousin's *Origin of the Species*, Galton began a parallel project: studying human intellectual capacity with the goal of showing that success in life was due to superior qualities passed down through biological heredity. In order to proceed toward his goal, Galton began by assuming—this is a key point—that intelligence is *one thing*, "general mental ability."

139

A decade after his cousin's paradigm-shattering publication, Galton published *Heredi-tary Genius*, in which he posited that genius is biologically inherited. This finding was based on Galton's analysis of the lineage of eminent Europeans, descriptions of whom he had studied in two sources: one was a ". . . biographical handbook, lately published by Routledge and Co., called 'Men of the Time,'" and the other was the obituaries of leading figures who had died during 1868, published in the January 1, 1869, issue of the London *Times*.[6]

Galton is the originator of three terms that soon passed into popular use in relation to intelligence. The first is *eugenics*, rarely heard nowadays but often discussed during the late 19th and early 20th centuries.[7] Eugenics is a deliberate plan to increase the proportion of a human population believed to have inherited superior traits, and to decrease the proportion believed to have inherited inferior traits. Its most objectionable outcome was Nazi concentration camps. Galton founded the Eugenics Education Society.[8]

In wide use today is a second term coined by Galton: *nature/nurture*. This is associated with the question of whether the behavioral and intellectual traits of any individual are more the outcome of inheritance (nature), or more the outcome of environment (nurture). As used by Galton and the eugenicists, of course, the answer was virtually always "na-ture."[9]

Galton's most enduring impact is found in Galton's third term: *gifted*. Even now, 150 years after Galton was in his prime, one cannot have a sustained conversation about the education of the young without using this word. "Gifted" refers to some type of "given" innate intelligence.[10]

Galton viewed natural selection as teleological, as *proactive* and *purposeful*, conveying humans toward an ever higher plane. This was emphatically not the conclusion that his famous cousin had reached.[11] One possibility is that Galton had read Spencer (see chapter 9) before trying to digest *Origin of the Species*. In any case, Galton's lifelong passion was to support and hasten the (wrongly) presumed march of evolutionary natural selection to-ward a society blessed with an ever higher proportion of people with superior inherited gifts.[12]

Charles Spearman (1863–1945), a British psychologist and statistician, admired Gal-ton's concept of "general mental ability."[13] It appealed to him because he and others could not agree on a definition of "intelligence." Was it a facility for logical reasoning? Spatial visualization? Mathematical abstraction? Physical coordination? Spearman wrote, "In truth, 'intelligence' has become a mere vocal sound, a word with so many meanings that finally it has none."[14]

In 1904, Spearman published an article[15] that reported his discovery of a single "gener-al intelligence," which he later termed "g," an inborn, centralized repository[16] that couldn't be measured directly but could be detected via a complex formula correlating measures of school marks, teachers' subjective assessments, peers' assessments of com-mon sense, the opinion of the school rector's wife, etc. As quoted at the beginning of this chapter, Spearman wrote that, ". . . a person can no more be trained to have ["g"] in higher degree than he can be trained to be taller."

Spearman claimed that identification of "g" as the critical factor in human intelligence was one of the most significant discoveries in the entire history of science! He described his finding as having derived from research among the children of one village school in Berkshire, England.

Binet Designs the Prototype for All Intelligence Testing

Spearman himself did not develop an intelligence test.[17] But during the same year in which his article appeared, the French government asked a Sorbonne-based psychologist,

Alfred Binet (1857–1911), to develop a way of identifying mentally "defective" children; the intent was to remove them from regular classrooms in order to give them special instruction.

Binet and his collaborator, a physician named Simon, collected from everyday life a diverse group of brief tasks that were not dependent on school learning (for example, reading was not assessed): naming objects in pictures, repeating number sequences, comparing two weights, and so forth. These tasks were administered in a quiet room by one test administrator to one child.

Binet and Simon sequenced the tasks into what they believed to be steps from the easiest to the most difficult.[18] The child's "mental age" was based on the most difficult tasks that he or she was able to perform. So if a girl of four was able to perform tasks that most five-year-olds were able to complete, she was said to have a mental age of five.

This one-on-one test has survived (with minor adjustments) into our 21st century as the Binet-Simon Intelligence Scale, the model for the testing of younger children. The idea of dividing the mental age by the chronological age, yielding a "quotient,"[19] was added due to the suggestion of a German psychologist; thus, the term "Intelligence Quotient," or "IQ," entered our language.

Binet viewed his test as no more than a diagnostic tool with a narrowly defined practical goal. He believed that a low-scoring child could be helped to improve by means of *exercices d'orthopédie mentale*, which he prescribed.[20]

Binet explicitly feared what today is called a "self-fulfilling prophesy," the situation in which a label applied to a child subtly influences adults' attitudes and behavior toward him, making it more likely that the child enacts the expected behavior. Binet wrote two sentences that became his second enduring legacy: "[Some] assert that an individual's intelligence is a fixed quantity which cannot be increased. We must protest and react against this brutal pessimism."[21]

Mendel's Findings Are Rediscovered and Misapplied

At the time of Binet's death in 1911, his name and the Binet-Simon Scale were household words among psychologists and interested laypeople beyond his native France. One reason for the growing interest in measuring the level of people's intelligence was that at the turn of the century there reemerged from obscurity the findings of the Austrian pea-plant experimenter, Gregor Johann Mendel[22] (1822–1884).

During the middle of the 19th century, Mendel had studied varieties of yellow peas, each with an easily observed trait (for example, tall and dwarf). Simply stated, he found that each plant had two hereditary inputs ("dominant" and "recessive") for each trait, one inherited from each parent plant. These inputs are now called "genes." Observing plants across numerous generations, he found that all possible outcomes were formed in mathematically predictable ratios.

Mendel reported his findings in all the right venues, but he was largely ignored. Then, in 1900, researchers working separately in The Netherlands, Germany, and Austria arrived at identical findings, after which they were astonished to find Mendel's 35-year-old publications. The field of genetics thereupon acknowledged Mendel's brilliance and quickly burgeoned.

It's important to note that Mendel investigated simple, narrowly definable properties of peas such as color, size, and wrinkling. His research and that of those who followed him demonstrated that, *within that narrow range of specificity*, single genes directly accounted for observed outcomes. This discovery reappeared in 1900, which is significant because the turn of the century was the era of rapidly growing enthusiasm for studying human intelligence.

Because of that enthusiasm, professionals and laypeople alike glossed over the fact that Mendel had studied narrowly defined traits of plants, not vastly complex behavioral capacities of mammals. So it was widely—and erroneously—*assumed* that Mendel's work supported the notion that complex human characteristics were unilaterally determined by single genes.

With the exception of Alfred Binet and possibly a few others, the majority of psychologists concluded that (a) each one of numerous, enormously complex human traits—for example, whether one's temperament is placid or domineering—was traceable in Mendelian fashion to a single gene and that (b) socially undesirable traits therefore could be reduced and eliminated by selective breeding (the eugenicist solution). As Stephen Jay Gould comments, "[These ideas] represented orthodox genetics for a brief time, and had a major impact on America."[23]

AMERICAN RESPONSES: INTEREST IN GENERAL INTELLIGENCE TAKES ROOT IN THE UNITED STATES

It is within this context of professional excitement about a Mendel-inspired breakthrough that the story we're following picks up in the United States. Facing challenges similar to those that Binet had addressed, New Jersey-based Henry H. Goddard[24] (1866–1957) was director of research at the Vineland Training School for Feeble-Minded Girls and Boys. Inventor of the word "moron," Goddard had a doctorate from Clark University, where he had studied under G. Stanley Hall.[25] Goddard was the first psychologist in the United States to use the Binet-Simon Intelligence Scale; he arranged for translation into English of both the scale and several of Binet's publications, and he encouraged American colleagues to take notice.

But in spite of his knowledge of and admiration for Binet's perspective, Goddard deviated from it in one critical respect: He treated each child's score as a complete measure of innate general intelligence. Note as well that Goddard also was an active advocate for eugenics.[26] Concerned for the racial purity of white Americans and fearful of indiscriminate breeding that involved immigrants and the feebleminded, Goddard advocated in favor of "segregation and colonization."[27] He saw Binet's Scale as an efficient method for identifying mental defectives.

Goddard also advocated for the belief that innate general intelligence was life-limiting and that environmental factors (parenting, schooling, travel, etc.) were not relevant. He wrote that

> . . . the chief determiner of human conduct is a unitary mental process which we call intelligence: that this process is conditioned by a nervous mechanism that is inborn: that the . . . consequent grade of intelligence or mental level for each individual is determined by the kind of chromosomes that come together with the union of the germ cells: that it is but little affected by any later influences except such serious accidents as may destroy part of the mechanism."[28]

Note how nicely this declaration by Goddard resonates with the ancient teachings of Aristotle.

Goddard attributed antisocial and immoral behavior to inherited mental deficiency. And he forcefully advocated for a point of view that we first encountered in chapter 12, that "scientific" ways of attaching numbers to human abilities made it easy to "sort" individuals into their proper economic and social roles. ". . . The people who are doing the drudgery," he wrote, "are, as a rule, in their proper places."[29] Addressing Princeton undergraduates in 1919, Goddard said:

> Now the fact is, *that workman* may have a ten year intelligence while you have a twenty. To demand for him such a home as you enjoy is as absurd as it would be to insist that every laborer should receive a graduate fellowship. How can there be such a thing as social equality with this wide range of mental capacity?[30]

Goddard used his wards at the Vineland Training School to study inherited intelligence, advancing the notion that "Normal intelligence seems to be a unit character and transmitted in true Mendelian fashion."[31] But he had doubts: "The writer confesses to being one of those psychologists who find it hard to accept the idea that the intelligence even *acts like a unit character*. But there seems to be no way to escape the conclusion from these figures."[32]

Most influential, though, was Goddard's book *The Kallikak Family: A Study in the Heredity of Feeblemindedness* (1912), read by Americans beyond the narrow community of psychologists. As related by Gould, the pseudonymous Martin Kallikak was said to have fathered a child by a feebleminded woman before he married a nice Quaker girl and produced more children. Over generations the progeny of the first union suffered social and mental disorders, while the progeny of the second union were all completely respectable. Goddard's book includes photographs in which the visages of the feebleminded descendents clearly had been altered. Gould notes that the "Kallikak family functioned as a primal myth of the eugenics movement for several decades."[33]

Goddard brought the Binet-Simon Scale to the United States; Lewis M. Terman[34] (1877–1956) popularized it. An Indiana farm boy whose fascination with mental ability was initiated at age 10 by a practitioner of phrenology (see chapter 11), Terman completed a dissertation in 1906—also at Clark under G. Stanley Hall—in which he reported examining "bright" and "stupid" boys and described what he found using racial and national stereotypes popular at that time. He concluded: "While offering *little positive data* on the subject, the study has *strengthened my impression* of the relatively greater importance of endowment over training as a determinant of an individual's intellectual rank among his fellows."[35]

Terman's professional career took him to Stanford University. He became well known when, in 1916, he made two major contributions. First, he revised the Binet-Simon Scale by adding dozens of new items and extending its application from children to "superior adults"; the result was the Stanford-Binet Intelligence Test, the model for many subsequent intelligence tests.

Second, Terman wrote *The Measurement of Intelligence* (1916), which outlined dozens of potential uses for tests of general intelligence. He said that the feebleminded, delinquents, criminals, schoolchildren, and job seekers all were ideal subjects, and predicted that "high-grade defectives" soon would be "brought under the surveillance and protection of society," resulting in "curtailing [their] reproduction" and "the elimination of an enormous amount of crime, pauperism, and industrial inefficiency."[36]

Terman's editor, the influential educator Elwood P. Cubberly, opined that the Stanford-Binet's scientific precision would unambiguously confirm any suspected defects in a person.[37]

INTELLIGENCE TESTS ENTER THE MAINSTREAM: SORTING RECRUITS FOR WAR SERVICE

As overviewed in chapter 12, the trend toward intelligence testing for educational purposes was already underway in the United States as the 20th century entered its first decade. Then, in 1917, the United States entered the tragic and protracted war in Europe.[38] Tens of thousands of mobilized young men soon appeared at the gates of army facilities. All needed to be assigned to different specialties, and a few needed to be funneled into officer training. How to proceed?

Into the breach stepped Robert M. Yerkes (1876–1956), professor of psychology at Harvard University and president of the American Psychological Association. He saw that the army's immediate need presented a transformative opportunity to his profession: to test the intelligence of a huge number of people. The Army gave Yerkes a commission. Col. Yerkes then traveled to Canada to learn to what extent its military authorities were applying psychological methods. There he met Carl C. Brigham (1890–1943) and persuaded him to become his assistant.

By May of 1917, Yerkes had gained the active support of a half-dozen leading American psychologists, including Henry Goddard and Lewis Terman. All of these "Army psychologists" were advocates, in varying degrees, of the eugenicist and hereditarian perspectives.[39]

Within two months, Yerkes and Brigham's Committee on the Psychological Examination of Recruits had produced three tests. Recruits who appeared able to read were given a group-administered written exam, the "Army Alpha." Those who failed the Alpha, together with illiterates, were given a group-administered pictorial test, the "Army Beta." Those who failed the Beta were given a one-on-one exam similar to the Binet-Simon Scale. By the close of World War One, well over a million recruits had been tested. The principal benefit of this testing program appears to have been in the identification of recruits for officer training.[40]

After the war, extensive information on all aspects of the army testing program became publicly available. Yerkes himself wrote an 890-page description[41]; included were 300 pages of statistics.[42] Yerkes's account reveals major flaws—in the tests' content, how the findings were interpreted, and the often difficult practical conditions within which the Alpha test was administered to recruits (tested 50 at a time). A full discussion of these flaws is beyond the scope of this account,[43] but here is one glimpse. Consider five items from the Alpha:[44]

Table 16.1.

The Panama Canal was built by . . .	Russia	England	Mexico	United States
The Leghorn is a kind of . . .	horse	chicken	fish	cattle
The forward pass is used in . . .	tennis	hand-ball	chess	football
The author of the "Scarlet Letter" is . . .	Poe	Hawthorne	Cooper	Holmes
The color of chlorine gas is . . .	red	blue	brown	green

To paraphrase questions posed by Gould,[45] how could a low score on items such as these be attributed to a deficiency in general intelligence when the test taker was a recent immigrant? How could a conclusion be drawn about someone's heredity when virtually every question assessed the impact of the environment on the test taker, including courses taken at school?

Another book based on the findings of the wartime testing program appeared two years later, written by Yerkes's former assistant, Carl C. Brigham. Far shorter and more accessible to the public than the tome edited by Yerkes, *A Study of American Intelligence* (1923) argued with dark foreboding that if appropriate steps were not taken soon, the overall intelligence of the American people would be permanently degraded by the continuing immigration of people termed "Mediterraneans" and "Alpines," and by racial mixing involving Negroes as well as others including Jews from the largely feeble-minded country of Russia.[46]

Most interesting for our inquiry is how the army psychologists dealt with data that ran directly counter to their hereditarian expectations. In a 1923 article in *The Atlantic Monthly*, Yerkes discussed the finding that, among the recruits, those with the least education got the lowest scores and those with the most education got the highest scores. Some people might look at that fact and conclude that intelligence is enhanced by schooling. No, said Yerkes, the data "flatly contradict" that idea. Instead, the data demonstrate that "the main reason that intelligence status improves with years of schooling is the elimination of the less capable pupil." The purpose of schooling is to select those who are most intelligent. [47]

In his 1923 book Carl C. Brigham addressed the following findings: The longer an immigrant had lived in the United States, the higher his score. Each five years of residency was associated with a significant increase in scores. At 20 years of residence the scores of immigrants were virtually identical to those of native men; after more than 20 years, the scores of foreign-born whites were *slightly higher* than those of native-born whites! The difference between the scores of new immigrants and the longest resident ones was 2.5 years in mental age. [48]

Brigham's interpretation: Long-term exposure to American culture and environment does not explain this. Rather, these data "forced" him to conclude that there had been a gradual deterioration over time in the average intelligence of immigrants, which Brigham related to the historical decrease in immigration from northern and western Europe and simultaneous increase in immigration from southern and eastern Europe. [49, 50]

INTELLIGENCE TESTS JOIN THE ESTABLISHMENT: SORTING APPLICANTS TO COLLEGES

Recall that in 1893, the National Education Association's Committee of Ten had issued a report stating that the appropriate objective for secondary schools was academic excellence for *all* students. In preparing its report, the committee had held a series of meetings in various parts of the country, each devoted to one high school subject area and the topics that it should cover.

One of the committee's goals was to standardize the various colleges' requirements for admission regarding *what* knowledge was expected and *when* they scheduled their exams. Committee chairman Charles W. Eliot, supported by headmasters, pushed for standardization. But the leaders of the colleges resisted; they were wary of being told what to do by outsiders.

The issue came to a head late in 1899 at a meeting in Trenton, New Jersey, of a regional educational association. Thanks to the personal intervention of Eliot, who reassured the college leaders, the attendees voted to establish the "College Entrance Examination Board." During June 1901, the CEEB administered its first exams at 67 centers in the United States and two in Europe. [51]

Those 1901 "College Boards" were standardized *achievement* tests of content knowledge; answers were in the form of written essays, which were graded by hand, one at a time. Grading was rigorous; more than 40 percent of the first test takers received a failing grade. [52]

By 1920, much had changed. The war was over. The army psychologists were returning to their campuses, enthusiastic about the promise of mass intelligence testing. Supported by the Rockefeller Foundation, three former army psychologists and Edward L. Thorndike developed "National Intelligence Tests" for students in grades three through eight, and 400,000 copies were quickly sold. Other intelligence tests were prepared; the market was eager for them. [53]

In 1924, a CEEB blue-ribbon commission recommended that the board take steps to prepare "psychological tests."[54] The Board named three experts to develop a procedure for preparing the tests, including Carl C. Brigham and Robert M. Yerkes. Brigham proved able to reassure a group of New England headmasters who were deeply suspicious of the new type of examination.

In 1925, a committee headed by Brigham prepared the test and a way of scoring its multiple-choice items; the impactful switch to multiple-choice[55] was driven by the need to lower costs.[56] This committee selected the name we all know so well: Scholastic Aptitude Test, or SAT.[57]

All accounts point to Brigham as the force behind the SAT's development. For example, it was he who dropped the traditional 0 to 100 grading scale, which emphasized subject mastery, then adopted the 200 to 800 range, which highlighted comparative ranking of all test takers.[58]

Of more social significance is the question of the extent to which Brigham's eugenicist views were being played out as an element in his indefatigable efforts on behalf of the SAT. Journalist David Owen, who extensively researched these matters, offers this conclusion:

> To say that Brigham and the College Board created the SAT to keep blacks and recent immigrants out of college would be quite misleading. . . . Brigham and the Board did not think of either group (or of women) as a threat to the Ivy League. The point of the SAT was to extend the Alpha standard to what [was] viewed as mainstream American culture. Brigham intended his test to establish a "scale of brightness" on which the "native capacity" of the nation's best and brightest young men could be measured and compared. The SAT was to be the cornerstone of a new American social order—the aristocracy of aptitude, the meritocracy.[59] [60]

THREE PROPONENTS OF GENERAL INTELLIGENCE RECANT THEIR VIEWS

Three leading proponents of general intelligence as an inborn "given" later changed their minds.

Carl C. Brigham, the principal force behind the SAT, recanted his views in a *Psychological Review* article published in 1930. His actual words were, "[The Army] study with its entire hypothetical superstructure of racial differences collapses completely." He went on to add:

> For purposes of comparing individuals or groups, it is apparent that tests in the vernacular must be used only with individuals having equal opportunity to acquire the vernacular of the test. This requirement precludes [comparing] individuals brought up in homes in which the vernacular of the tests is not used, or in which two vernaculars are used. Comparative studies . . . may not be made with existing tests. . . . One of the most pretentious of these comparative studies—the writer's own—was without foundation.[61]

Lewis M. Terman also recanted his views, but only privately. In his 1932 autobiography, *Trails to Psychology*, he had written that ". . . the major differences in intelligence test scores of certain races . . . will never be fully accounted for on the environmental hypothesis." In his personal copy of the book, Terman wrote next to that sentence in 1951, "I am less sure of this now." Four years later he added, "And still less sure in 1955!"[62]

Henry H. Goddard publicly, if partially, recanted. In a 1928 address to the American Association for the Study of the Feebleminded, he stated that "The problem of the moron is a problem of education and training," adding that "when we get an education that is entirely right there will be no morons who cannot manage themselves and their affairs and compete in the struggle for existence." In an article published that same year, Goddard stated his two new views as "1. Feeble-mindedness (the moron) is *not incurable*. 2. The feeble-minded do not generally need to be segregated." He added, "As for myself, I think I have gone over to the enemy."[63]

The Scholastic Aptitude Test was first administered to students during 1926. It went on to become the most widely recognized test of any kind in the United States—and, ironically, one of the most prepared-for. Thus, a millennia-old assumption regarding innate "givens" became not only a deeply embedded element in the mindset of Americans but also an indelibly institutionalized feature of American educational practice.

MUSINGS AND SPECULATIONS

A young person's version of the story contained in chapters 12 and 16 might read like this: Certain wise men said, "Adults are smart, or not, because of how well their brains formed inside their mothers. So let's measure people's smarts while they're still young. There's no need to wait until they grow up." The wise men went away and planned an easy way to do that, and they did it. Then they came back and told everyone else what they'd discovered, using lots of numbers on impressive tables and charts. They said, "Look at all this! It tells us exactly how smart each child is. And because we know that, we can foresee each child's future. And because we know *that*, we can help each child get ready for his or her future. Let's not waste time helping children get ready for futures other than the ones they'll have."

WHY CHAPTER 16 IS IMPORTANT

We are at the end of the long and complex story of how belief-based notions about the human mind's "given" contents and capabilities, most of which originated 2,500 years ago, became the foundation of many 21st century beliefs and practices of American education.

Chapter 16 has given us a fresh opportunity to review the activities of people who advocate belief-based points of view, and who turn for verification to evidence-based methods.[64] In the story told in this chapter, the believers ostensibly gained the support they craved; for many onlookers, the imprimatur of "science" settled the matter once and for all.

Significantly, however, the evidence-based methods themselves were fundamentally flawed: They attributed the data thus gathered to a single, fixed, internal factor instead of to a complex and shifting amalgam of factors, *one* of which was internal and the rest of which—many of them!—were external (familial, cultural, social, and others of an experiential and environmental nature). When this was pointed out to the believers, they found clever ways to reinterpret and reinforce their original conclusion.

Chapter 16 also is important because of something that does *not* appear in it. The believers rarely considered (nor were they obliged by others to consider) the role in children's learning of newly awakened interests, of "will power" and self-discipline, of sheer perseverance leading to sustained study and practice, or of guidance and support from the child's family. These factors usually aren't thought of as being innately "given" and (except for family guidance and support) they cannot be categorized as external or environmental. They belong to a hybrid third category that we could provisionally name "Internal But Not Innate."

"Internal But Not Innate" factors are capable of making a significant difference in how much, how well, and how fast an individual can master learning content, whether in a school classroom or during daily life. More will be said about this in the Conclusion (chapters 17 and 18).

At TheAptitudeMyth.info are the genealogical chart and "What to Remember" list for chapter 16.

NOTES

1. Ian J. Deary, Martin Lawn, and David J. Bartholomew, "A conversation between Charles Spearman, Godfrey Thomson, and Edward L. Thorndike; The International Examinations Inquiry Meetings, 1931–1938," *History of Psychology*, vol. 11, no. 2 (May 2008), 128. Cited by David Shenk, The Genius in All of Us (Doubleday, 2010, 32, endnote 167–68.

2. For this chapter, I've relied primarily on Stephen Jay Gould, *The Mismeasure of Man* (W. W. Norton, 1981), chapter 5; Diane Ravitch, *Left Back* (Simon & Schuster, 2000), chapter 4; and Peter Sacks, *Standardized Minds* (Perseus Books, 1999), chapter 2. Also useful has been Nicholas Lemann, "A History of Admissions Testing," in Rebecca Zwick, ed., *Rethinking the SAT* (RoutledgeFalmer, 2004), 5–13; Michael P. Riccards, *The College Board and American Higher Education* (Fairleigh Dickenson, 2010), chapters 1 and 2; David Owen, *None of the Above: Behind the Myth of Scholastic Aptitude* (Houghton Mifflin, 1985), especially 18–204; and Shenk, *op. cit.*, chapters 1 and 2.

3. These two assumptions would seem to be related because both arose out of fascination with consciousness. The result is that consciousness often has been understood either as part of an otherworldly ultimate reality, or as in communication with such an ultimate reality. See chapter 2.

4. In preparing this section, I relied on Gould, *op. cit.*; Sacks, *op. cit.*; and Shenk, *op. cit.*, 31–32. See also the Human Intelligence website at www.indiana.edu/~intell.

5. Human Intelligence website (*ibid.*), page on Francis Galton. The quote is attributed to G. Allen, "The Measure of a Victorian Polymath: Pulling Together the Strands of Francis Galton's Legacy to Modern Biology," *Nature*, vol. 145 (2002), 19–20. The website's page on Galton states that "Galton estimated from his field observations in Africa that the African people were 'two grades' below Anglo-Saxons' position in the normal frequency distribution of general mental ability."

6. Francis Galton, *Hereditary Genius: An Enquiry into its Laws and Consequences* (Macmillan, 1869), 9–10.

7. "Eugenics" was first discussed by Galton in his 1883 book, *Inquiries into Human Faculty and its Development* (Macmillan, 1883); see footnotes on pages 24–25.

8. The Eugenics Education Society was founded in the United States and met regularly at the American Museum of Natural History in New York. It counted famous people as adherents: H. G. Wells, George Bernard Shaw, Sidney and Beatrice Webb, among others. Jim Holt, "Measure for Measure: The Strange Science of Francis Galton," *New Yorker*, 24–31, January 2005, 90; Holt's article is extensively quoted by Shenk, *op. cit.*, 165–67. In 1989, the Society changed its name to the Galton Institute.

9. Galton explained the nature/nurture distinction is his 1875 book, *English Men of Science: Their Nature and Nurture* (D. Appleton, 1875), 9: "When nature and nurture compete for supremacy on equal terms in the sense to be explained, the former proves the stronger. It is needless to insist that neither is self-sufficient; the highest natural endowments may be starved by defective nurture, while no carefullness [sic] of nurture can overcome the evil tendencies of an intrinsically bad physique, weak brain, or brutal disposition."

10. "Gifted" is used repeatedly by Galton throughout *Hereditary Genius, op. cit.*, and it appears as well in his *English Men of Science, ibid.*

11. However, in 1871 Darwin wrote that ". . . we now know through the admirable labors of Mr. Galton that genius, which implies a wonderfully complex combination of high faculties, tends to be inherited"; and ". . . that insanity and deteriorated mental powers likewise run in the same families." Charles Darwin, *The Descent of Man, and Selection in Relation to Sex* (D. Appleton, 1871), 106–7.

12. For example, on page 1 of *Heredity Genius, op. cit.*, Galton writes, "I conclude that each generation has enormous power over the natural gifts of those that follow, and maintain that it is a duty we owe to humanity to . . . exercise it in a way that . . . shall be most advantageous to future inhabitants of the earth." See also the Galton Institute's website [www.galtoninstitute.org.uk].

13. This paragraph draws heavily on Sacks, *op. cit.*, 19–21, and Shenk, *op. cit.*, 31–32.

14. Charles Spearman, *The Abilities of Man: Their Nature and Measurement* (Macmillan, 1927), 14.

15. "General intelligence, objectively determined and measured," *American Journal of Psychology*, vol. 15 (1904), 201–93.

16. Sacks, *op. cit.*, offers on pages 21–22 a critique of the validity of Spearman's "g." The Human Intelligence website, *op. cit.*, overviews Spearman's calculation of "g," which was derived by factor analysis, a statistical procedure invented by Spearman for this purpose. Factor analysis demonstrated that

scores on separate measures of intelligence were positively correlated with each other, thus suggesting that an individual's degree of intelligent behavior had a single source, which Spearman labeled "g."

17. This paragraph and the next two draw heavily on Sacks, *op. cit.*, 22–25, and Gould, *op. cit.*, 148–54. See also Alfred Binet and Th. Simon, *The Development of Intelligence in Children* (*The Binet-Simon Scale*), translated by Elizabeth S. Kite (The Training School at Vineland, New Jersey), no. 11, May 1916.

18. The page on Alfred Binet at the Human Intelligence website (www.indiana.edu/~intell) provides examples of many of Binet's tasks.

19. For example, the girl of four who could perform tasks that most five-year-olds had been found able to complete would be assigned a "quotient" of 125 ($5 \div 4 = 1.25$ or, simplified, 125).

20. Some details of Binet's "mental orthopedics" are found in Gould, *op. cit.*, 154.

21. Binet, *Les idées modernes sur les enfants* (Flammarion, 1909), 105; reprinted in Andrew Elliot and Carol Dweck, eds., *Handbook of Competence and Motivation* (Guilford, 2005); cited by Shenk, *op. cit.*, 160.

22. Basic information about Mendel is from Edward O. Dodson, "Gregor Johann Mendel," *Collier's Encyclopedia* (Collier's, 1997), vol. 15, 683–86. The interpretation of Mendel's impact relies on Gould, *op. cit.*, 162.

23. Gould, *ibid.*

24. Information about Henry H. Goddard is based on Gould, *ibid.*, 158–63, and on Diane Ravitch, *op. cit.*, 133–34, 158. See also the Goddard page at the Human Intelligence website, *op. cit.*.

25. Ravitch, *ibid.*, 133.

26. Ravitch, *ibid.*, 134, points out that "Historians later saw the eugenics movement as 'closely related to the other reform movements of the Progressive era,' drawing support from many of the same people." She cites Mark H. Haller, *Eugenics: Hereditarian Attitudes in American Thought* (Rutgers University Press, 1963), 5.

27. The Goddard page at the Human Intelligence website, *op. cit.*, includes a quote in which Goddard discusses the benefits of segregation and colonization. Also recounted is Goddard's government-invited activities at Ellis Island, which sharply increased the number of immigrants sent back home because they were mentally defective.

28. Henry H. Goddard, *Human Efficiency and Levels of Intelligence: Lectures delivered at Princeton University April 7, 8, 10, 11, 1919* (Princeton, 1920); 1.

29. Henry H. Goddard, *Psychology of the Normal and Subnormal* (Dodd, Mead, 1919), 246.

30. Goddard, *Human Efficiency, op. cit.*, 101.

31. Henry H. Goddard, *Feeblemindedness: Its Causes and Consequences* (Macmillan, 1914), ix.

32. *Ibid.*, 556.

33. Gould, *op. cit.*, 168; Gould's discussion includes photographs of the two lines of Kallikaks.

34. My information about Lewis M. Terman is based on Gould, *ibid.*, 174–92, and on Ravitch, *op. cit.*, 133–34, 158. See also the Terman page at the Human Intelligence website, *op. cit.*; Owen, *op. cit*, 180–81; and Shenk, *op. cit.*, 25–27.

35. Gould, *ibid.*, 175; italics added. Gould cites Terman's 1906 dissertation, 68.

36. Terman (1916), 6–7. Diane Ravitch notes that "Terman maintained that low IQs (in the 70–80 range) were 'very, very common among Spanish-Indian and Mexican families in the Southwest and also among negroes. Their dullness seems to be racial, or at least inherent in the family stocks from which they come.'" She cites Terman (1916), 91–92. On the other hand, Terman's *The Measurement of Intelligence* also includes on pages 48–50 a discussion of "some avowed limitations" of the Binet test.

37. Cubberly's comment is reported without attribution by Sacks, *ibid.*

38. My principal source for World War One testing has been Gould, *op. cit.*, 192–224; also consulted has been Owen, *op. cit.*, 181–84, and Ravitch, *op. cit.*, 135–37.

39. I say "in varying degrees" because I've found data on another participant, Walter V. Bingham, who had little interest in debating the nature/nurture question and otherwise emerges as a relatively modest hereditarian and eugenicist. Human Intelligence website (*op. cit.*), page on Bingham.

40. Robert M. Yerkes, ed., "Psychological Examining in the United States Army," *Memoirs of the National Academy of Sciences*, vol. 15 (Government Printing Office, 1921), 86, 154.

41. Yerkes, *ibid.*

42. Yerkes's account claimed that (1) the average mental age of white American men was 13.08 on a scale that classed anyone with a mental age between 8 and 12 as a moron; (2) immigrants from northern and western Europe were far more intelligent than those from southern and eastern Europe; (3) negroes were the least intelligent with an average mental age of 10.41. Gould, *op. cit.*, 196–97.

43. For details, see Gould, *ibid.*, 199–222.

44. Yerkes, *op. cit.*, 206.

45. Gould, *op. cit.*, 199, adds that an item in the Beta Test's complete-a-picture section was of a house with something missing from the roof; the test taker was scored correct if he added a chimney. Anthropologist Franz Boas told of a Sicilian recruit who completed the house with a crucifix, as he was accustomed to seeing in his native land. This response was marked wrong.

46. Sacks, *op. cit.*, 31; it is not clear if "from the largely feeble-minded country of Russia" is a quote of Brigham. *A Study of American Intelligence* is also discussed at length by Ravitch, *op. cit.*, 142–46, and Gould,

op. cit., 225–30. Ravitch notes that Brigham's book was published as a "companion volume" to Charles W. Gould's *America: A Family Matter* (Scribner's, 1920), which advocated purebred races. Brigham acknowledged relying on Madison Grant, *The Passing of the Great Race; or, The Racial Basis of European History* (Scribner's, 1916). Grant warned of the influence of racial groups such as Polish Jews, "whose dwarf stature, peculiar mentality, and ruthless concentration on self-interest are being engrafted upon the stock of the [American] nation"; Grant, 14.

47. Ravitch, *ibid.*, 145–46. Yerkes's article is "Testing the Human Mind," *The Atlantic Monthly*, March 1923, 358–70. During the early 20th century, public schools still were functioning to a considerable extent on an elitist model in which students with lower achievement dropped out while those with higher achievement continued on.

48. This paragraph draws on Sacks, *op. cit.*, 30; Ravitch, *op. cit.*, 144; and Gould, *op. cit.*, 226–27. Gould notes (226) that "Even Yerkes had expressed agnosticism—the only time he considered a significant alternative to inborn biology—on the causes of steadily increasing scores for immigrants who had lived longer in America."

49. My recounting of Brigham's explanation is based on Ravitch, *op. cit.*, 144. For a more technical account that includes references to statistical procedures, see Gould, *op. cit.*, 226–30.

50. A 1922 Ph.D. dissertation reexamined the army data and found, among other things, that the States with the highest proportion of native-born whites were home to the lowest-scoring Army recruits. The author concludes that the Army test appeared to be "a test of what *had* been learned rather than what *can* be learned." Ravitch, *op. cit.*, 152. She cites Herbert B. Alexander, "A Comparison of the Ranks of American States in Army Alpha and in Social-Economic Status," *School and Society*, 30 September 1922, 388–92 [italics in original].

51. Michael P. Riccards, *The College Board and American Higher Education* (Fairleigh Dickinson, 2010), 27–33. Eliot "intervened" because, though not a member of the association, he traveled from Boston to attend, perhaps because he thought it would bring his signature issue to a head.

52. *Ibid.*, 32–33, 34.

53. Details about postwar activities are from Ravitch, *op. cit.*, 137. Owen adds that intelligence tests were the wave of the future; several colleges were developing their own; *op. cit.*, 185.

54. This paragraph draws heavily on Fuess, *ibid.*, 104–6.

55. Essay responses test *recall*, whereas multiple-choice responses merely test *recognition*. A switch from essay to multiple-choice renders any examination significantly less rigorous.

56. Throughout its quarter-century of existence, the CEEB had lost money every year, due in part to the high cost of hiring teachers and others to hand-score the written tests. Riccards, *op. cit.*, 34.

57. "In their preface [to the SAT manual] they very wisely introduced a paragraph" saying that the new test "should be regarded merely as a supplementary record." Fuess, *op. cit.*, 107.

58. Riccards, *op. cit.*, 42. See also Owen, *ibid.*, 189.

59. Owen, *op. cit.*, 189. Owen cites "scale of brightness" as from Brigham, "Intelligence Tests," *Princeton Alumni Weekly*, 5 May 1926, 1; he cites "native" as from Brigham, "Psychological Tests at Princeton," *Princeton Alumni Weekly*, 28 November 1923, 185.

60. For another view of the SAT's origins, plus an impassioned argument that meritocracy is not good for the United States, see Nicholas Lemann, *The Big Test* (Farrar, Straus and Giroux, 2000).

61. Carl C. Brigham, "Intelligence Tests of Immigrant Groups," *Psychological Review*, 37 (March 1930), 158–65. The quotes are from Gould, *op. cit.*, 233. Owen notes that Brigham does not dismiss the *idea* of racial and national differences; he only questions "existing tests"; *op. cit.*, 187.

62. Ravitch, *op. cit.*, 159. Ravitch cites Paul Davis Chapman, *Schools as Sorters: Lewis M. Terman, Applied Psychology, and the Intelligence Testing Movement, 1890–1930* (New York University Press, 1988), 193.

63. Ravitch, *op. cit.*, 158; Gould, *op. cit.*, 172, 174. Gould cites Goddard, "Feeblemindedness: A Question of Definition," *Journal of Psycho-Asthenics*, vol. 33 (1928), 222–25 [italics in original]. The "As for myself . . ." quote appears on 224.

64. This same tendency appeared in the much-discussed 1996 book, *The Bell Curve*, by Richard J. Herrnstein and Charles Murray, at least insofar as it applied the methods of science in a fresh attempt to establish that there are stable differences in intelligence at the ethnic-group level.

III

Tomorrow's Opportunities

CAN WE TRANSCEND OUR INHERITED MINDSET TO GIVE MASTERY THE HIGHEST PRIORITY?

In the final portion of this book, I urge parents, teachers, and other caretakers of American children to recognize that the values and beliefs many of them think *with* do not necessarily represent 21st century evidence-based conclusions about children, learning, teaching, and parenting. Instead, they represent an inherited past. They represent the belief-based ideas of people who needed to solve problems that had little or no relation to children's acquisition of mastery of the skills and knowledge taught in schools. Our problem *today* concerns mastery. We won't be able to decisively solve it if we apply the solutions of long-bygone eras to our 21st century problems.

Chapter 17 begins by unpacking the meanings of the western-contemporary paradigm's value propositions about children's learning and classroom teaching. Notably absent is concern about mastery. Then, I unpack our views about mastery and effort, focusing on the fact that our inherited mindset leads us to fear that intense and sustained mental effort by a child is debilitating. *We must rid ourselves of that old belief.* Finally, I offer a suggestion about how we can best proceed.

Chapter 18 offers a transformative new paradigm, a fresh set of conceptual tools to think *with*, to enable us to overcome the educational challenge that we're compelled to think *about*. The new paradigm comprises seven assertions about how *today's* world works best with respect to children, parenting, learning, and teaching. This paradigm makes it possible for every American with responsibility for a child to positively contribute to a redirected and reinvigorated national effort to improve children's mastery of the skills and knowledge taught in schools.

SEVENTEEN

Which Problems Are *Now* More Significant to Solve?

Since no paradigm ever solves all the problems it defines and since no two paradigms leave all the same problems unsolved, paradigm debates always involve the question: Which problems is it more significant to have solved?

—Thomas S. Kuhn[1]

Aided by the revealing historical inquiry that we have undertaken throughout the preceding sixteen chapters, we can now "unpack" (undertake an analysis and elaboration of) the elements that comprise our current western-contemporary paradigm for thinking about children's learning and classroom teaching. Unpacked, those value propositions reemerge as *nine declarative statements of belief*—nine inherited assumptions—about "the way things work" regarding learning and teaching:

1. Each child at birth is endowed with, or "given," a set of mental capacities—preferences, strengths and weaknesses, preset pathways for future growth and development—that will very largely determine future performance when encountering learning tasks.
2. Latent at birth, these mental capacities inevitably and spontaneously emerge from within the child to give rise to a unique mental profile, similarly to the manner in which the child's physical body instinctively emerges and attains maturity. Note also that:

   a. This emerging-from-within process, analogous to the botanical growth and flowering of a plant, is natural and "organic" and consequently is beneficial and desirable;
   b. Implicit is that mental development is fixed in its preset course, very largely incapable of flexibility or adaptation, and is bounded and limited in its scope and power; and
   c. Implicit is that mental development is passive. Because it's organic, it simply *happens to* a child, who needs to assume little or no active role in, or responsibility for, the process.

3. Important for a growing child's optimal mental development is that he or she be enabled to freely enact, build upon, and eventually express a natural set of capacities and preset pathways. Therefore, parents, classroom instructors, and other caretakers should:

153

a. Remain alert in order to detect what those emerging preset pathways actually are;

b. Provide the young, growing child with a wide and well-rounded set of experiences and learning options, so as to enable these preset pathways to emerge early on;

c. Encourage and support the child along whatever pathways show signs of emerging;

d. Design learning methods that are responsive to, and guided by, the child's pathways;

e. Insure that the child is not impeded or discouraged from following his or her own pathways; and

f. Defend and approve of factors that support the child's growing independence in terms of being able to creatively express his or her "given" unique capacities and pathways.

4. A child is precious in terms of inherent value, and thus is fragile, delicate, and susceptible to damage; this applies to the child's developing mind even more than it applies to his or her physical body. Parents, classroom instructors, and other caretakers should:

a. Avoid expecting any mental performance that might exhaust the child or upset his or her mental/emotional composure, which can undermine the child's mental capacities;

b. Avoid expecting any mental performance that might exceed the child's spontaneously attained level of ability. Expect from the child performances that, in terms of quantity and quality, are "the best that you can do" or "up to the limits of your ability"; and

c. Hesitate to criticize or punish the child for an inferior mental performance, as doing so risks damaging, discouraging, or embarrassing the child; use only positive incentives.

5. Superior learning processes are those toward which the child, at least in the moment, feels some degree of curiosity, interest, or positive motivation. Note also that:

a. Motivation is most desirable when it arises spontaneously from within the child, but it also may be induced or incentivized by parents, classroom instructors, and others;

b. Motivation is enhanced by the expectation of pleasure, entertainment, or fun; insure that, as much as possible, learning tasks have, and are seen to have, these qualities; and

c. Learning tasks perceived as highly demanding or difficult risk demotivating the child; employ tasks that are only *slightly* challenging, thus requiring only a tiny "stretch."

6. Superior learning processes are those describable using the prefix "self-": self-directed, self-discovered, self-expressive, self-constructed, etc.; such processes are said to involve active learning, with "active" implying *visible* child participation and activity. Therefore:

a. Any learning process is highly suspect if it compels or allows a child to remain visibly passive for even a short duration of time, i.e., one measured in just a few minutes;

    b. A learning process that attempts in some way to elicit skill or knowledge from within the child is more desirable than one that delivers external skill or knowledge to the child; and

    c. Any hint or overt expression of creativity, even if poor in quality, is highly desirable and should be encouraged, for it demonstrates that the child is actually becoming self-directed, self-expressive, etc. Encourage, elicit, and reward creativity early and often.

7. Authoritative and directive behavior toward a child from parents, classroom instructors, and others, in reference to learning goals and performances, is undesirable. Note that:

    a. Such behavior risks undermining the child's progress toward creative expression;

    b. Such behavior risks upsetting or damaging the child's mental/emotional composure;

    c. Such behavior risks diverting the child from establishing creative independence; and

    d. Directiveness in pursuit of *physical* performance goals (e.g., in athletics) *is* desirable.

8. A child's mental performances, for better or for worse, are always primarily attributable to his or her "native ability" or "aptitude," i.e., to the child's "given" mental capabilities. Inferior performances are "not up to your level of ability," implying a *preset* level.

9. A child's mental performances may be secondarily attributable to factors in his or her environment such as cultural context, parenting/teaching, formative experiences, etc. Rarely are such factors seen as enabling a child to transcend his or her "given" abilities.

MISSING FROM OUR UNPACKED BELIEFS AND VALUES: *MASTERY* AND *EFFORT*

The most important fact about those nine unpacked beliefs is what is missing from them:

- The importance of skill- and content-*mastery*, about which the nine beliefs are neutral.
- The possibility of a child's attaining mastery through his or her own dogged effort and patient perseverance, about which the nine beliefs are hostile (see especially belief 4).

Mastery and effort are related, two sides of the same coin. Mastery almost always requires effort—patient perseverance. Effort in sufficient quantity usually leads to mastery.

What is mastery? It is *not* proficiency.[2] Mastery refers to the value, process, and goal of *thoroughly learning*—"mastering"—whatever skill or knowledge is set to be learned.

Most Americans do not oppose the goal of mastery. But many judge mastery—and the persistent effort needed to attain it—to have relatively low priority in comparison with the value and goal of enabling children to become self-directing, self-expressive individuals able to freely enact, build upon, and express their innate mental capacities and preset pathways.

Why do many Americans give mastery a lower priority? The historical record provides an answer: The American mindset with its associated values and beliefs is grounded in a tradition of some 2,500 years in which the mastery of knowledge and skills was rarely the principal concern.

It's possible that skill and knowledge was a high-priority concern of educated people during the 15th and 16th centuries when the scholastics and Jesuits were the leading educators (see chapter 3), and perhaps also during the 16th and 17th centuries when Sense Realism, Humanism, and Rationalism were worldviews espoused by many among the educated elite (see chapter 4).

Then mastery slowly declined in relative importance—but not because it came to be judged as useless. *Mastery declined in relative importance because it was eclipsed by enticing new values and goals, many of which were driven by deepening or emerging concerns about innate "givens."* Advocates wanted to extend those new values and goals to benefit their children.

The Eclipse of Mastery in Our Historical Record

Here is the accumulated evidence:

- During the pre-Christian Greek era, one of the critical problems to be solved by leading thinkers was epistemological: how to understand the nature of the human mind and the process by which it develops and gains knowledge. They came to imagine that the most valuable knowledge already is *inside* each individual, having been acquired by, or "given" to, him or her before birth. Socrates claimed to be drawing out this pre-packaged knowledge. Plato claimed to know how that knowledge came to reside in each individual's mind.

  The enduringly influential Aristotle taught that human beings' biological *and mental* development inexorably occurs, a process depending neither on external support *nor the individual's own effort*. This seed-time of Western thinking clearly was not conducive to elevating mastery to top priority. It had precisely the opposite effect. *The Greeks laid the foundation for all of the subsequent preoccupations with inborn "givens"* (see chapter 2).
- During the 15th and 16th centuries when Original Sin (a "given") was a preoccupation, a critical problem to be solved by Christians was how to preserve children's innocence and purity. The solution required virtue to trump mastery as the main goal of instruction. During 19th century's Romantic era, admiration of children's innocence and purity transformed into a focus on their preciousness, which then evolved into concern about their presumed mental fragility and ease of exhaustion, which in turn led to the widespread belief that perseverance in pursuit of mastery would be permanently debilitating (see chapters 5, 7, 10, and 11).
- During the 16th, 17th, and 18th centuries, one of the critical problems to be solved by thought leaders was how to overcome humans' dependent fatalism and move toward individual self-direction. A piece of the solution was the exhilarating idea that authorities deserved neither obedience nor deference by ascription. Applied to the authority figure in each classroom, this mindset shift not only reduced his being automatically accepted as *in authority*; it also engendered a reduction in his being seen as *an authority* regarding knowledge and skill. Not only was the teacher devalued; what he taught became devalued as well (see chapter 6).
- During the 18th century after the publication of *Émile*, a critical problem to be solved by educated parents was how to insure that their children could fully benefit from "organic" development (which emerged from within). Drawn to Rousseau's ideals, these parents sought "negative education," a solution that deliberately side-stepped former expectations of mastery (see chapters 5 and 7). Note that the foundational assumption in operation here was Aristotelian: mental growth *inexorably occurs* if there is no impediment (see chapter 2).

- During the 18th and early 19th centuries, once again it was many educated parents, now joined by many educators, who decided that their critical problem to be solved was how to insure that children were free to enjoy the developmental ideal being popularized by the literary Romantics: spontaneous growth and flowering, portrayed as a "given" emerging from within. That image, for many, was far more appealing than the previously common one: the child's toiling in a dingy classroom to memorize externally delivered skills and knowledge.

  Keep in mind two significant facts. The Romantics specifically denigrated learning from books and in school classrooms. And the organic principle, also known as the botanical model (championed by the Romantics) is *passive*. This principle says: Mental development does *not* happen because I direct it or I work at it; it automatically happens (see chapter 7).

- By the mid-19th century, under the influence of Rousseau and the Romantics, and more specifically Pestalozzi and Spencer, the principal problem to be solved by educators in the United States and Europe was not how to attain mastery. Rather, it was how to plan and deliver instruction in accordance with a child's inner life (a "given"), i.e., how to "psychologize instruction." Their solution needed to respect a widely accepted "fact" about children: their mental fragility and the constant danger of exhaustion due to study (see chapters 8 and 10). Similar views also arose in the United States, due in part to European influences and in part as a drawing away from the harsh child-rearing practices of the Calvinists (see chapter 11).

- During the late 19th century in the United States, municipal, industrial, and educational leaders struggled with a massive problem that needed immediate solving: how to cope with unprecedented waves of immigrants flooding American cities. But if mastery of skill and knowledge played any role in their educational solutions, it was merely in terms of the most menial of skills and the most rudimentary of knowledge. The decision makers "knew" that the immigrants' congenital mental capacity was *very* limited. So as a matter of public policy, an academic education was denied to millions of newcomers (see chapters 12 and 14).

- Around the turn of the 20th century in Europe and the United States, a problem that awaited solving by those with scientific training and an interest in the mind was how to measure intelligence, assumed in those days to be a single "given" trait. Their paths to solutions and the findings they yielded, which we now recognize as fundamentally flawed, confirmed what municipal, industrial, and educational leaders already "knew"—that almost all children could learn only the most rudimentary knowledge and basic manual skills (see chapters 13 and 16).

- Around the turn of the 20th century in Europe and especially the United States, interest in what was "given" at birth to each child soared, propelled by the recapitulation hypothesis and the popular child study movement. The problem to be solved—more precisely, the research goal—was to figure out in detail what those "givens" were. The solution is of less interest to us than two side effects of all that effort. They were a confirming of the belief that whatever had been "given" was beyond anyone's control, and an intensifying of the demands for child-centered—*pedocentric*—instruction in which meeting children's "needs" became the focus of decision making, not children's mastery of skills or knowledge (see chapters 10 and 15).

What One Has Been "Given" Is All that One Has Got

None of these historical trends had room for mastery. None of them promoted perseverance as the route to mastery; on the contrary, some of them darkly warned against perseverance. The cumulative effect has been to counsel passivity. *Whatever one has been "given" is all that one has got, and talk of "potential" is actually talk about assumed limits beyond which one simply cannot go.*

The historical story told by this book ends in 1926, when the first administration of the Scholastic Aptitude Test marked the institutionalization of an ages-old belief: that a child's "given" intelligence is the best predictor of his or her future performance.

After 1926, was concern about mastery eclipsed in the same way that it had been during so many previous historical eras? If you're reading this book, it's possible that you've also done related reading, and are already aware of trends such as the post-World War Two life adjustment movement[3] and the more recent campaign to abolish homework.[4]

20TH CENTURY WAKE-UP CALLS ABOUT OUR NEGLECT OF MASTERY

During the subsequent three quarters of the 20th century, there were two widely publicized "wake-up calls" to the American public about the dangers of giving mastery a low priority.

No event was more impactful than the launching of Sputnik by the Soviets in October 1957. It occasioned an enormous outpouring of public debate, self-criticism, and action-planning. Next in significance was the report of the National Commission on Excellence in Education, *A Nation at Risk: The Imperative for Educational Reform*, which in 1983 declared this:

> If an unfriendly foreign power had attempted to impose on America the mediocre educational performance that exists today, we might well have viewed it as an act of war. As it stands, we have allowed this to happen to ourselves. We have squandered the gains in student achievement made in the wake of the Sputnik challenge, which helped make those gains possible. We have, in effect, been committing an act of unthinking, unilateral educational disarmament.

Why did we squander the gains in student achievement made after Sputnik?

We squandered those gains because of the reigning beliefs—unpacked above—about what's best for children's learning. Those beliefs were deeply felt, widely shared, and credible because during two dozen centuries of Western history they emerged, reinforced each other, and gained familiarity and legitimacy. For many of us, those beliefs are the bedrock of our core values with respect to the raising and educating of children. Those beliefs comprise the principal component of our received cultural heritage, our foundational web of assumed "Truths."

Our historical inquiry into this received cultural heritage has shown that these were *belief-based ideals* that paid scant attention to children's attainment of mastery. The outcome today is that, as a nation, we tend to be, at best, passively positive about mastery. Yes, Sputnik was a major shock. *A Nation at Risk* was troubling. Today, awareness of the decades-long decline of most measures of students' mastery is, for at least a few of us, an unmistakable danger signal.

But within each one of us, the preemptive stance is this: When it's the future of *my own children* that's at stake, I instinctively revert to the guidance of my foundational values and assumptions, the ones that emerged over millennia. Those values resonate with the ideals espoused by other parents like me, by members of my extended family, by many teachers and other educators known to me, and by the members of my community whom I respect. Therefore, acting in accordance with these values *must* be the superior way to raise and educate children!

OUR VALUE PROPOSITIONS ABOUT MASTERY AND EFFORT, UNPACKED AND ELABORATED

It's time to get down to details about our western-contemporary paradigm's stance with respect to mastery and effort, a 10th element that is awaiting unpacking.

10. Content mastery and other superior mental performances may be attributable to a child's hard work and perseverance; some adults believe this is highly admirable. *However:*

   a. Hard work and perseverance, because they tend to be exhausting, are rarely recommended as a way for a child to transcend his or her limited capabilities for learning.

   b. Hard work and perseverance, because they are seen as likely to impede the organic flowering of the child's uniquely creative self-expression, are rarely recommended.

   c. Hard work and perseverance are *not* admirable when viewed as so time- and energy-consuming that the child has little opportunity for socializing, free play, and learning non-academic skills. Many adults very highly value a child's becoming "well-rounded."

   d. Hard work and perseverance, for the reasons cited above, are demotivating. Rapid, easy learning is motivating, and is claimed for many learning methods and materials.

   e. Perseverance and hard work in pursuit of learning goals, when seen being required of *other* people's children by *their* caretakers, are criticized as destroying the freedom of those children to become self-expressive, socially adept, emotionally secure, etc. The fact that they learn and perform in school with high superiority carries little weight. Ironically . . .

   f. Perseverance and hard work are *frequently* called into action as a way for a child to transcend his or her limitations in terms of physical capabilities (e.g., in athletics).

Fascinating and troubling to me—and to many other commentators besides me—is the fact that Americans have historically taken enormous pride in hard work and perseverance, in our "can-do" spirit as demonstrated so impressively by the impoverished immigrants who first settled on our shores, by those freezing rag-tag soldiers who secured our independence, by the tenacious pioneers who plunged ever farther westward, by the indefatigable builders of the transcontinental railroad, by our courageous armed service members today, and on and on.

Our willingness and ability to work hard and persevere isn't merely a historical oddity. Americans here and now have every expectation that athletes—on professional teams, in colleges and secondary schools, and even in elementary schools and children's leagues—will drill, practice, build endurance and strength, learn from errors, and ceaselessly strive to win. Interviews with athletes are broadcast and published without ceasing; listen to what they say. Most of their talk references willpower, perseverance, hard work, and often-repeated drills.

On the street and in public places, one often observes clothing with messages such as:

Sweat & Steel Gym: No guts, no glory. [5]

If only we could extend that all-American value, which is as alive and well today as it ever was, to the mastery of the skills and knowledge taught in classrooms!

But in the amalgam of beliefs and values that many of us share, mastery of school subjects has been walled off from the game-changing power of hard work and perseverance.

We inherited that western-contemporary paradigm from distant European forebears. But today, the problems *we* need to solve are different from the problems *they* needed to solve way back when. The paradigm they willed to us is not working. To solve our problems today, we must . . .

- rid ourselves of the irrational fear that intense mental effort damages children,[6] and
- replace several other features of the ancient paradigm we inherited (see chapter 18).

CONFRONTING THE INEVITABLE OUTCOME OF OUR INHERITED BELIEFS AND VALUES

Given that, for many of us as earlier for those who preceded us, children's mastery of knowledge and skill has been a secondary priority at best, why are we so disappointed to learn that a sizeable majority of American children are falling short of mastery?

Actually, most of us recognize that mastery *is* important. "Secondary priority" does *not* mean "of no value at all." We know that mastery is critical for our nation in the global arena as well as for our children's futures. So we're collectively unhappy upon confronting study after study that concludes that American children's academic skills are mediocre . . . and declining.

But when on behalf of each of our beloved children we face *this* uncomfortable dilemma . . .

Our children's becoming
self-directing, self-expressive
individuals able to freely enact and
build upon their innate mental
capacities and preset pathways

Our children's attaining
mastery of skill and
knowledge

Figure 17.1.

. . . we find it difficult to give higher priority to the option on the right. And even if we *say* that we'll favor the attainment of mastery, we find that, within the context of our adult peer group, it's difficult to act day after day with unwavering purpose to insure that outcome.

Perhaps you're thinking now, "This is *not* either-or! It's way more complicated than that!"

It's well known that we Americans have a powerful tendency to think in dichotomies about all sorts of things. And it looks like the figure above is just one more stark either-or dichotomy, presenting a binary choice that actually resides within a highly complex, emotion-laden, subtly nuanced amalgam of inputs and factors that, all together over 18–20 years, constitute the raising and educating of each of our children. No room for a simplistic dichotomy there! So if you're thinking, "This is *not* either-or," then a great many Americans would agree with you.

This chapter was drafted during the same week that Amy Chua's book, *Battle Hymn of the Tiger Mother* (2011), gained fame almost overnight. Chua addresses the same issues that we've been discussing in historical perspective. Her perspective is that of a parent with roots in Chinese culture. Simply stated, Chua confronted what above was called "this uncomfortable dilemma" and selected the option on the right: "Our children's attaining mastery of skill and knowledge." Her book ignited a firestorm of commentary, most of which dealt in this dichotomy: Demanding, unforgiving Chinese tiger moms versus supportive, self-esteem-building American loving moms.

What does such dichotomizing accomplish? It barricades people defensively and resolutely inside their familiar, comforting paradigms. It's simple: Right versus Wrong!

If it's true that most of us actually *do* accept that mastery is desirable—not only for our own children's future but also for our nation in the global arena—then it's imperative that we get this discussion far away from either-or dichotomizing and the vituperative anger it breeds.

The historical research presented in the foregoing sixteen chapters presents us with this fact: The predicament in which we find ourselves today—the seemingly irreversible decline of our children's mastery—is the inevitable outcome of our beliefs and values, of what this book has labeled the "western-contemporary paradigm," which you and I did not invent. *We inherited it.*

The western-contemporary paradigm is an ancient, belief-based invention that we assimilated without awareness during our upbringings. It expressed "the way things are done around here." We learned to live with it. We accepted it "as-is." It effortlessly became our Truth.

We need not continue to accept that ancient paradigm "as-is."

LEARNING TO THINK ON A GRADUATED SPECTRUM

Leaving aside the question of whether Figure 17.1 above presents a simplistic dichotomy, you might have responded to the dilemma by thinking, "We can have *both* outcomes!" That is, we can attain *both* mastery *and* self-directed, self-expressive individualism along lines envisioned by Parker, Spencer, Pestalozzi, Rousseau, and a host of lesser lights.

Two features of the American mindset are relevant here. The first is that we have a "can-do" attitude coupled with a willingness to persevere through strenuous effort to attain goals that, to ordinary mortals, seem beyond realization. The second is that, to a degree scarcely matched by any other national group known to history, we've come close to "having it all" (at least that's our reputation, which helps explain the continuing attraction of our nation to would-be immigrants). Thus, we're conditioned to viewing highly challenging goals as attainable.

But the goals we usually have in mind are material in nature (conquering the physical environment, inventing and building things, gaining daily comfort and convenience, etc.). Our present discussion is about something very different: the raising and educating of our children. In *that* highly complex realm, attaining *both* outcomes, *each in full measure*, occurs so rarely that it's useless for that possibility to guide our expectations and actions.

Therefore, it's far more practical for us to think of the two choices—mastery on the one hand, self-expressive individualism on the other—as the end points of a *continuum*, a *graduated spectrum* of alternative possibilities. In aid of that goal, here is the figure above, slightly altered:

Our children's becoming self-directing, self-expressive individuals able to freely enact and build upon their innate mental capacities and preset pathways	1...2...3...4...5...6...7...8...9...10 ← graduated spectrum →	Our children's attaining mastery of skill and knowledge

Figure 17.2.

Envisioning the issue as a graduated spectrum gives this debate a different flavor and trajectory, opening possibilities for our resolving to *adaptively shift* the overall emphasis of our child-rearing and education toward the right—*toward* it, but not all the way to 10.

Applying this 10-point spectrum as a discussion aid, many American parents and educators are somewhere on the left side of the spectrum, around 3 . . . 4. In contrast, Amy Chua's Tiger Mother parenting method, much of which was about never settling for less than mastery, is a 9.

Are you thinking that Chua should be a 10? Here are two examples of a genuine 10:

- In January 2011, *The Wall Street Journal* on its front page told of immigrant parents, Slavic Christians living in Oregon, who routinely beat their children. One of their children testified in court "that he was once 'whipped' so badly with a leather strap by his father that he had to skip school to allow the injuries to heal."[7] That's a genuine 10.
- In May 2011, *The New York Times* revealed the atrocious academic demands made on students in South Korea. Focusing on suicides among college-level students at the Korea Advanced Institute of Science (think of it as Korea's M.I.T.), it also discussed competition at lower levels. The Education Ministry reported that 2010 alone witnessed 146 student suicides, including 53 in junior high and 3 in elementary school. [8] That's a genuine 10.

LEARNING TO SHIFT MODERATELY BUT SIGNIFICANTLY TOWARD THE GOAL OF MASTERY

Let's not conduct this discussion as though it's about precipitously leaping from 1 . . . 2 all the way rightwards to 9 . . . 10. Very few of us are hard-left at 1 . . . 2 (parents and teachers who are blindly accepting). And only a tiny percentage of us would even *think* of raising children at 9 . . . 10 (furiously and relentlessly demanding parents and teachers). A huge leap to the right is totally unrealistic for Americans. And in any case, this book is *not* recommending the 9 . . . 10 solution.

Instead, let's learn how to think, discuss, and act in terms of a more realistic possibility: shifting from wherever we are on the spectrum's left (perhaps most of us are at 3 or 4) just a few clicks rightward until we settle somewhere around 7 or, more ambitiously, around 8:

Our children's becoming self-directing, self-expressive individuals able to freely enact and build upon their innate mental capacities and preset pathways  Our children's attaining mastery of skill and knowledge

Figure 17.3.

Sounds simple, right? Don't kid yourself. Adapting to a new, unfamiliar set of values and attitudes, and to the required day-to-day, hour-to-hour behavioral differences, is difficult. Most people have no experience doing that. They have no one else who's done it to be their model.

Many people feel morally obligated to maintain intact all the beliefs, values, and patterns of behavior that they absorbed during childhoods. When one feels a *moral obligation* to maintain as-is all features of his or her received world view, making a major transformation is impossible.

Similarly, if you feel a moral obligation to maintain intact all the ways and means that you employ to raise and support the education of your children—the sum of all you deliberately do and don't do, day after day, over 18–20 years—so that you would feel *wrong* about making the shift rightwards to 7 . . . 8, then the message of this book simply is not for you.

But if you view your activities for the raising and educating of children as guided by the *long-range outcomes* that can be expected to result, and if you're apprehensive about your children's failure to attain mastery of the skills and knowledge taught in classrooms, then please consider the possibility of *moderately shifting* your behavior rightwards, toward 7 or even 8.

The Aptitude Myth does not come with an accompanying parenting guide or teacher-training manual. But in the following chapter you will find a transformational paradigm for you to think *with* whenever you're thinking *about* parenting, children, learning, and teaching. It's a paradigm that recognizes which problems are *now* more significant for us to solve.

NOTES

1. Thomas S. Kuhn, *The Structure of Scientific Revolutions*, 3rd ed. (University of Chicago, 1996), 110.

2. Proficiency refers to a level of demonstrated competence that authorities have judged to be acceptable as a minimum level.

3. The life adjustment movement is chronicled by, among others, Lawrence A. Cremin, *The Transformation of the School: Progressivism in American Education* (Alfred A. Knopf, 1961), 332–38; and Diane Ravitch, *Left Back* (Simon & Schuster, 2000), 327–35.

4. Arguments for and against the abolition of homework are recounted by James W. Noll, ed., *Taking Sides: Clashing Views on Controversial Educational Issues*, 13th ed. (McGraw-Hill/Dushkin, 2005), 328–43. For up-to-the-minute arguments against homework, visit StopHomework.com. For information about a similar effort, visit RaceToNowhere.com.

5. This was the actual message on a sweatshirt I observed in my Brooklyn neighborhood.

6. Presumably it is clear that I accept that, at *some* point, additional intense mental effort by a child is unwise and, ultimately, dangerously unhealthy. But the expectations and demands of most American parents, teachers, and other caregivers stop far short of that danger point.

7. Miriam Jordan, "Abuse Case Sparks Clash Over Limits of Tough Parenting," *The Wall Street Journal*, 22–23 January 2011, A1–A12. The article does not specify that these punishments concerned school performance.

8. Mark McDonald, "Suicides at a Major University Stun a Nation Consumed by Competitive Pressure," *The New York Times*, 23 May 2011, A8. The article specifies that, within South Korea, there is a broad consensus that the suicides are directly related to school performance pressures. It also reports that "South Korea as a whole ranks first among O.E.C.D. nations in suicide and is routinely among the leaders in developed nations."

EIGHTEEN

Toward a New Paradigm: Seven Assertions to Think With

**Mastery of Science Eludes Most
Students, NAEP Scores Indicate**

Fewer than a third overall deemed "proficient"

—Erik W. Robelen, *Education Week*,
2 February 2011, 10 [headline]

Recipients of *Education Week* in February, 2011, found the above headline. The article reported recent findings from the National Assessment of Educational Progress, drawn from students in the 4th, 8th, and 12th grades. "Proficiency" in science had been attained by 34 percent, 30 percent, and 21 percent, respectfully, of students. Mastery (or "Advanced") had been attained by 1 percent, 2 percent, and 1 percent.[1]

A PARADIGM TO SOLVE THE PROBLEM THAT, HERE AND NOW, IS MOST SIGNIFICANT FOR US

There's much about the western-contemporary paradigm that's beautiful and inspiring, and some of the practical outcomes to which it probably led us are desirable and admirable. One that's often cited is the innovativeness of American graduates, said to be a key explanation for the high proportion of Nobel Prizes going to Americans. There might well be truth to this.

But since the late 1950s, more and more of us have come to feel alarmed by the repeatedly measured and seemingly irreversible decline in the extent to which the vast majority of our youth falls short of mastering anything taught in school. We are so removed from bringing our youth to mastery that, nowadays, we wring our hands over whether children are attaining *proficiency*.

Mere proficiency is now our goal!

The virtual absence of mastery is the problem that, *here and now*, is most significant for us in reference to our children's, and our nation's, future.

We need a new paradigm[2] —new concepts and values to think *with*—that enables us to think *about* today's problem, the near total absence of mastery, realistically and therefore productively.

Below you'll find a new paradigm, one deliberately crafted to address the problem that's most significant for us today. This paradigm will help to point the way for both parents and educators to make a *moderate shift rightward* on that graduated spectrum illustrated in chapter 17, moving from the 3 . . . 4 range over toward 7 or maybe even all the way to 8.

As noted in the Introduction, a paradigm is a set of assertions about what people believe to be "the way things work" (or *should* work). Such assertions additionally can be understood as value propositions and as guidelines for thought and behavior. Herbert Spencer would have called them "first principles." Here, now, are seven fresh assertions to help things work better.

1. ACCOUNTABILITY FOR LEARNING RESTS MORE WITH THE PARENTS THAN WITH THE TEACHER

Among the many people with prominence in the life of a child, none has greater capacity to support and steer that child toward the mastery of critical skills and knowledge than his or her parents or guardians. Parents can fulfill this role through the application of precepts, examples, expectations, monitoring, supporting, insisting, and *not* settling for less.

They Thought Then

During medieval times, most features and expectations of parenting that we are familiar with today did not exist. It has been argued that the whole idea of "childhood" emerged within the 200 years following the invention of the printing press. Before then, skills and knowledge had been transmitted to the young via speaking, observing, and imitating; schools were rare. We don't know to what extent parents felt responsible for children's learning.

All that began to change during the Renaissance. Concepts such as "childhood," "parenting," and "development" began to gain attention. Thought leaders put forward competing ideas about parenting. The Calvinist and Romantic views, poles apart in all other ways, were both anchored by "givens." The belief in "givens," aided by the public's interest in new ideas such as personal autonomy and self-determination, created fertile ground for new views of children and parenting.

One perspective came from the Catholic Church, which focused on children's precious innocence. A newer perspective came from secular thought leaders, who claimed that children were model humans, that their development was steered by a "given" inner principle, and that their minds were fragile. (The expectation that parents inculcate virtue remained alive and well.)

Knowledge-mastery was another matter. Increasingly accepted was the idea that sustained intellectual effort damages children, which led parents' to discourage academic perseverance.

For Us to Think with Now

With respect to a child's gaining virtue, there is no need to change our expectation that *parents* will instill their own ideals. With respect to a child's gaining *knowledge*, there's no need to change our expectation that *teachers* have a key role to play.

But when it comes to a child's gaining knowledge-*mastery*, we must accept that *parents are more important than teachers* in terms of insuring that mastery is attained, that mere proficiency isn't settled-for. Nobody is better positioned than parents to expect, reward, encourage, and insist on mastery, and to create in the home conditions that support mastery as the Number One goal.

When children's attainment of mastery becomes the unrivaled main goal of parents and guardians, *the intentional pursuit of mastery will occupy far more of each child's time than it does today*. What does that look like? Readily available are first-person accounts of what childhood looks like when mastery is the Number One goal of caring parents. [3] There are no shortcuts. Be especially wary of entrepreneurs' claims that their new, more efficient study methods will yield mastery when used over relatively short amounts of time. [4]

No one has, or potentially can gain, more direct influence over the development and learning of a child than his or her parents or guardians. Parents who activate their capacity to influence mastery-acquisition will see their child's mastery increase. (See the Postscript to this chapter.)

2. ACCOUNTABILITY FOR LEARNING RESTS MORE WITH THE STUDENT THAN WITH THE TEACHER

The determining role in any individual's learning process belongs to none other than to *that* individual. No one else bears ultimate accountability for successful learning and its retention.

They Thought Then

It is clear what "child-centered" meant to those who shepherded into wide public acceptance the western-contemporary paradigm and its ideal of the child-centered classroom. Fundamentally, it meant this: Each child arrives among us having been "given" a fixed set of mental abilities, which then follow a purposeful internal principle as they direct the child's mental development. This is a natural ("organic") process that inexorably moves to completion. The child's caretakers need to understand that process, defensively protect it, and subserviently cater to it. Mental growth *happens to* a child; neither the child nor the caretakers can intentionally play a positive role. Passivity prevails in all quarters.

During recent times, child-centeredness also came to comprise the idea that caretakers—especially teachers—may, and should, entice and motivate the child's natural inclinations, hastening the emergence of "givens" that, it is hoped, are slumbering inside him or her.

For Us to Think with Now

It's fine for parents and teachers to discover and promote a child's natural inclinations. It's fine for them to try to entice and motivate. But if the adults' efforts are expended largely to make learning fascinating, entertaining, and fun, [5] then ironically the adults are the enablers of a reactive, "show me," intention-free role for students. It's a strategy that treats students as mere consumers, those who must be pleased. [6] We allow and even encourage them to have fun attending our performances. Can mastery result from this?

Writes Texas-based classroom teacher Paul A. Zoch: "For learning in the broadest, most general sense, only two things are absolutely necessary: the learner, and the thing to be learned. Teachers are helpful but by no means absolutely necessary." [7] And as we've seen in previous chapters, when teachers strive long and hard to "lubricate things" [8] for the child, the effect on the child is to confirm passivity and undermine capacity for intentional self-determination.

Only the learner can accomplish learning. Ultimate accountability for the success of any learning effort always belongs to the learner, *never* to his or her assistants.

3. A CHILD'S MENTAL APPARATUS IS VIGOROUS, ROBUST, RESILIENT, CURIOUS, AND ABSORBENT

The minds of human children are strong, resilient, and able to absorb huge inputs. Their minds are open, uncomplicated by prior prejudices and beliefs. Their brains are growing, forming synapses and other connections for the first time. Treating a normal child's mind as fragile, lacking capacity to rebound, and endangered by challenging applications of his or her intellectual capacity, is inaccurate; worse, it results in numerous lost learning opportunities.

They Thought Then

The belief that a child's mind is frail, severely exhausted by overuse of its intellectual capacity, began emerging in the West over 500 years ago. Church leaders understood that a child's ignorance was important to address. But more important to their values was the preservation, for as long as possible, of a child's miraculous innocence. That led people to think of children as precious, which in turn came to imply that their minds were delicate and easily damaged by more than modest effort.

These beliefs were then adopted by non-religious authors, especially Rousseau and Spencer; it was only 150 years ago that the latter devoted 22 pages of his blockbuster book on education to the awful danger of requiring anything beyond pleasant engagement from the minds of youth.

For Us to Think with Now

Children are learning much about their world; they're learning it fast. They are busy making sense of, flexibly adapting to, and internalizing a great many inputs from their environment. Their relentlessly curious minds have malleability and stamina. Future-oriented, caring adults can harness a child's propensity to learn, expanding it to encompass greater mastery, both qualitatively and quantitatively.

Most children are capable of learning far more at a very young age than we Americans believe possible . . . or, more to the point, advisable. One reason why America's youth have long been bested in international comparisons is that, in many other cultures, parents and teachers expect far more mastery of knowledge and skills by young children than we do.

To remain aware that a child's mind is strong, resilient, and able to absorb huge inputs is *not* to conclude that he or she can never become mentally exhausted. Rather, it requires us to act with the knowledge that children's minds are not *easily* damaged and therefore are not in need of protection from all challenges and stress associated with directed learning, including directed learning with the objective of gaining genuine mastery.

4. A CHILD'S MENTAL DEVELOPMENT INVOLVES INTENTIONAL ADAPTATION TO ITS ENVIRONMENT

Mental development is about a child's gaining the competence to adapt to, and thrive in, his or her external environments: natural, human-made, social, economic and, yes, intellectual.

They Thought Then

Aristotle taught that a human being's attainment of his or her mature form necessarily occurs, driven by a purposeful *internal* (i.e., "given") principle that inexorably moves to completion if there is no impediment. That image may apply reasonably well to the growth of a plant and to the maturation of a human's physiological body. It's seriously misleading when applied to human mental and intellectual development.

Aristotle's image was popularized by Rousseau, who advocated "negative education," and by the literary Romantics, who envisioned mental development as spontaneously emerging in organic fashion in the same way that a plant grows and flowers. Such visions of mental development portrayed the child as one to whom mental development happens; he or she plays no volitional role. Adult caretakers were viewed, like the child, as passive. Adults were counseled to stand back out of the way, taking care only that environmental impediments were minimized.

In modern times, the expectation of adult caretakers became that they should creatively try to motivate and entice the child to strive to reach his or her "given," fixed potential. The influential Herbert Spencer pronounced that nothing could alter what had been foreordained. The loveable, grandfatherly Francis Parker said, "Thus far shalt thou go and no farther." Such views are not only inaccurate but also dangerous. They created and support the belief that each individual's intelligence is a limited quantity that no amount of effort can transcend.

For Us to Think with Now

A child's mind is busy striving to acquire the competence to understand, navigate, adapt, and thrive in its natural, human-made, social, economic, and intellectual environments. That intentional effort can be actively promoted and assisted by the complementary efforts of supportive adults, who can draw on their own experience and accumulated wisdom, marshal other available inputs, and make informed decisions about what is critical for the child to become aware of, and what is critical for him or her to master.

For adults to intentionally select what a child will learn does *not* require them to dictate the focus of that child's every waking hour. Adults are not choosing between either standing back out of the way or dominating all of the child's waking hours. Imagining that choice as bipolar insures an unfavorable outcome. Adults can intentionally select how the child will use *much*, but not all, of his or her time. Their guidance can *and should* insist that activities and blocks of time routinely be devoted to gaining mastery of whatever is being taught in the child's classroom.

5. A CHILD'S COMPETENCE GROWS MORE STRONGLY AND SWIFTLY WITH AUTHORITATIVE GUIDANCE

Mental development is about gaining competence in the external world, of which the child knows nothing at birth. Parents and other adults well know this world and its ways.

Their supportive guidance, authoritatively applied, yields vital long-term benefits for the child.

They Thought Then

The belief that adults should hesitate to take authoritative, directive roles vis-à-vis children arose during the 16th, 17th, and 18th centuries as a derivative of (1) political ferment over the abuse of political and religious authority, and (2) philosophical questioning of the age-old assumption of dependent fatalism, which had been fostered by deference to ascribed authorities. The trend toward less authoritative behavior concerned the civil arrangements of adults; it had nothing to do with pedagogical objectives. Nevertheless, that trend came to be applied to the raising of children and to their instruction in school classrooms.

Today, acting with overt authority toward a child continues to be viewed negatively by many Americans because (a) children are still regarded as fragile; (b) an adult's exercising power over a child is seen by some as disempowering the child,[9] and (c) the media are quick to publicize cases in which adults truly have been unnecessarily harsh or overtly cruel. Some members of the public conceive of a bipolar choice: callous authority vs. uncritical acceptance. Not considered is adult behavior that is *both* confidently authoritative *and* warmly supportive.

For Us to Think with Now

When viewed in the context of one's first 18–20 years of life, authoritative adult guidance is one of the most developmentally beneficial factors that any child could have. Like any other exercise of power, an adult's authoritarian stance can easily shade into excess. The goal is to temper authority with positive respect and evident caring.

When a widely-recognized challenge facing our nation is our children's lack of mastery, a resolutely authoritative stance toward how children use their time could make a significant difference. To require sustained effort toward gaining mastery is to show more concern about both the child's and the nation's future than about the child's momentary contentment.

If an adult withholds directive guidance out of a conviction that doing so will undermine the child's capacity for self-determination, or that doing so will exceed the child's developmental "readiness" for this or that learning activity, the child's development is diminished by being denied the benefit of that adult's acquired competence and wisdom.

6. LEARNING ATTAINMENT IS DETERMINED FAR MORE BY PERSEVERANCE THAN BY "GIVENS"

A child's "givens" *do* influence his or her pathways of intellectual attainment.[10] But to accept presumed "givens" as the determining factors in the child's development of competence and mastery is fatalistic, inaccurate, and unnecessary. And it denies an intentional role to the child.

They Thought Then

The idea that "givens" are components of an infant's mind (soul, spirit, essence, *psychê*, or form) originated 2,500 years ago. Thereafter, questions arose about what "givens" are and to what extent they affect one's life. The focus of curiosity drifted away from religious issues and toward educational issues, especially the question of one's learning capacity.

In our nation, the question about learning capacity rose to prominence during the arrival of millions of immigrants. It was *assumed* that their intellectual "givens" were low in quantity and quality. Measurements of mental capacity were devised, based on an *assumed* fact that innate intelligence was *one* factor; thus was confirmed immigrants' modest endowments. The role of culture was overlooked or denied; the wishes of the immigrants were not solicited and not respected.

For Us to Think with Now

Historically down to our present day, a celebrated feature of American cultural values has been self-improvement through determination, hard work, and perseverance. The "rags to riches myth" still draws to our shores immigrants with high aspirations. Every day, these values are relentlessly discussed and applied in our world of athletics. It's tragic that, because of historical factors such as those revealed in this book, this set of all-American values has been, by many, kept apart from mastery in school classrooms.

Anthropologists of education know that, in many other cultures, aptitude is given little weight.[11] What *is* accepted in some cultures as the infallible indicator of a student's ability is the *product* of his or her effort. *Product tells the full story of what any student can do.* Would things be different in the United States now if we had been conditioned to evaluate children in that way?[12]

Recently a young woman told me, with deep admiration, of one of her secondary school teachers. At that point in her young life, she said, she was feeling convinced that she simply was deficient in her aptitude for understanding several academic subjects. She shared this conclusion with her teacher. *The teacher treated this information as irrelevant.* She insisted that only excellent work would be accepted. The message was that the young woman's own hard work and perseverance would enable her to overcome her assumed "givens." It did.

Children do have "givens" and "givens" do have impacts. But children also have, or can be taught and helped to gain, the determination to work long and hard in pursuit of mastery. *The product of that persevering pursuit is the one and only arbiter of how good the child really is.*

7. INCREASING MASTERY OF SKILLS AND KNOWLEDGE DEPENDS ON SKILL- AND KNOWLEDGE-FOCUS

Whenever the attainment of mastery by children is indisputably the Number One intention and focus of a school and its classrooms, then the children there are more likely to attain mastery. But when child-centered intentions, methods, and goals—worthy though many of them may be![13]—eclipse mastery as the undisputed Number One goal of a school, then those children's attainment of mastery is much more likely to remain flat or begin a downward slide.[14]

They Thought Then

Child-centered intentions, methods, and goals emerged hundreds of years ago, not merely as an emotional response to the notion of children as precious and fragile but also, and equally significantly, as a corrective to the demeaning and demotivating expectations and conditions typical of most classrooms of that era. Child-centeredness was a needed solution.

As the 18th century turned into the 19th, the child-centered perspective gradually gained credibility in the thinking of more and more educators. The tipping point might have been reached when the influential Johann Pestalozzi wrote that his purpose was to "psychologize instruction," to purposely regulate teaching to match the child's "given" developmental pattern. From then on, child-centeredness overreached.

Among the overreaching but persuasive forces were Herbert Spencer, who insisted that adults *must* cater to children's every need; and the child-study movement, which drew thousands of educated adults to try to record children's patterns of development. Mastery further receded in importance. Its retreat was aided by professionals cloaked in scientific authority, who told of how they had tested masses of the young and found the vast majority of them sorely lacking in intelligence. So why should anyone even bother trying to help all those youths gain mastery?

The drive to "psychologize instruction" continues unabated. It is still led by professionals cloaked in scientific authority. They direct many people's attention to (a) using methods that children are familiar with, and/or (b) motivating children to learn, and/or (c) understanding what is going on inside each child's head—i.e., understanding the child's "givens"—so that the teacher can then align her efforts with that child's learning style, culture, interests, and so forth.

Currently emphasized are differentiation, brain research, and technology (i.e., computers). Books, videos, events, and gurus galore support these trends! Yes, it's possible that some of this might actually help children attain mastery. [15] But all of it together shows just how persistent is that old western-contemporary paradigm. It's all about *catering to children* in the hope that, eventually, the adults will learn to cater to each unique child with such precision that he or she, almost effortlessly, *will* learn. Eventually. Well, this cater-to-the-child effort has been going on for hundreds of years—while mastery has all but slipped beyond our grasp.

For Us to Think with Now

Today our challenge is to swiftly reverse the distressingly low levels of mastery among our youth. In no way does this require the abandonment of every benefit brought to instruction by child-centered thinking. *It does require* that no feature of child-centered thinking, regardless of its subjective appeal, developmental benefit, or social worthiness, be allowed to eclipse mastery as our Number One intention, focus, and goal.

Example: Drill has been denigrated over decades for child-centered reasons related to children's pleasurable contentment. Drill is a way for learners to gain confident command of basic facts and processes, enabling them to advance efficiently through higher level material. [16, 17] Drill is a litmus test: To spurn drill is to reveal that mastery is not one's Number One goal.

Children's mastery of skills and knowledge will attain significantly higher levels if, and only if, adults abandon the paradigm we inherited from ancient European sources and adopt a new paradigm in which mastery is the unrivalled Number One priority. Mastery cannot be, must not be, the *sole* objective of child development. But our own experience teaches us unmistakably what happens when mastery is somewhere in the middle of that long list of worthy objectives and priorities. Our children's opportunities *and* our nation's competitiveness visibly wither.

The ages-old paradigm we inherited has failed. Now is the time to think *with* something new.

POSTSCRIPT: BEYOND THINKING *WITH*,
AN OUTSTANDING RESOURCE FOR *DOING*

These seven assertions can lead to high-impact changes in the behavior of parents, teachers, and children. But some readers will want, in addition, guidelines for day-to-day life with children.

A set of guidelines exists. It's a book by two sisters, Soo and Jane Kim, one a surgeon, the other an attorney, who were raised by their Korean parents, Jae and Dae Kim, who immigrated to the United States before the girls were born. Their mother became a seamstress to help support their father as he was completing a master's degree; he also brought in money as a janitor and gas-station attendant. He eventually rose through the ranks of Nortel Networks.

Soo and Jane Kim wrote *Top of the Class: How Asian Parents Raise High Achievers—And How You Can Too*, published by Berkley in 2006. It's a how-to book for parents, with each of the 17 chapter titles written as an imperative such as "Clearly Define Your Child's Role as a Student" and "Limit Extracurricular Activities That Interfere with Schoolwork." This little paperback explains to parents—and teachers—how to guide children toward mastery.

In their Foreword, Soo and Jane rehearse some of the all-too-familiar statistics about the disproportionately high percentages of Asian students who are studying at top universities and graduating with advanced degrees such as M.D., Ph.D., J.D., etc. They point out that in 2002, the median household income for Asian and Pacific Islanders was $10,000 higher than for the rest of the population. Then on page two comes this paragraph (italics in the original):

> *The reason that Asian students outperform their peers in the classroom has nothing to do with how they are born and everything to do with how they are raised. This book is for all parents and children who want to discover (or rediscover) a love for learning and develop the discipline to use this love to build knowledge and indispensable skills in the classroom and beyond.*

Top of the Class describes how to raise children day-after-day as though aptitude hardly matters. It's about working hard, persevering, and not being deflected from a goal.

Has reading *The Aptitude Myth* deepened your determination not only to think *with* assumptions that make mastery Number One, but also to *do* something that will transform a child you know? Then get out there and purchase *Top of the Class* by Soo and Jane Kim.[18]

Perhaps in addition to, or instead of, advice to parents, you'd like to find advice or inspiration for doing something to transform your *own* intellectual performances. In that case, I recommend that you get out there and purchase *Mastery*, by Robert Greene, published by Viking in 2012.

NOTES

1. Hope of children's attaining "mastery," or "advanced" understanding, is fading. In 2011 *The Wall Street Journal* reported: "In fourth-grade reading . . . 35 states set passing bars that are below the 'basic' level on the national NAEP exam. 'Basic' means students have a satisfactory understanding of material, . . . 'proficient' . . . means they have a solid grasp of it. Massachusetts is the only state to set its bar at 'proficient'—and that was only in fourth- and eighth-grade math." "The data help explain the disconnect between the relatively high pass rates on many state tests and the low scores on the national exams [NAEP]." Stephanie Banchero, "States Fail to Raise Bar in Reading, Math Tests," 11 August 2011, A2. Banchero doesn't even mention "mastery."

2. In reference to scientific paradigms, Thomas Kuhn writes: "To reject one paradigm without simultaneously substituting another is to reject science itself." *The Structure of Scientific Revolutions*, 3rd ed.

(University of Chicago Press, 1996), 79. Chapters 1–17 of *The Aptitude Myth* reject a 2,500-year-old paradigm. This final chapter substitutes a new paradigm.

3. For example, see Amy Chua, *Battle Hymn of the Tiger Mother* (Penguin Press, 2011). See also this chapter's Postscript.

4. Consider advertisements claiming that foreign language "fluency" is attainable by briefly using the seller's new method. Possible? Yes—if "fluency" no longer means language mastery.

5. Of the many hundreds of books and other professional development opportunities that show educators how to entice and motivate students, my favorite title is this: Frank Sennett, *101 Stunts for Principals to Inspire Student Achievement* (Corwin, 2004).

6. Comparisons of students with consumers have been offered by James G. Hutton, *The Feel Good Society* (Pentagram, 2005), chapter 4; and Lisa Delphit, *Other People's Children* (The New Press, 1995), 37–38.

7. Paul A. Zoch, *Doomed to Fail* (Ivan R. Dee, 2004), xi. He adds, "The role of the teacher is to help students by providing them with crucial information which they might otherwise find only with the greatest difficulty . . ." xiv.

8. This phrase "lubricate things" belongs to William James; the full quote is in chapter 13.

9. Delpit, *op. cit.*, 32.

10. I have *not* argued that children have no "givens." I have revisited the historical record to show that "givens" and their alleged determining power have *largely* been the product of imagination.

11. See Harold W. Stevenson and James W. Stigler, *The Learning Gap* (Touchstone, 1992), chapter 5.

12. In Asian cultures, persevering effort is viewed as the path to egalitarian outcomes, a belief traceable directly to Confucius: "If someone [else] does it once, do it a hundred [times]; if someone does it ten [times], do it a thousand. By truly doing it this way, though unintelligent one becomes bright; though weak one becomes strong." Confucius, *Doctrine of the Mean*, XX, stanzas 20–21; translated for the author by Anthony Pan and Kay M. Jones.

13. I'm aware that a wide variety of goals are competing for inclusion in the curriculum, methods, and purposes of classrooms. To cite one example, in August, 2011, New York City announced renewed emphasis on sex education. There are numerous worthy objectives that arguably should be pursued in American classrooms. My point is this: Our Number One educational challenge is the seemingly irreversible decline in children's mastery of basic subjects; unless we make and maintain mastery as our unrivalled Number One priority, that challenge cannot, will not, be met.

14. Another distraction from mastery comes from the high value placed by many parents, teachers, and colleges on children's being "well-rounded," leading to some teenagers' being scheduled non-stop for extracurricular activities. This is especially true in the case of families with college aspirations. For a thoughtful exploration of the complex factors affecting the lives of middle-class teenagers, see the documentary film "Race to Nowhere." Visit RaceToNowhere.com.

15. For some mastery-supporting findings from brain research, see Annie Murphy Paul, "The Trouble With Homework," *The New York Times*, 11 September 2011, Sunday Review section, 6.

16. See Daniel T. Willingham, *Why Don't Students Like School* (Jossey-Bass, 2009), chapter 5.

17. See an article in the Science Times section of *The New York Times* of 7 June 2011, entitled "Brain Calisthenics for Abstract Ideas." Discussed is a breakthrough way of enabling students to learn, and to retain and use, what they learn. Excerpt: "Experts develop such sensitive perceptual radar the old-fashioned way, of course, through years of study and practice. Yet there is growing evidence that a certain kind of training—visual, fast-paced, often focused on classifying problems rather then [sic] solving them—can build intuition quickly." I wonder whether Benedict Carey, the journalist, realizes that his erudite article was actually describing drill.

18. An example in chapter 17 of child-rearing and education at the "genuine 10" level concerned "the atrocious academic demands made on students in South Korea," which is the homeland of Soo and Jane Kim's parents. This fact highlights the importance of *carefully calibrating our expectations* regarding young people's efforts to attain mastery. The expectations often characteristic of South Koreans appear to be beyond the endurance of some young people, i.e., a "genuine 10," which I do not support or admire. The expectations of Soo and Jane Kim's parents appear to not have reached the "genuine 10" level; their expectations illustrate a level 8 or, perhaps, level 9. Regardless of whether we assign an 8 or a 9 to the Kim parents, my view is that they got it right. That's why *Top of the Class* opens with this statement: "This book is dedicated to our parents, Jae and Dae Kim. Thank you for everything."

Appendix

Table A-1.   The Calvinist Perspective (see discussion in chapter 11)

Principal focus of proponents' attention	UPwards toward God, heaven, afterlife, importance of salvation
Perspective on the newborn child	Innately depraved and invariably prone to evil
Key objective of child-rearing	Compel child to become Good as soon as possible
Basic process in a child's education	Behavioral discipline: instill right conduct guided by Godly knowledge
What about a child must get the most attention	His or her soul, which must be "saved" as soon as possible
Expected approach in dealing with children	Prescribe, demand, and punish to quickly internalize virtue
Where what-is-to-be-gained is found	In the holy book, which focuses BACKwards to the past (and UPwards)
Presumed value of the learning experience	Learner is saved from hell; society is saved from evil-doers
To be *avoided* during the learning experience	Backsliding (flagging interest in, or turning away from, virtue)
Typical classroom teaching styles	Didactic, punitive; require extensive memorization and recitation
Approach and role of the teacher	Authoritarian dispenser of virtue, also of knowledge
Often associated images or sayings	"Break the will"
Associated trend in American thought	Evangelical and Fundamentalist Protestantism
Historical thought leaders	John Calvin; in the U.S., preachers such as Jonathan Edwards
Historical trajectory	18th century: the strongly dominant parenting and instructional style Early 19th century: increasingly regarded as questionable Late 19th century: enters a sharp and permanent decline Early 20th century: maintained only by fringe religious groups
Significance for us	The Calvinist perspective reaches conclusions starkly different from those of the Romantics (Table A-2). But *both* perspectives attend to the child as a unique individual, and *both* are based on the assumption that each child has innate, "given" factors in his or her nature.

Table A-2. The Romantic Perspective (see discussion in chapter 11)

Principal focus of proponents' attention	INwards on each child as precious, able to "organically" flower…
Perspective on the newborn child	Pure, innocent, full of potential, precious: the ideal human
Key objective of child-rearing	Shield the child from an evil world; allow his/her potential to flower
Basic process in a child's education	Nurturing: maintain the child's "state of nature" as much as possible
What about a child must get the most attention	His or her personality, which must come to reveal uniqueness
Expected approach in dealing with children	Insure that early experiences enable inborn potential to emerge
Where what-is-to-be-gained is found	Inside the child [reminiscent of ideas tracing back to Platonic Realism]
Presumed value of the learning experience	Learner realizes his or her unique potential
To be *avoided* during the learning experience	Demands that the child work hard, because he/she is mentally fragile
Typical classroom teaching styles	"Negative education," i.e., very few didactic methods, or none at all
Approach and role of the teacher	A developmentally sophisticated arranger of experiences for the child
Often associated images or sayings	"State of nature" and "organic growth"; more recently, "readiness"
Associated trend in American thought	Romanticism; Transcendentalism
Historical thought leaders	Jean-Jacques Rousseau, Johann Pestalozzi, the Romantic Poets, Herbert Spencer; in the U.S., Francis W. Parker, G. Stanley Hall. (In deep history, derived in part from the thinking of Plato and especially Aristotle.)
Historical trajectory	18th century: scarcely recognized within North America Early 19th century: beginning to find acceptance and an audience Late 19th century: steadily gaining (due to Spencer's influence) Early 20th century: becoming the orthodox paradigm of instruction
Significance for us	The Romantic perspective reaches conclusions starkly different from those of the Calvinists (Table A-1). But *both* perspectives attend to the child as a unique individual, and *both* are based on the assumption that each child has innate, "given" factors in his or her nature.

Table A-3. The Practical Perspective (see discussion in chapter 11)

Principal focus of proponents' attention	OUTwards to the local community; FORwards to a near-future time
Perspective on the newborn child	A blank slate (Locke's *tabula rasa*) and morally neutral at birth
Key objective of child-rearing	Deliberately guide and shape the child to bring about a better society
Basic process in a child's education	Additive: fill the blank slate with socially and personally useful material
What about a child must get the most attention	His or her character, which must be morally molded to fit society
Expected approach in dealing with children	Use rewards/punishments to teach and establish socially useful habits
Where what-is-to-be-gained is found	External to oneself, in one's contemporary and near-future environment
Presumed value of the learning experience	Learner becomes capable, useful; society reaps the benefits
To be *avoided* during the learning experience	Corporeal punishment (but lesser punishments were acceptable)
Typical classroom teaching styles	Directive but with gentleness; build habits via repeated actions
Approach and role of the teacher	A representative of society who is forming useful new citizens
Often associated images or sayings	"Tabula rasa" and, more recently, "improve the race"
Associated trend in American thought	Empiricism; Pragmatism; Objective Psychology
Historical thought leaders	Francis Bacon, John Comenius, John Locke, Johann Herbart; in the U.S., Horace Mann, William James, John Dewey, E.L. Thorndike
Historical trajectory	18th century: known about, but overshadowed by the Calvinist view Early 19th century: starting to find an audience/acceptance Late 19th century: steadily gaining (via Mann and "common schools") Early 20th century: more influential in practice than in people's thought
Significance for us	The Practical perspective has very little in common with either the Calvinist or Romantic perspectives: It attends to the needs of society more than it attends to the child; it views the child as *tabula rasa* instead of an heir of "givens"; its focus is environmental and practical.

Table A-4.   The Classical Perspective (see discussion in chapter 13)

Principal focus of proponents' attention	BACKwards in time to era of unsurpassed human excellence, and INwards to the reasoning and processing capabilities of each individual's mind
Perspective on the newborn child	not applicable
Key objective of child-rearing	not applicable
Basic process in a child's education	Mental discipline: exercise, train, and strengthen the child's mental powers
What about a child must get the most attention	His or her mind, which must be sharpened through exercise and discipline
Expected approach in dealing with learners	Teachers provide texts and guidance that will train, exercise, and discipline the learner's mental "faculties" and processes. [Parenting is not a concern.]
Where what-is-to-be-gained is found	Very largely in classical and humanist texts in Latin and Greek. Mathematics and philosophy are sometimes included as well, as is the Christian Bible (as a classical text). These are the elements of a "classical" or "liberal" education.
Presumed value of the learning experience	The learner trains and disciplines the various "faculties" of his/her mind, which then will be capable of performing well in handling any and all mental challenges that might be encountered subsequently. "Transfer of training."
To be *avoided* during the learning experience	Usually, any concession to learners' tendency to explore, play, and socialize.
Typical classroom teaching styles	Didactic, heavy memorization and recitation, sometimes punitive. Not clear is the extent to which scholastic methods—e.g., the disputation—were in use.
Approach and role of the teacher	Authoritative repository of materials and guidance that will enable learners to exercise and train their mental "faculties" and attain mental discipline
Often associated images or sayings	"Transfer of training"
Associated trend in American thought	Classical humanism; dualistic humanism; faculty psychology
Historical thought leaders	During the 15th, 16th, and 17th centuries, classical humanists, scholastics, and Jesuits; during the 18th century, René Descartes and other rationalists. (In deep history, derived in part from the thinking of Pythagoras.)
Historical trajectory	18th century: classical humanistic studies widely revered Early 19th century: still revered; growth of faculty psychology Late 19th century: under increasing attack from evidence-based philosophies Early 20th century: rapid and ultimately terminal decline
Additional discussion	The Classical Perspective differs from the other three in that it did not arise out of concerns about the nature of children. Grounded in reverence for classical languages and literature, it saw these as necessary and sufficient for training the mind so that, going forward, it could adroitly handle *any* mental challenge. This perspective is about *mental process excellence*, not about subject mastery.

Index

About the Author

Cornelius N. Grove is an independent educational researcher whose day job is managing the global leadership consultancy he founded in 1990, GROVEWELL LLC.

Grove's parents were educators. He attended a classic one-room schoolhouse in his native Pennsylvania during part of his third-grade year, graduated from high school in Chattanooga, attained an M.A.T. from Johns Hopkins and, 15 years later, an Ed.D. from Teachers College.

Grove's graduate school interest was in understanding, *at the level of assumptions, values, and practices*, worldwide differences among instructional styles and classroom cultures. (His dissertation compared U.S. and Portuguese classrooms.) As an adjunct at Teachers College and New School University, he designed and taught "Cross-Cultural Problems in Classroom Communication." In 1986 he taught at Beijing Foreign Studies University, after which he coauthored, with that institution's vice chancellor, *Encountering the Chinese* (3rd ed., 2010).

During the mid-1990s, GROVEWELL was asked to train corporate trainers facing learners from abroad. Designing and facilitating "Dr. Grove's Framework for Effective Presentations to Nationally Mixed Audiences" reignited Grove's earlier interest. In 2005, he delivered in Singapore a major conference paper, "Understanding the Two Instructional Style Prototypes: Pathways to Success in Internationally Diverse Classrooms," which was later published. That paper became his starting point for a book project intended to give parents and teachers a comprehensive framework for understanding classroom learning in cross-cultural perspective.

While working on that book, Grove became curious about the historical wellsprings of the beliefs that many Americans *think with* when they think about children's learning. Intending to include in his book one chapter from a historical perspective, he redirected his research. One chapter, however, proved far too short. That chapter grew to become *The Aptitude Myth*.